Mysteries
of the
BIBLE
Now Revealed

Mysteries
of the
BIBLE
Now Revealed

James Combs • Robert Faid • Frank Harber
Ed Hindson • Thomas Ice • Grant Jeffrey
David Allen Lewis • Chuck Missler
Elmer Towns • Clifford A. Wilson

Edited by David Allen Lewis
and Jim Combs

New Leaf Press

First printing: March 1999

ISBN: 0-89221-459-7
Library of Congress Number: 99-70075

Cover by Lee Fredrickson

Printed in the United States of America.

To the

One

whose return

we await.

Contents

The Grand Classic of History

The Best-Selling Book of the Past Millennium

O f all the billions of books produced since the printing of the Gutenberg Bible in the 15th century, the Bible is the most fabulous volume of all. It is a book of truth, history, wisdom, poetry, prophecy, ethics, biographies of common and uncommon people, of whom the greatest is the Master-Teacher of all time, Jesus Christ, who is declared to be the Son of God and the Savior of all men.

And it is a book of mysteries, addressing the greatest issues of life, time, and eternity.

Many approaches have been taken toward the sacred Scriptures, this compendium of 66 books produced by some 40 Jews (Israelites) and 1 Gentile (Luke). Some believe it implicitly; some scoff at the foolishness of those who follow old sagas, legends, and out-of-date religious philosophies; others regard it as interesting but not necessarily divinely inspired.

This volume attempts to present a dozen aspects of the Bible's uniqueness. All who have contributed have spent literally decades researching, reading, absorbing, and practicing the truth of this book. Not every one of the contributors necessarily is in perfect agreement with all the others, but every chapter is thought-provoking and examines a different facet of this mysterious and influential book.

Mysteries of the Bible is an appropriate title. The very word *mysteries* in English is derived from the Greek word *musterion*, which conveys the idea of being initiated (*mueo*) into secret or unknown mysteries. "In the New Testament, it denotes that which, being outside the range of unassisted natural apprehension, can be made known only by divine revelation, and is made known in a manner and a time appointed by God, and only to those illumined by the Spirit."[1]

In ordinary English a mystery indicates knowledge withheld, but in its scriptural significance it is *truth revealed*.

Archaeologist and contributing writer to this volume Clifford Wilson writes:

> The Concise Oxford Dictionary defines the word "mystery" in a number of ways. One of these is this definition: "Religious truth divinely revealed especially one beyond human reason."
>
> The revealed Word of God, the Christian's Bible, certainly fits that definition. Here is a book whose writings stretch over more than 2000 years, crossing national, social and linguistic barriers. Its writers came from a large number of varied backgrounds with occupations as diverse as nomadic cattlemen in the wilderness to kings in palaces. Its subjects cover national history, personal success and failure, law and politics, love and sex, music and poetry, miracles of God and activities opposing evil forces plus much more!
>
> The book takes its place as number one in all of the world's great literature. But it is far more than a wonderful collection of literature, for this Book stands alone as God's unique Word of truth, His revelation of himself.
>
> In all this, it has been subjected to malicious criticism, to deliberate lies, to charges of plagiarism, and to many other nonsensical accusations. Yet, through the centuries it has endured beyond the expectations of its critics, sustaining a place of reverence, affection, and acceptance beyond any other book. Unique in its design, amazing in the way it has proved itself to be beyond legitimate criticism, the Bible continues to be "right after all."

Long-time pastor, evangelist, and educator W. Kenneth Connolly well observes:

> Nearly every branch of knowledge and every sphere of human endeavor has had its masters who have submitted to the supremacy of this book. David Livingstone, the great explorer, died kneeling at a cot in the heart of Africa. He had just finished reading his Bible.

Napoleon Bonaparte once commented to three generals who were in his room: "That Bible on the table is a book to you; it speaks to me; it is as if it were a person."

When he was on his death bed, Scotland's great literary giant, Sir Walter Scott, asked his friend Lockhart to read to him from the book. Scott had a library of 20,000 volumes, so Lockhart asked him, "What book would you like?" Scott replied: "Need you ask? There is but one."

George Mueller, the builder of the huge 19th century orphanage in Bristol, said: "I have read the Bible through one hundred times and found something new and inspiring every time."

England's King George V, as he promised his mother, read his Bible every day.

William Gladstone, four times prime minister of Great Britain, wrote a book which he entitled *The Impregnable Rock of Holy Scripture*. He professed to know 95 great men in the world of his day, and 87 of them, he said, "were followers of the Bible."

Men who publicly professed allegiance to the Bible and served as president of the United States include George Washington, Thomas Jefferson, Abraham Lincoln, and Franklin Roosevelt. The Bible is in every courtroom. Every hospital is a monument to its moral influence.

Turn the coin over and look at the subject from the other side. Take the Bible out of literature, and what is left? Tennyson used over 300 quotations from the pages of the Bible. It has been calculated that Shakespeare has over 500 ideas and phrases taken directly from the pages of the Bible. Charles Dickens said: "It is the best book that ever was or ever will be in the world."

Or look at its contribution to the world of music. Take the Bible from Bach, Handel, and Mozart, and what is left? Would we have ever heard of Handel, had it not been for his Bible? Look at the world of art. Where would the names of Leonardo da Vinci, Michelangelo, Donatello, Rembrandt, and Raphael be found, if they had not been inspired by the themes of the Bible?

Look back to the early days of many educational institutions and you will see they are inseparably linked with the church. Harvard, Yale, William and Mary, and Dartmouth were all founded for the express purpose of training religious ministers. Dr. William Phelps, once principal of Yale University, the third oldest educational institution in the United States, is quoted as saying: "I believe that a knowledge of the Bible without a college course is more valuable than a college course without a knowledge of the Bible."

Grant Jeffrey, whose curious and controversial presentation of the "incredible secret letter codes of the Bible" leads off in chapter 1 of this volume, has long pondered the mysteries of sacred Scripture, as well as the plain gospel the Book proclaims, and draws an intriguing analogy to the famous "Seven Wonders of the World." Read on:

We have all heard of the Seven Wonders of the World that have fascinated mankind through the centuries. Yet, for those who will examine the evidence, the Scriptures should hold an equal fascination. The Bible also manifests Seven Wonders of the Word of God.

1. The Wonder of Its Formation
The marvelous manner in which the Scriptures grew from the first 5 books of Moses to include all 39 books of the Old Testament and, then, the addition of the 27 books of the New Testament in the first century of our era, is one of the greatest mysteries of the ages.

2. The Wonder of Its Unity
The Bible is a complete library composed of 66 books, written by 44 different authors over a period of 1,600 years. The authors came from different backgrounds — including kings of Israel, warriors, shepherds, poets, a physician, and fishermen. However, the Bible is the most unified book in the world, containing a progressive revelation of the message of God without any real contradictions.

3. The Wonder of Its Age
The Bible is without doubt the oldest and most ancient book in the world, beginning with its first section of five books written by Moses 35 centuries ago. What other ancient writing is read daily by hundreds of millions of people who find answers to their most immediate problems and concerns?

4. The Wonder of Its Sales
Despite the fact that it is the oldest and most popular book in the world, its continuing sales year after year are the greatest wonder in

the field of book publishing. Scholars have estimated that there are far more than two billion Bibles published throughout the globe. Incredibly, the American Bible Society printed its two billionth Bible in 1976 and presented it to President Ford. Despite the phenomenal number of Bibles that exist, it continues to outsell every other book with several hundred million in annual sales worldwide.

5. The Wonder of Its Popularity

Despite the fact that the Bible was written over two thousand years ago by ancient inhabitants of the Middle East in an oriental form of literature, the Bible remains the most fascinating and intriguing book on earth. Every year the Bible is read by over a billion adults and young people representing every nation and class of people on the planet.

6. The Wonder of Its Language

The Scriptures were written in three languages: Hebrew, Aramaic, and Greek, by some 44 writers. Most of these writers were not well-educated, nor did most of them know each other. Yet the wisest men of every age have acknowledged the Bible as the world's greatest literary masterpiece.

7. The Wonder of Its Preservation

There is no other book in history which has suffered more opposition, hatred, persecution, and outright burning. Yet, after thousands of years of opposition, the Bible has not only survived, it has triumphed over emperors, kings, and dictators who sought to silence its message of salvation through the blood of Jesus Christ."

"Come now and let us reason together . . ." (Isa. 1:18). We shall now examine 12 facets of this marvelous jewel of a Book and by doing so, we shall not exhaust this treasure trove of eternal wisdom or discover all there is to know about God's Word. You may not concur totally with every writer or every aspect of our examination. But, we ask, are all of these things separately and cumulatively only the product of blind chance and random coincidences? Or is this a supernatural book, containing a mighty revelation from our great God and Father?

Survey this evidence! Examine the witnesses to the Word! Draw your own conclusion!

We close with this quotation from a great Bible expositor of yesteryear, A. T. Pierson:

> The Bible is not a worn-out Book. The Statue of Liberty in the harbor of New York lifts its great light for the

guidance of mariners, and though the birds of the night fling themselves madly against its crystal, as to put out the flame, they only beat themselves into insensitivity, and fall dead at last at its base; so whatever antagonism there may be to this Book, God's beacon light, those who assault it will only damage themselves, while the light shines on, safe and se-rene.

Maranatha!

David Allen Lewis and James (Jim) Combs

Foreword Endnote

1 W.E. Vine, *Vine's Expository Dictionary of New Testament Words* (Grandville, MI: World Bible Publishers, Inc., 1987).

1

The Incredible Secret Letter Codes of the Bible

Grant Jeffrey

everal years ago computer scientists in Israel discovered a staggering phenomenon — encoded words hidden within the text of the Bible. Within the Hebrew text of the Old Testament they found hidden codes that revealed an astonishing knowledge of future events and personalities. The existence of these codes can only be explained if God inspired the writers to record His precise words.

An Astonishing Discovery

Rabbi Michael Dov Weissmandl, a brilliant Czechoslovakian Jewish scholar in astronomy, mathematics, and Judaic studies, found an obscure reference to these codes in a book written by a 14th-century rabbi, Rabbeynu Bachayah. This reference described a pattern of letters encoded within the Torah, the first five books of the Bible. This discovery during the years before World War I inspired Rabbi Weissmandl to search for other examples of codes hidden within the Torah. During the war years, he found that he could locate certain meaningful words, phrases, and word pairs, such as "hammer" and "anvil," if he found the first letter and then skipped forward a certain number of letters to find the second one, and the same number again to find the third one, and so on. As an example, he found the letter tav (ת), the first letter of the word Torah תורה, the Hebrew word for "law," within the first word of Genesis 1:1, "Beginnings" Bereishis בראשית. Then, by skipping forward 50 letters, he found the second letter vav ו. He continued to skip forward 50 letters and found reysh ר and finally the last letter hey ה, completing the spelling of the word Torah תורה.

The rabbi was astonished to find that many significant words were hidden within the text of the Torah at equally spaced intervals. These intervals varied from every two letters up to hundreds of letters apart.

Although Rabbi Weissmandl found many encoded names by manually counting the letters in the text, he did not record his code discoveries in writing. Fortunately, some of his students did. Over the following decades, students in Israel who had heard about his research began searching the Torah for themselves to ascertain whether or not such codes actually existed. Their discoveries ultimately resulted in research studies at Hebrew University that have proven the validity of the codes, now known as Equidistant Letter Sequence (ELS) codes. In the last decade, the introduction of sophisticated high-speed computers has allowed Jewish scholars at Hebrew University to explore the text of the Torah in ways that were unavailable to previous generations.

In 1988 three mathematics and computer experts at Hebrew University and the Jerusalem College of Technology (Doron Witztum, Yoav Rosenberg, and Eliyahu Rips) completed an astonishing research project that followed up Rabbi Weismandl's original research. As a result, they published a paper in August 1994 called "Equidistant Letter Sequences in the Book of Genesis" in one of the most prominent mathematical and scientific journals in the world, the American mathematics journal *Statistical Science*.

In one experiment, the scientists arbitrarily chose three hundred Hebrew word-pairs that were logically related in meaning, such as "hammer" and "anvil," or "tree" and "leaf," or "man" and "woman." They asked the computer program to locate any such word pairs anywhere in the Genesis text. Once the computer found the first letter in the Hebrew word for "hammer," it would look for the second letter at various intervals or spaces between letters. If the program could not locate the second letter of the target word "hammer" following the first letter at a two-letter interval, it would search at a three-letter interval, then a four-letter interval, and so forth. Once it located the second letter at, say, the 12-letter interval, it would then skip forward at the same 12-letter interval looking for the third letter, and so on through all 78,064 Hebrew letters in the Book of Genesis. The computer also looked for coded words by checking in reverse order.

After the program had examined the text for each of the three hundred word pairs, the researchers were astonished to find that every single word pair had been located in Genesis in close proximity to each other. As mathematicians and statisticians, they were naturally astounded because they knew it was impossible for humans to construct such an intricate and complicated pattern beneath a surface text, such as Genesis, which tells the history of the beginnings of the Jewish people. The odds against the three hundred word pairs occurring by random chance in the text of Genesis was staggering! The bottom line is that only a supernatural intelligence, far beyond our human ability, could have produced the intricate pattern of secretly coded words found in the Bible.

More Surprises

As they studied this pattern the scientists discovered that many of the coded words described future events and personalities in human history, from ancient times until today. When they looked at the string of Hebrew letters in Genesis 1:1, they counted forward 49 letters from the letter ת, the first letter (תּשׁה) of the Hebrew word Torah and found the second letter in the word. Skipping forward another 49 letters they found the third letter of the word Torah. Incredibly, the Hebrew word Torah was spelled out using every 50th letter of the text.

To their surprise they found that the opening verse of Exodus, the second book in the Bible, contained the same word Torah, once again spelled out at the same 50-letter intervals beginning with the first appearance of the letter ת. However, when they examined the opening verses of the third book of the Bible, Leviticus, they did not find Torah encoded. However, they did discover the word God was spelled out when they skipped forward every eighth letter from the first letter י yod that appeared in the book.

Upon examining the initial verses of Numbers and Deuteronomy, the fourth and fifth books of the Bible, the scientists again found that the word Torah was encoded. In the Book of Numbers, the word Torah is spelled out in reverse at a 50-letter interval. However, to their surprise, while the word Torah was also found to be spelled out in reverse order in the Book of Deuteronomy, it appeared at a 49-letter interval beginning with the fifth verse of the book.

Mathematicians calculated that the odds were more than three million to one against the word Torah being encoded by chance alone within the opening verses in the first five books of the Bible. Bible students know that the number 50 is very significant in Scripture. For example, God commanded Israel to free their slaves and return family lands that had been pledged to a lender on the 50th year of Jubilee. In addition, the Bible reveals that law itself, the Torah, was presented to the Jewish people at Mount Sinai by God precisely 50 days after their miraculous Exodus from Egypt.

These coded words are interlaced in intricate patterns at evenly spaced intervals in the text reading both forward and backward. The scientists realized that these coded letters formed words and associations of such complexity and design that it is absolutely impossible that the patterns could have occurred by chance.

It is fascinating to observe that the key word "Eden" is encoded repeatedly 16 times within the relatively short Genesis 2:4-10 passage of only 379 Hebrew letters dealing with the Garden of Eden. The odds against 16 "Edens" occurring by chance in such a short passage is one chance in ten thousand.

Thousands of detailed and precise patterns and codes such as these were discovered hidden in the Hebrew text of the ancient Scriptures. Mathematical and computer statisticians, after exhaustive statistical analyses, concluded that this pattern of coded words could not have occurred by chance nor could a human writer have purposely produced this phenomenon. Their conclusion is that only a divine intelligence could have directed Moses to record this precise text containing such complex codes thousands of years ago.

The Bible Codes Speak of Future Events

That was only the beginning of the story. In a 1994 follow-up paper, the team of researchers recorded the results of a new experiment involving their search for pairs of encoded words that related to events that occurred thousands of years after Moses wrote the Torah. They selected the names of 34 of the most prominent rabbis and Jewish sages who lived from the beginning of the 9th to the end of the 18th century. These Jewish sages had the longest biographies found in the *Encyclopedia of Great Men in Israel*[1], a well-respected Jewish reference book. They asked the computer program to search the text of the Torah for close word pairs coded at equally spaced intervals that contained the names of the famous rabbis, paired with their dates of birth or death (using the Hebrew month and day). The Jewish people celebrate the memory of their famous sages by commemorating the dates of their deaths. Incredibly, the computer program found every single one of the 34 names of these famous rabbis embedded in the text of Genesis. Each name of a rabbi was paired in significantly close proximity to the actual date of his birth or the date of his death. The odds against this occurring by chance were calculated by the Israeli mathematicians to be only one chance in 775,000,000!

The scientists and editors at the *Statistical Science* journal who reviewed the experimental data were naturally amazed. They demanded that the Israeli scientists run the computer test program again on a second sample group. This time they searched for the names of a second group of 32 prominent Jewish sages listed in the encyclopedia. To the astonishment of the skeptical reviewers, the results were equally successful with the second set of famous sages. The combined test revealed that the names and dates of the births or deaths of every one of the 66 most famous Jewish sages were encoded in close proximity within the text of Genesis.

Despite the fact that all of the science journal reviewers previously denied the inspiration of the Scriptures, the overwhelming evidence from the data was so strong that the journal editors reluctantly agreed to publish the article in its August 1994 issue under the title "Equidistant Letter Sequences in the Book of Genesis." Robert Kass, the editor of *Statistical Science*, wrote this comment about the study: "Our referees were baffled: their prior beliefs made them think the Book of Genesis could not possibly contain meaningful references to modern day individuals, yet when the authors carried out additional analyses and checks the effect persisted. The paper is thus offered to *Statistical Science* readers as a challenging puzzle." After three years of careful analysis by many scholars throughout the world, the experiment remains credible.

In October 1995, an article in *Bible Review* magazine by Dr. Jeffrey Satinover, reported that the mathematical probability that these 66 names of Jewish sages paired with their dates of birth or death occur by chance in an ancient text like Genesis is less than 1 chance in 2.5 billion!

The *Bible Review* article provoked an onslaught of letters (mostly critical) to the editor. Dr. Satinover responded to his critics as follows: "The robustness of the Torah codes findings derives from the rigor of the research. To be published in a journal such as *Statistical Science*, it had to run, without stumbling, an unusually long gauntlet manned by some of the world's most eminent statisticians. The results were thus triply unusual: in the extraordinariness of what was found; in the strict scrutiny the findings had to hold up under; and in the unusually small odds (less than 1 in 62,500) that they were due to chance. Other amazing claims about the Bible, Shakespeare, and so forth, have never even remotely approached this kind of rigor, and have therefore never come at all close to publication in a peer-reviewed, hardscience venue. The editor of *Statistical Science*, himself a skeptic, has challenged readers to find a flaw; though many have tried, none has succeeded. All the [basic] questions asked by *Bible Review* readers — and many more sophisticated ones — have therefore already been asked by professional critics and exhaustively answered by the research. Complete and convincing responses to even these initial criticisms can get fairly technical" (*Bible Review*, November 1995).

ELS Bible Code Analysis Using Computer Programs

The primary method used by researchers to find the coded words is called equidistant-letter sequence (ELS). During the last six years I have analyzed the Hebrew Scriptures using this method with several computer programs I obtained in Jerusalem during the 1991 War in the Persian Gulf. These computer programs enable a researcher to discover various Bible Codes for themselves through the examination of particular Hebrew letters that are distributed at equal intervals, (i.e., 5th, 10th, 17th letter, throughout the text). I use the Torah Codes computer program that allows a researcher to personally search for any encoded word within the first five books of the Old Testament. In addition, the Bible Scholar computer program will print out the text of any passage of the Old Testament in Hebrew or English from Genesis to Malachi. This will allow a researcher with a MacIntosh or IBM-compatible computer to verify a particular code discovery reported by any other researcher.

These computer programs are allowing thousands of Bible students to begin searching the biblical text to both verify the code discoveries of others and to conduct independent research on their own. Anyone familiar with computers who is fascinated by this research project can personally participate by acquiring such a computer program. In addition, they will find that a Hebrew-English Interlinear Bible and a Hebrew-English dictionary are helpful in their research.

The Bible Codes: Equidistant-Letter Sequence

The Hebrew word for "equidistant sequence" is *shalav* שלב, which means either "equally spaced rungs on a ladder" or "several objects equally spaced from one another," such as letters in a text.

Let's examine the real issue. Are the Bible Codes valid? The answer is yes. Do these coded words appear in the biblical text in a manner that is beyond the statistical possibility that this is simply a random-chance occurrence? Anyone who spends a few hours studying the scholarly articles in *Statistical Science* journal (Aug. 1994), and *Bible Review* magazine (Nov. 1995), will conclude that the phenomenon is real. Dr. David Kazhdan, head of the mathematics department of Harvard University confirmed, "This is serious research carried out by serious investigators."

I have studied the phenomenon of the Bible codes for the last ten years. In the last seven years, I have used the computer programs to find new codes as well as to verify the discoveries by the scientists at Hebrew University and my friend Yacov Rambsel. I believe that the Bible contains a number of significant proofs that it is inspired by God. The Bible codes are simply one additional proof that is especially meaningful to our generation in that they could not have been discovered or analyzed until the development of high-speed computers in our lifetime.

Why would God have placed hidden codes in the Bible that would not be discovered until the final generation of this millennium? Only God knows. However, I would suggest that God knew that our generation would be filled with skepticism and doubt more than any other generation in history. The Bible has suffered relentless attacks in the last 80 years that have caused many pastors and laymen to abandon their confidence in the authority and inspiration of the Scriptures. If these codes are genuine, and I believe they are, they were placed there by God to speak to this generation, to those who deny the supernatural inspiration of the Scriptures.

No human could have produced these incredibly complex codes. In addition, they glorify and lift up the name of Jesus Christ. Therefore, I conclude that they are powerful evidence of the inspiration and authority of the Bible. Together with the standard apologetic evidences, including the archeological and historical evidence, the advanced scientific and medical statements in the Bible, and the evidence from fulfilled prophecy, the Bible codes will motivate many in our generation to consider the claims of the Bible about Jesus Christ. If we use this material wisely and carefully, in conjunction with these other evidences, we will fulfill God's command to us as revealed in 1 Peter 3:15: "But sanctify the Lord God in your hearts: and be ready always to give an answer to every man that asketh you a reason of the hope that is in you with meekness and fear."

More Bible Code Discoveries

I will share a number of the most fascinating codes that provide evidence of the supernatural origin of the Bible as the Word of God.

Twenty-five Trees Encoded in Genesis 2

In my book *The Signature of God* I pointed out that the Israeli code researchers had discovered the encoded names of 25 trees within the Hebrew text of Genesis 2, which contains the story of God's creation of Adam and Eve as well as the plants and animals in the Garden of Eden. Every one of the 25 trees that are mentioned by name in the rest of the Old Testament appear encoded within this short chapter (635 words in English).

Obviously, this encoding of the Hebrew names of the trees is not prophetic. However, it is an incredibly complicated thing for any human to attempt to write a short story about any topic while, at the same time, encoding 25 names of trees at ELS intervals within the text. My estimate is that it would take the better part of one year for someone to accomplish this in Hebrew or English. In addition, the researchers found that the name of the garden "Eden" was also encoded 16 times in this same chapter.

The Names of Twenty-five Trees Encoded in Genesis 2

Encoded Name	Hebrew
vine	גפן
grape	ענב
chestnut	ערמן
dense forest	עבת
date	תמר
accacia	שטה
bramble	אטד
cedar	ארז
nut	בטן
fig	תאנה
willow	ערבה
pomegranate	רמון
aloe	אהלים
tamarisk	אשל
oak	אלון
poplar	לבנה
cassia	קדה
almond	שקד
mastic	אלה
thorn bush	סנה
hazel	לוז

olive	זית
citron	הדר
fir	גפר
wheat (related to tree of knowledge)	חטה

In my own recent computer code research on this fascinating portion of the Bible, I found that God had also encoded in this same chapter, Genesis 2, the Hebrew names of 17 animals that are named throughout the balance of the Old Testament. Furthermore, the name *Torah* is encoded five times, and the name *Yeshua* is found ten times in this same chapter. These incredibly complex codes appear embedded in a text that flows quite naturally in the Hebrew and English language. In other words, there appears to be nothing artificial or contrived in the choice of words that the author has used to express the story of God's creation of mankind in the Garden of Eden. I believe that it would be virtually impossible for a human or a computer program to produce a short passage such as Genesis 2 and place as many encoded words hidden at ELS intervals within the text.

Among the most fascinating code discoveries made in recent years is the discovery that God has encoded the names of Jesus and His disciples, together with numerous other individuals involved in the life and ministry of our Lord, in two different portions of the Old Testament. In this chapter I deal with the Messiah codes, wherein you will find overwhelming evidence that these codes describe virtually every significant person in the life of Christ in the Old Testament, written many centuries before Jesus of Nazareth was born. This will reveal Bible code discoveries about Jesus Christ that will provide powerful evidence of the supernatural origin of the Scriptures as well as the identification of Jesus as the true Messiah.

The Hebrew Aleph-bet
Sefardi Pronunciation

Numerical Value	Phonetics	Letters Form	Final Form
1	aleph	א	
2	bet, vet	ב	ב
3	gimmel	ג	

4	dalet	ד	
5	hey	ה	
6	vav	ו	
7	zayin	ז	
8	chet	ח	
9	tet	ט	
10	yod	י	
20	kaf	כ	ך
30	lamed	ל	
40	mem	מ	שׁ
50	nun	נ	$
60	samek	שׂ	
70	ayin	[	
80	pey, feh	פ	ף
90	tzadi	c	#
100	qof	ק	
200	resh	ר	
300	shin, sin	f	שׁ
400	tav	ת	

Note: Hebrew is written and read from right to left.

The Messiah Codes Found

The Names of Jesus the Nazarene and His Disciples Encoded in Isaiah 53

The central theme of the prophecies of both the Old Testament and the New Testament is God's inspired revelation of Jesus of Nazareth as the Messiah and the Son of God.

Special Note

While we cannot use the codes to predict future events, once a historical event such as the life, death, or resurrection of Jesus has occurred, we can examine the text of the Bible to see whether or not there are ELS-encoded words that reveal God's foreknowledge of that event. In this manner, only God receives the glory from our examination of these fascinating codes.

After my book *The Signature of God* and Yacov Rambsel's book *YESHUA* were released in 1996, they quickly became international best sellers. However, some scholars challenged the significance of Yacov's discovery of the name *Yeshua* encoded in virtually every major messianic prophecy in the Old Testament, as presented in our books. Some critics claimed that since the name "Jesus" *Yeshua* יֵשׁוּעַ was a relatively short name with only four Hebrew letters, it could be found by random chance almost anywhere in Hebrew literature. However, they could not explain why the name *Yeshua* would appear encoded at small ELS intervals within so many major messianic prophecies throughout the Old Testament. We have not found any other significant names of historical individuals appearing repeatedly in small ELS intervals within these major messianic passages. These particular messianic prophecies where we found the name *Yeshua* encoded are considered significant messianic prophetic passages by most Christian students of the Bible. In addition, many of these same prophecies are identified as messianic by the Jewish sages in their writings.

Do the Yeshua Codes Point to Jesus of Nazareth?

However, the skeptics dismissed Yacov's discovery of the *Yeshua* codes and declared that the encoded word *Yeshua* did not refer to Jesus of Nazareth. While they acknowledge that the word *Yeshua* appears repeatedly within these messianic passages, as our books claimed, they reject our claim that these codes are significant and meaningful. The skeptics claim that you can find *Yeshua* encoded in ELS intervals in almost any Hebrew literature, including the Israeli phone book or Woody Allens's writings translated into the Hebrew language. While you can find random or accidental ELS letters showing the name *Yeshua* and other names in Hebrew literature, the skeptics have not explained why the name *Yeshua* appears repeatedly in virtually every significant messianic prophecy. Our research indicates that no other name of any other historical personality turns up repeatedly in these messianic verses. However, the real question to be determined is this: Do the ELS codes showing the name *Yeshua* in messianic passages actually refer to the historic Jesus of Nazareth, or is this just a coincidence as the skeptics suggest? After thinking about this question for a while, I thought of an experiment that should settle the issue.

In 1996 I asked Yacov to complete an exhaustive analysis of the famous "Suffering Servant" messianic prophecy in Isaiah 52:13 through Isaiah 53 to search for other codes that would identify Jesus of Nazareth. This well-known messianic prophecy predicts many incredible details about Jesus Christ's death on the Cross that were precisely fulfilled seven centuries later. If there was any particular passage in the Old Testament that one might anticipate that God would place ELS codes about Jesus Christ and His disciples, most Christians would assume that Isaiah 53 would be the logical place to look.

Yacov made an astonishing discovery that God has encoded the names of Jesus Christ and virtually everyone that was involved in His tragic crucifixion two thousand years ago. He found the encoded names of Jesus, the Nazarene, Messiah, the three Marys, the two High Priests, Herod, Pilate, and many of Christ's disciples in one prophetic passage — Isaiah 53. Furthermore, these names were encoded in Isaiah's prophecy written in 740 B.C., more than seven centuries before Jesus was born. Can any unbiased observer of this evidence honestly claim that these codes refer to anyone other than Jesus of Nazareth?

The prophet Isaiah wrote a powerful passage known as the "Suffering Servant" prophecy that depicts Israel's Messiah suffering and dying for our sins. This famous passage is found in the messianic chapters of Isaiah 52-53. Isaiah 52 reveals God's promise of blessing. Isaiah 53 depicts the sacrificial price of the blessing. These two chapters in Isaiah should be read together as a complete passage. Beginning with Isaiah 52:13 and continuing through Isaiah 53:12, the prophet Isaiah provides a powerful description of the Messiah as the Lamb of God, as prophesied by His death, His burial, and His resurrection to life.

Throughout these vital chapters, God has hidden many astonishing ELS codes that reveal historic events and names of key individuals. Every one of these events and the role of the named people were fulfilled in the life of Jesus as recorded in the New Testament precisely seven centuries after the prophecy of Isaiah was written. Within these prophetic Scriptures, God encoded the name of His Messiah, Jesus *Yeshua*, together with the names of almost every single person involved in the crucifixion of Jesus the Messiah. In addition, Isaiah 53 reveals the names of both of the chief priests at the time of the crucifixion, as well as the names of Herod, Caesar, and many others involved in the crucifixion of Jesus of Nazareth.

"*Yeshua* is My Name" ישרע שמי

One of the most astonishing discoveries mentioned in my book *The Signature of God* was the fact that the name of Jesus *Yeshua* was found encoded within the Hebrew text of the messianic passages of the Old Testament. Yacov Rambsel wrote an extraordinary book, *Yeshua*, that documented his incredible discovery of the name of *Yeshua* Jesus encoded in the major messianic prophetic passages throughout the Old Testament from Genesis to Malachi. The name "Jesus" in Hebrew is *Yeshua* יְשׁוּעַ. *Yeshua* is spelled with four Hebrew letters (right to left) as follows: yod (י); shin (שׁ); vav (וּ) and ayin (עַ). I was delighted when I verified by computer and through manual examination of my Hebrew-English Interlinear Bible that my friend Yacov Rambsel had found the name *Yeshua* encoded in Isaiah 53:10. This famous prophecy foretold the grief of the suffering Messiah and His atoning sacrifice when He offered himself as the Lamb of God, a perfect sacrifice for our sins by His death on the cross: "Yet it pleased the Lord to bruise him; he hath put him to grief: when thou shalt make his soul an offering for sin, he shall see his seed, he shall prolong his days, and the pleasure of the Lord shall prosper in his hand" (Is. 53:10).

The words *Yeshua Shmi* "*Yeshua* [Jesus] is My Name" שְׁמִי יֵשׁוּעַ are encoded in this messianic verse beginning with the second Hebrew letter yod (י) in the phrase "He shall prolong" *ya'arik* יַאֲרִיךְ and counting every 20th letter left to right. Yacov's discovery of the name *Yeshua* encoded in Isaiah 53 and in dozens of other well-known messianic prophecies has thrilled hundreds of thousands of readers of the books *The Signature of God* and *Yeshua*.

However, I challenged Yacov to continue his research and complete an in-depth investigation of additional codes related to the life of Jesus of Nazareth in Isaiah 53. As a result of hundreds of hours of detailed research, I would like to share Yacov's incredible new discovery. Over 40 names of individuals and places associated with the crucifixion of Jesus of Nazareth are encoded in Isaiah's Suffering Servant passage, which was written seven centuries before the birth of Jesus. I hope that you will be as thrilled with this astonishing discovery as I am. Yacov's complete research on this project is documented in his latest book entitled *His Name Is Jesus*, published recently by our ministry, Frontier Research Publications, Inc. I highly recommend his book to anyone who is fascinated by the phenomenon of the Bible codes. With Yacov's permission, I will share a portion of his research on the incredible codes found in Isaiah 53 together with my own discovery of a similar code in Exodus 30:16.

The Names of Jesus and His Disciples

Within these key chapters of Isaiah, God has secretly encoded the names of the people, the actual locations, and events in the life of Jesus Christ that are recorded in the New Testament. Incredibly, the precise details of the people, the places, and the precise history of Christ's crucifixion were encoded in the Old Testament Scriptures seven centuries before the events took place. God clearly is in charge of human history. The Lord has revealed His supernatural prophetic knowledge of future events to our generation through the extraordinary discovery of the Bible codes. This unprecedented phenomenon is a forceful reminder of the words recorded by Moses thousands of years ago: "The secret things belong unto the Lord our God: but those things which are revealed belong unto us and to our children for ever, that we may do all the words of this law" (Deut. 29:29). Let us examine the details of this remarkable series of Bible codes about Jesus Christ and His crucifixion.

First, we need to review the words of Isaiah's remarkable prophecy about the Messiah who would suffer for the sins of mankind. The full passage from Isaiah 52:13 through chapter 53 reads as follows:

> Behold, My Servant shall deal prudently, He shall be exalted and extolled, and be very high. As many were astonied at Thee; His visage was so marred more than any man, and His form more than the sons of men: So shall He sprinkle many nations; the kings shall shut their mouths at Him: for that which had not been told them shall they see; and that which they had not heard shall they consider" (Isa. 52:13-15).

> Who hath believed our report? and to whom is the arm of the Lord revealed? For he shall grow up before him as a tender plant, and as a root out of a dry ground: he hath no form nor comeliness; and when we shall see him, there is no beauty that we should desire him. He is despised and rejected of men; a man of sorrows, and acquainted with grief: and we hid as it were our faces from him; he was despised, and we esteemed him not. Surely he hath borne our griefs, and carried our sorrows: yet we did esteem him stricken, smitten of God, and afflicted. But he was wounded for our transgressions, he was bruised for our iniquities: the chastisement of our peace was upon him; and with his stripes we are healed. All we like sheep have gone astray; we have turned every one to his own way; and the Lord hath laid on him the iniquity of us all. He was oppressed, and he was afflicted, yet he opened not his mouth: he is brought as a lamb to the slaughter, and as a sheep before her shearers is dumb, so he openeth not his mouth. He was taken from prison

and from judgment: and who shall declare his generation?
for he was cut off out of the land of the living: for the transgression of my people was he stricken. And he made his
grave with the wicked, and with the rich in his death; because he had done no violence, neither was any deceit in his
mouth. Yet it pleased the Lord to bruise him; he hath put
him to grief: when thou shalt make his soul an offering for
sin, he shall see his seed, he shall prolong his days, and the
pleasure of the Lord shall prosper in his hand. He shall see
of the travail of his soul, and shall be satisfied: by his knowledge shall my righteous servant justify many; for he shall
bear their iniquites. Therefore will I divide him a portion
with the great, and he shall divide the spoil with the strong;
because he hath poured out his soul unto death: and he was
numbered with the transgressors; and he bare the sin of many,
and made intercession for the transgressors (Isa. 53:1-12).

13. הנה ישכיל בדי ירום ונשא ונבה מאד.

14. כאשר שממו ע ליך רבים כן-משחת
מאיש מראהו ותארו מבני ארם:

15. כן יזה גוים רבים ע ליו יקפצו מלכים פיהם כי אשר
לא-ספר להם ראו ואשר לא-שמע ו התבוננו.

1. מי האמין לשמcעתנו וזרוcע יהוה ע ל-מי נגלתה.

2. כיונק לפניו וכשרש מאר# צcיה לא-תאר
ריעcל לו ולא הדר ונראהו ולא-מראה ונחמדהו.

3. נבזה וחדל אישים איש מכאבות וידו
חלי וכמסתר פנים ממנו נבזה ולא חשבנהו.

4. אכן חלינו הוא נשא ומכאבינו סבלם
ואנחנו חשבנהו נגוע מכה אלהים ום ענה..

5. והוא מחלל מפשעינו מ דכא מעונתינו
מוסר שלומנו ע ליו ובחברתו נרפא-לנו..

6. כלנו כצcאן תע ינו איש לדרכו
פנינו ויהוה הפגי בו את ע ון כלנו..

7. נגש והוא נ ענה ולא יפתח-פיו כשה לטבח
יובל וכרחל לפני גזזיה נאלמה ולא יפתח פיו..

8. מעצcר וממשפט לקח ואת–דורו מי ישׂוחח
כי נגזר מארץ# חיים מפשׁcע עמי נג ע למו..

9. ויתן את–רשׁע ים קברו ואת–ע שׁיר במתיו
על לא–חממס ע]שׁה ולא מרמה בפיו..

10. ויהוה חפץ# דכאו החלי אם–תשׂים אשׁם נפשׁו
יראה זרע יאריך ימים וחפ#ץ יהוה בירו יצ cלח..

11. מעcמל נפשׁו יראה ישׂבע בדעתו יצcדיק
cצדיק עcבדי ל רבים ועונתם הו יס בל..

12. לכן אחלק–לו ברבים ואת–cעצומים יחלק
שׁלל תחת אשׁר הערה למות נפשׁו ואת–
פשׁעים נמנה והוא חטא–רבים נשׂא ולפשׁעים יפגיע..

Jesus of Nazareth

Christ was called Jesus of Nazareth because He was raised in the city of Nazareth with His family until commencing His public ministry when He was 30 years of age: "And He [Jesus] came and dwelt in a city called Nazareth: that it might be fulfilled which was spoken by the prophets, He shall be called a Nazarene" (Matt. 2:23). Some of the critics of the *Yeshua* codes have challenged our conclusion that the name *Yeshua* found encoded in Isaiah 53 and other passages actually refers to the historical Jesus of Nazareth. However, if the critics examine the encoded words we have discovered in this messianic prophecy, they will find over 40 encoded names identifying virtually everyone who was present at the crucifixion of Jesus Christ. The odds against finding these precise words naming each of these important people, places, and events in the life of Jesus of Nazareth by random chance in a similar sized non-biblical Hebrew text are simply astronomical.

A Challenge to the Critics of the *Yeshua* Code

When my book *The Signature of God* and Yacov Rambsel's book *Yeshua* were published in 1997, hundreds of thousands of readers rejoiced in this discovery about the Bible codes. Many students of the Scriptures were especially fascinated with Yacov's research that revealed the encoded name of Jesus in well-known messianic prophecies. However, a number of Bible code researchers in Israel and North America, as well as orthodox Jewish rabbis, have disputed the significance of this discovery of *Yeshua*'s name. They have pointed out that the name *Yeshua* יעשׁו is a relatively small word with only four letters and two common vowels. Some of these critics have contemptuously challenged the significance of the *Yeshua* codes and declared that one could find the name *Yeshua* יֵשׁוּעַ in virtually any passage in Hebrew literature (from a novel to the Israeli phone book). However, the critics ignore the fact that the name *Yeshua* appears at very small ELS intervals (i.e., every 5th, 9th, or 20th letter, etc.) in dozens of familiar messianic prophecies. We have not found significant names of any other historic personalities encoded at small ELS intervals in dozens of messianic prophecies.

One critic claimed on the Internet that the name of the false messiah Rev. Sung Yung Moon appears frequently in these same messianic prophecies. However, this is false. While the short three-letter Hebrew word for "moon" does appear frequently including some places near some of these messianic passages, the word "moon" does not identify the Rev. Sung Yung Moon of South Korea, who formed the Unification Church. The encoded words do not reveal "Rev. Sung Yung Moon" as the critics falsely imply; it is only the three letter word "moon" that appears frequently. This criticism is without merit.

Yacov's astonishing discovery of over 40 names of individuals and places associated with the crucifixion of Jesus of Nazareth in this Isaiah Suffering Servant messianic passage is unprecedented. I would like to issue a challenge to the critics who reject the *Yeshua* Codes to find any other passage of similar length (15 sentences) in Hebrew literature outside the Bible that contains 40 ELS codes, including the names of Jesus, the Nazarene, Messiah, Passover, Herod, Mary, and the names of Christ's disciples. A partial list of Yacov's code discoveries found in this prophecy from Isaiah 52:13 through Isaiah 53 is provided at the end of this chapter to help the reader realize the astonishing amount of detailed information encoded in this remarkable prophecy. The critics claim that these codes about *Yeshua* can be found by random chance in any Hebrew literature, and, therefore they reject the significance of this discovery.

Here is a challenge from Yacov and myself to the critics. Let them produce any other Hebrew literature of the same length as or shorter than this Isaiah passage that also contains all of the encoded names listed in the summary that follows. If they cannot discover these names encoded in any passage outside the Bible, and we believe it will be impossible, we will have additional evidence that these codes about *Yeshua* the Nazarene, and His disciples, are truly unprecedented.

Jesus and His Disciples Found Encoded in Isaiah 53

NameBegins	Word	Letter	Interval	
Yeshua Shmi	Isa. 53:10	11	4	(-20)
Nazarene	Isa. 53:6	11	3	(47)
Messiah	Isa. 53:11	1	1	(-42)
Shiloh	Isa. 53:12	21	4	(19)
Passover	Isa. 53:10	13	3	(-62)
Galilee	Isa. 53:7	1	2	(-32)
Herod	Isa. 53:6	4	1	(-29)
Caesar	Isa. 53:11	7	4	(-194)
The evil Roman city	Isa. 53:9	13	2	(-7)
Caiaphas - High Priest	Isa. 52:15	7	3	(41)
Annas - High Priest	Isa. 53:3	6	5	(-45)
Mary	Isa. 53:11	1	1	(-23)
Mary	Isa. 53:10	7	3	(6)
Mary	Isa. 53:9	13	3	(44)
The Disciples	Isa. 53:12	2	3	(-55)
Peter	Isa. 53:10	11	5	(-14)
Matthew	Isa. 53:8	12	1	(-295)
John	Isa. 53:10	11	4	(-28)
Andrew	Isa. 53:4	11	1	(-48)
Philip	Isa. 53:5	10	3	(-133)
Thomas	Isa. 53:2	8	1	(35)
James	Isa. 52:2	9	3	(-34)
James	Isa. 52:2	3	4	(-20)
Simon	Isa. 52:14	2	1	(47)
Thaddaeus	Isa. 53:12	9	1	(-50)
Matthias	Isa. 53:5	7	4	(-11)
Let Him Be Crucified	Isa. 53:8	6	2	(15)
His Cross	Isa. 53:6	2	2	(-8)
Pierce	Isa. 52:10	15	3	(-92)
Lamp of the Lord	Isa. 53:5	5	7	(20)
His Signature	Isa. 52:7	8	4	(49)
Bread	Isa. 53:12	2	3	(26)
Wine	Isa. 53:5	11	2	(210)
From Zion	Isa. 52:14	6	1	(45)
Moriah	Isa. 52:7	4	5	(153)
Obed	Isa. 53:7	3	2	(-19)
Jesse	Isa. 52:9	3	1	(-19)
Seed	Isa. 52:15	2	2	(-19)
Water	Isa. 52:7	9	1	(-19)

Levites	Isa. 54:3	3	6	(19)
From the Atonement				
Lamb	Isa. 52:12	12	2	(-19)
Joseph	Isa. 53:2	1	2	(210)

New Code Discoveries Revealing Jesus of Nazareth in the Torah, Exodus 30:16

After the astonishing code discovery by Yacov Rambsel of the 41 names related to the ministry and crucifixion of Jesus of Nazareth in Isaiah 53, I wondered if God had encoded this prophetic information confirming the identity of Jesus as His Messiah in any other place in the Bible. Using my Torah codes computer program, I began a systematic search through the Hebrew Bible, focusing especially on the Torah, to see if this information was encoded there as well. To my amazement, I found the following series of codes naming everyone who was significant in the ministry of Jesus Christ, including the three Marys, the names of every disciple, including the replacement for Judas Iscariot, the disciple Matthias, and much more. The following list of codes will enable anyone with a Hebrew-English Interlinear Bible to confirm my discovery.

Significantly, phenomenal codes were found in Exodus 30:16 that deal with God's commands to Moses regarding the atonement price for Israel's sins.

> And thou shalt take the atonement money of the children of Israel, and shalt appoint it for the service of the tabernacle of the congregation; that it may be a memorial unto the children of Israel before the Lord, to make an atonement for your souls (Exod. 30:16).

Jesus of Nazareth and His Disciples in Exodus 30

Name	Begins	Word	Ltr	Interval	Ends	Word	Ltr
Yeshua	Ex. 30:16	19	1	(12)	Ex. 30:18	1	2
Nazarene	Ex. 30:16	15	3	(8)	Ex. 30:16	20	4
Messiah	Ex. 30:13	12	3	(60)	Ex. 30:18	3	2
Shiloh	Ex. 30:14	7	1	(40)	Ex. 30:16	12	2
Passover	Ex. 30:9	7	4	(-9)	Ex. 30:10	1	3
Galilee	Ex. 29:19	7	3	(-39)	Ex. 29:21	8	3
Mary	Ex. 30:15	7	2	(60)	Ex. 30:18	11	1
Mary	Ex. 30:16	13	1	(61)	Ex. 30:20	8	2
Mary	Ex. 30:17	5	3	(92)	Ex. 30:23	14	2

Peter	Ex. 30:16	2	2	(32)	Ex. 30:17	1	2
Matthew	Ex. 30:20	8	2	(20)	Ex. 30:21	6	2
John	Ex. 29:19	9	1	(14)	Ex. 29:20	12	2
Andrew	Ex. 29:27	15	4	(115)	Ex. 29:36	7	4
Philip	Ex. 29:24	9	4	(50)	Ex. 29:27	4	5
Thomas	Ex. 30:18	14	4	(11)	Ex. 30:19	7	2
James	Ex. 30:7	6	2	(-59)	Ex. 30:10	14	5
Simon	Ex. 29:19	7	3	(-39)	Ex. 29:21	8	3
Nathanael	Ex. 30:4	8	2	(-100)	Ex. 30:12	8	2
Judas	Ex. 29:13	9	2	(24)	Ex. 29:15	2	1
Thaddaeus	Ex. 30:16	2	2	(32)	Ex. 30:17	1	2
Matthias	Ex. 30:20	8	2	(20)	Ex. 30:21	6	2
Let Him Be Crucified	Ex. 30:20	1	1	(8)	Ex. 30:20	8	1

In this passage we find 21 signficant codes naming virtually every significant person in the minstry of Jesus of Nazareth. The fact that these codes were found in the Torah is especially important. The Bible established the principle that the truth was confirmed in the word of two witnesses. Moses wrote, "At the mouth of two witnesses, or at the mouth of three witnesses, shall the matter be established" (Deut. 19:15). Therefore, it is extremely significant that this complex series of codes revealing the identity of Jesus of Nazareth as the Messiah has been located in two separate portions of the Bible by two independent researchers using two different search methods. I believe that these Messiah codes are the most important code discoveries that have been found to date.

About Michael Drosnin

Michael Drosnin's book, *The Bible Code*, published in the late spring of 1997, caused a great sensation in the secular community and the Christian community. Although this book appeared almost one year after my book, *The Signature of God*, and the books of several Israelis about the codes, *The Bible Code* was extensively promoted by its publisher in virtually every major media outlet from CNN, to *TIME* magazine, to "The Oprah Winfrey Show." The result is that the whole world is now talking about the phenomenal *Bible codes*. On balance, I believe this publicity will prove positive in that it will create a curiosity about the phenomenon in the minds of tens of millions of readers who would otherwise never read about the codes in a Christian book like this. Perhaps God will use this secular approach to the Bible codes to draw many people into a closer examination of the Bible with the result that many will be introduced to Jesus Christ. Naturally, I have received many letters and questions on radio talk shows about my response to Drosnin's book *The Bible Code*.

Firstly, I believe the book is fascinating in its reporting of many additional code discoveries by Israeli code researchers. Unfortunately, author Michael Drosnin reveals that he is somewhere between an atheist and an agnostic in his rejection of the existence of God, despite the overwhelming evidence of the supernatural origin of the Bible that is obvious to any unbiased reader of the incredible code discoveries. While he admits that only a supernatural being could have produced the Bible codes three and a half thousand years ago, Drosnin firmly rejects the conclusion that the author of the codes is God.

Can the Bible Codes Allow Us To Correctly Predict the Future?

Many readers have written to ask if we could use the Bible codes to discover the name of the Antichrist or tell of any other future events. The answer is "no." A much greater objection to Drosnin's book is his false claim that the Bible codes can be used to accurately predict future events. One of his major claims is that he personally discovered the coded word "Yitzchak Rabin," the first letter of his name, beginning in Deuteronomy 2:33 and the second letter 4772 letters forward, in the text of Deuteronomy 4:42 where the letter appears in the Hebrew surface text which reads "will be assassinated." In the King James Bible this phrase is translated "kill his neighbour unawares." How could Drosnin "know" that this code actually meant that Rabin would be assassinated in advance of the event? I don't deny that the code is significant. That is why I wrote about the "Rabin" code in my earlier book. However, in advance of the tragic event, it was impossible to know that the encoded word meant that the assassination would definitely occur. The most Drosnin could do was make a guess. He was certainly aware of the growing public threats to Rabin's life that appeared in letters to newspapers and on signs held up at political rallies in the year proceeding the assassination.

In his press release criticizing Drosnin's attempts to prophesy future events, Eli Rips, one of the major Israeli code researchers, pointed out a place in the Bible where you can find the words "Winston Churchill" encoded close to the phrase "will be murdered." If Drosnin had found this code years earlier when Churchill was still alive, would he have flown to Britain to warn Winston that his life was in imminent danger? However, this guess would have proven to be mistaken because

Winston Churchill died peacefully. Therefore, the placement of Winston Churchill's name close to the phrase "will be murdered" was not a code foretelling the future. This illustrates the truth that we cannot and should not attempt to use the Bible Codes to predict future events. Significantly, the Israeli researchers, especially Eli Rips, who Drosnin quotes extensively, have publically repudiated Drosnin's sensational conclusions that the codes can be used to predict future events such as earthquakes or the next world war.

God forbids fortune telling and divination of any kind. The point is that the Bible codes can only be interpreted accurately and confidently after an event has occurred to determine if the Bible contains encoded words that reveal God's supernatural prophetic knowledge thousands of years in advance. When the codes are interpreted after an event, we can verify that the codes are prophetically accurate. These discoveries support the Bible's claim to be supernatural in its origin, and God receives the glory, not the researcher. We need to remember the words of the prophet Isaiah: "For mine own sake, even for mine own sake, will I do it: for how should my name be polluted? and I will not give my glory unto another" (Is. 48:11).

An Invitation and a Challenge

Some Christian writers have rushed to judgment on the Bible codes phenomena and mixed together the mystic concepts of Michael Drosnin with the original research of the Jewish scientists and statisticians and the studies of Christian scholars, firing broadsides against this whole field of investigation. Some have repeated the criticism of the Orthodox Jewish critics, who of course do not want to acknowledge the existence of the Messiah codes, the information about Jesus which we have found in nearly all Old Testament Messianic passages. Unfortunately, some have been content merely to repeat the criticisms of those who reject the inspiration of the Bible or do not believe in Jesus as the Messiah.

I invite you to search the Scriptures for yourself.

Obviously, much work remains to be done. My research team has decided to make our computer program available on the Internet to allow any interested researcher to personally examine the Greek text for Bible codes. This unique computer search program is designed to search for ELS patterns in both the Hebrew text of the Old Testament, as well as the Greek text of the New Testament. This Internet website will include all verified discoveries made by researchers to date, in both the Hebrew and the Greek Scriptures. For the first time, those who are fascinated by the Bible codes will be able to use this software search engine to personally search for Bible codes through the whole Bible, from Genesis to Revelation. After verification, genuine ELS code discoveries made by visitors to this website will be published on a page on our website for examination by other interested readers. By this means, we hope to build up a permanent library of recognized, verified, and significant Bible codes that have been discovered by both Jewish and Christian researchers.

In addition, we hope to interest mathematicians and statisticians to examine several of the Hebrew and Greek Bible codes to determine whether or not they can be statistically proven to be beyond the probability of random chance. By making our search engine, BibleFind Research Center, available to any interested researcher, we hope to expand interest in this phenomenon. The new program developed by our team is now available on the Internet to allow you to search for fascinating ELS patterns and to explore the discoveries of other students of the Bible. The URL address of the BibleFind Research Center Website is http://www.grantjeffrey.com.

Decide for yourself if what we have described here (and there is much more that space forbids we include in this chapter) are merely fantastic improbable coincidences, just random chance combinations, or if they are of divine design.

It is the glory of God to conceal a matter, but the glory of kings is to search out a matter (Prov. 25:2).

2

The Amazing Literary Structure of the Bible

Jim Combs

This entire volume and every chapter in it raises the question, "Is this book of supernatural origin?" Does it truly contain the revelation of God to mankind? Does its undeniable uniqueness result from a fantastically large number of fortuitous coincidences not applicable to any other book ever written, compiled, or edited by the human race? Or is this in truth and verity the Word of God?

During the 19th century a supposedly scientific approach to the study of the Bible resulted in what became known as "Higher Criticism." This skeptical approach to the Bible may have been rooted in some of the heretical movements during the early centuries of the Christian era, but were articulated by Rabbi Aben Ezra in 1168. Put forth by those scholars who questioned the historical accuracy and doctrinal truth of the Scriptures, the movement gradually spread, culminating in the 19th century. It sets forth a "liberal" interpretation of the Bible which is commonly presented, without much in class refutation from the conservative side, in most universities and seminaries in America today. An anti-supernatural mindset or *zeitgeist* in such institutions often results in ridicule of conservative positions.

Merrill F. Unger, prolific author and editor of *Unger's Concise Bible Dictionary*, well depicts the present situation:

> Although the most effective foes (of the Bible) are neglect and indifference, the Bible has undoubtedly endured greatest abuse and misunderstanding from rationalistic

higher criticism and skepticism. The tendency has been to narrow the science of Bible introduction to a consideration of purely critical questions. Too frequently the internal evidence of *order*, *symmetry*, *purpose* and *meaning* of the *books individually* and in their *collective* relationship has been completely set aside by radical hypotheses, based on unwarranted assumptions.

In brief, advocates of this position start with the presumptive premises that the Bible is not supernaturally inspired; Moses did not write the Pentateuch; the stories of the flood, the patriarchs, the exodus, the early history of Israel, and the whole account of God's dealing with Israel are late productions, based on ancient sagas, legends, campfire stories, and religious concepts of the Jewish priesthood brought together and collated a few centuries before the common era. Various authors developed the Torah (Pentateuch), who can be identified by their use of different names for God (J for Jehovah, E for Elohim, P for the compiling priests and D for Deuteronomy, a supposed late redaction and addition likewise performed by Jewish writers after the return and exile in the fifth century B.C.). Some prophetic books could have been published as late as 150 years before the birth of Christ, as in the Book of Daniel, some say.

This writing will demonstrate the amazing internal literary structure and style to be found in the Bible, as further evidence of divine inspiration.

Just Why Is This Book Called "The Bible?"

Merrill F. Unger rightly observes:

The development of the expression "The Bible" to denote the Book of books is evidently providential. As a quasi-technical term it would be difficult to find a more apt designation to capture the vital idea of the essential oneness of the sixty-six books. . . .

It is a matter of common knowledge that our English word "Bible" came originally from the name of the papyrus or *byblus* reed, used extensively in antiquity for making scrolls and books. Quite naturally the Greeks came to term a book *biblos* or small book *biblion*. The second century A.D. Greek Christians began to refer to their Sacred Scriptures under the designation *Ta Biblia*, "the books." When this title was subsequently transferred to the Latin, it was significantly treated as if it were a feminine singular *Biblia*, which reappears in English as *Bible*. Accordingly, this most appropriate name not only emphasizes the unity of the collection of books, but stresses their selection from a larger literature for their present position of pre-eminent authority.

The Unity of the Bible

Notwithstanding the fact that over three dozen writers during a millennium and a half wrote the 66 books of the Bible, they are drawn together by an amazing literary unity.

There is a logical beginning in Genesis and a logical conclusion in Revelation with a progress of doctrine, an increasing unveiling of truth, throughout the entire book. Usually the first mention of an important subject forecasts its general treatment throughout the Bible. As that subject is developed, other aspects that relate to it will appear, which may be called parallel mention, bringing together a whole body of information on that subject. There may be an extended passage discussing this subject as the doctrine is progressively presented.

As an illustration, think of the Holy Spirit. He is first mentioned in Genesis 1:2, set forth as "moving" or "hovering" or "brooding" over the dark waters at the dawn of creation. Thereafter, the Holy Spirit is depicted as moving, stirring, guiding human beings, an external power, and influence involving the guidance of God. He is said to "strive" with man (Gen. 6:3); "fill with wisdom" (Exod. 35:31); "to rest upon" the future Messiah (Isa. 11:2; Isa. 61:1); to bring about the virgin birth of Christ (Matt. 1:18, 20); "to baptize" (Matt. 3:11); to make possible the new birth (John 3:3,5); to indwell (John 20:22; 1 Cor. 6:19-20); to endue with power (Luke 24:49; Acts 1:8; 2:1-30); to "fill" (Eph. 5:18); and to "guide" (John 16:13). Finally in Revelation 22:17 the Spirit is mentioned for the last time: "And the Spirit and the brides say come. . ." an invitation to come to partake "of the water of life freely."

He is first seen moving upon natural water, essential to natural life; He is last seen inviting "whosoever will" to come to the spiritual water, the river of salvation, essential to spiritual life.

This brief paragraph has only skimmed the surface. There are hundreds of references to the Holy Spirit in the Bible, but they all fit together to provide the total truth about this wondrous person of the Trinity.

This same kind of first and last mention with a progress of doctrine and truth throughout the entire Bible can be applied to hundreds of ideas, principles, and teachings.

There is a wondrous structure and design in the teachings of this book, bespeaking both unity and variety; both simplicity and complexity. Truly, one mind is behind each doctrine and truth, though penned by two score different writers. In a half century of daily delving into this book, I have never plumbed all of its depths or learned all there is to know.

The Most Amazing Literary Design of All

Each book of the 66 in the Word of God is itself designed, and all in somewhat similar fashion, using a unique pattern never to be found in any other body of literature. Then specific passages appear most frequently throughout the Bible with this same intriguing literary pattern of comparisons and contrasts. Even verses often can be scrutinized carefully to reveal this same special patterning of ideas.

E. W. Bullinger in his *Companion Bible* speaks of "a symmetrical exhibition of the Word itself, which may be discerned by the humblest reader of the Sacred text" and may be "seen to be one of the most important evidences of Divine Inspiration of the words.

"For these structures constitute a remarkable phenomenon peculiar to Divine Revelation; and are not found in any other form of known literature.

"This distinguishing feature is caused by the *repetition of subjects* which reappear either in alternation (contrasts) or introversion (opposites), or a combination of both in many diverse manners. This repetition is called 'Correspondence.' "

What we have presented here is only a small sampling of the thousands of such structurally designed patterns of truth and narrative, ranging from the entire Bible, which is so symmetrically arranged, to sections of the books and chapters, paragraphs, verses, and sentences.

Each book has its own structure with comparisons, opposites, and similar ideas, thoughts or persons set forth symmetrically in *alternations* or *introversions*. In *The Companion Bible* you can find a comprehensive presentation of this unique quality and literary design. As the expositor notes, "The structure of the whole book is given at the commencement of each book; and the succeeding structures are the expansion of this. Each structure is referred back to the page containing the larger Member (the major thought or idea that introduces a section of the book), of which it is an expansion or development.

"The large Members (major points of truth) forming a telescopic view of the whole book are thus expanded, divided, and subdivided, until chapters and paragraphs, and even verses and sentences, are seen to form part of a wondrous whole, giving a microscopic view of its manifold details, and showing the fact, that while the works of the Lord are great and perfect, *the Word of the Lord* is the greatest of His works, and is 'perfect' also (Ps. 19:7)."

I first discovered this literary phenomenon years ago when Dr. Walter L. Wilson, founder of Calvary Bible College (in 1932), introduced me to *The Companion Bible*, prepared by E.W. Bullinger, (but not using his name in an obvious manner). Providentially in the 1950s I found one in a huge old book store in Long Beach, California, one published by Lamp Press early in this century. Most happily, Kregel Publications has copied and republished this treasure trove of biblical material, which with its 200 pages of fine print appendices has to be the most extensive and unusual study Bible published this century in one volume.

For those who are intrigued by the wonder of the sacred Scriptures, the acquisition of this masterpiece of biblical research and investigation should have high priority. It compiles and contains information and analyses of the Word, including the use of over 180 figures of speech (as catalogued by the Greeks for their language in which the New Testament was written); studious insights on typology; observations on prophecy, biblical linguistics, and chronologies; supplemental and often unique information both on the same page as the biblical text and in the huge supplement on every book in the Bible.

Ponder now this marvelously designed structure which forms a network of logical revelation of truth, symmetrically arranged with parallel or oppositive thoughts in a manner unknown among the ancients and unduplicated by moderns today.

Is this phenomena, which must be searched out but then becomes crystal clear, another fortuitous coincidence, another accidental confluence caused only by random chance?

Did the Holy Spirit in creating this Book incorporate this structure and include besides the insertion of thousands of equidistant letter codes in Hebrew names of persons, places, things, and events, as outlined in chapter 1?

Is there really an astounding pattern in the Bible of numerical or mathematical significance, as in chapter 11, or is this only a causeless and incidental combination of random factors?

Are we seeing something which is not there?

Or, again, is this mysterious one-of-a-kind and most ancient and most modern masterpiece the revelation of Almighty God to the human race, the living Word of God for us and for all peoples of all times?

There is more. Read on. . . .

Samples of Literary Structures

For your examination, here are a few outlines, which are drawn out of the ideas and truths in the text, which demonstrate the symmetrical presentation of corresponding concepts. As you see, these may be similar, nearly identical, opposites, or complements, alternates and inversions (reversals).

There are thousands of these symmetrical patterns in the Bible; a pattern for each book, many passages and pericopes and paragraphs. For all of this material and more, acquire *The Companion Bible*. The numbers and letters in these outlines may differ slightly from those in *The Companion Bible* for simplification.

The Literary Structure of the Account of the Fall of Man (Genesis)

I. Man before the fall, 1:26; 2:4-7

  A. The earth for man and woman, 2:4-7; 21-23

    B. For the ground, no man, 2:5

      C. The ground and vegetable creation, 2:6

        D. The formation of man, 2:7

          E. The Garden, 2:8

            F. The trees, 2:9

              G. The rivers, 2:10-14

          E. The Garden, 2:15

            F. The trees, 2:16-17

    B. For the man, no woman, 2:18

      C. The ground and animal creation, 2:18

        D. The formation of woman, 2:20-23

  A. The man and woman for the earth, 2:24-25

II. The Fall

  A. The serpent (Nachash): procuring man's death,

          in Adam 3:1-5

    B. The Tree of Knowledge — eating of it, 3:6

      C. Effect on both: the man and the woman, 3:7

        D. Human provision: man-made aprons, 3:7

          E. God's inquiry of the man, 3:12

F. God's inquiry of the woman, 3:13

  G. Sentence on serpent, 3:14

  G. Promise of seed of the
    woman, 3:15

F. God's sentence on the
  woman, 3:16

E. God's sentence on the man, 3:17-19

C. Effect on both: the man and the woman, 3:20

  D. Divine provision: God-made coats
  (sacrifice), 3:21

B. The Tree of Life. Expulsion from it, 3:22-24

A. The cherubim: preserving man's life, to be in
Christ, 3:24

III. After the Fall

A. Adam's sons: Cain and Abel, 4:1-16

B. Cain's son: Enoch, 4:17-24

A. Adam's son: Seth, 4:25

B. Seth's son: Enos, 4:26

The Structure of the Book of Job

A. Introduction. Historical background, 1:1-5

B. Satan's assault; Job stripped of everything 1:13-19

  C. The three friends, 2:11-13; Their arrival 2:11-13

    D. Job and his friends, 3:1- 31:40

      E. The ministry of Elihu: the Mediator,
        32:1-37:24

    D. Job and Jehovah, 38:1-42:6

  C. The three friends; the departure, 42:7-9

B. Satan's defeat — Job blessed with double 42:10

A. Conclusion: Historical information, 42:14-17

Notice again that ideas and events can be easily seen to form an "arc of truth," in this case an introversion of oppositive events. Note by this grand introversion, the ministry of Elihu the Mediator is placed in the middle, summing up the ministry of Job's three friends and introducing the ministry of Jehovah. Job may very well be the oldest book in the Bible, since it has no references to the Torah, which was formed in the 15th century B.C. It is unlikely that such a poetic drama on the theme "Why the righteous suffer" would exclude any allusions to the Law and the Prophets.

The Literary Structure of the Book of Isaiah

A. Exhortation: Reprehensory. Prophetic, 1:1-5:20
  B. The voice from the temple The scattering of
      Israel, 6:1-13
    C. The historic account: Events and prophecies
       (King Ahaz), 7:1-12:6
      D. Burdens alternated with Israel's blessings,
       13:1-27:13
      D. Woes, alternating with Jehovah's glories,
       28:1-35:16
    C. The historic account; events and prophecies (King
      Hezekiah)   36:1-39:8
  B. The voice from the wilderness; the gathering of
    Israel 40:1-11
A. Exhortation: promissory, prophetic, 40:12-66:24

Throughout this longest book in the Bible are many more illustrations of this symmetric design of truth with alternations and introversions.

The Structure of the Book of Mark

A. The forerunner, 1:1-8
  B. The baptism: with water, 1:9-11
    C. The temptation: in the wilderness, 1:12-13
      D. The Kingdom, 1:14-20
        E. The King, 1:21-8:20 — PROCLAIMED
        E. The King, 8:31-10:52 — REJECTED
      D. The Kingdom, 11:1-14:25
    C. The agony: in the garden, 14:20-42
  B. The baptism: of suffering death, burial and
    resurrection, 14:23-16:14
A. The successors 16:15-20

All four gospels have a similar structure with scores of sub-points in the same arranged arcs of truth within all chapters and pericope.

The Structure of the Epistle of James
Introversion and Alternation

A. Patience,1:1-4
  B. Prayer, 1:5-8
    C. The low exalted, the rich made low, 1:9-10

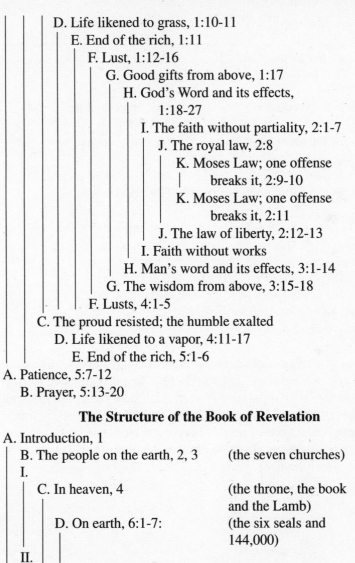

D. Life likened to grass, 1:10-11

E. End of the rich, 1:11

F. Lust, 1:12-16

G. Good gifts from above, 1:17

H. God's Word and its effects, 1:18-27

I. The faith without partiality, 2:1-7

J. The royal law, 2:8

K. Moses Law; one offense breaks it, 2:9-10

K. Moses Law; one offense breaks it, 2:11

J. The law of liberty, 2:12-13

I. Faith without works

H. Man's word and its effects, 3:1-14

G. The wisdom from above, 3:15-18

F. Lusts, 4:1-5

C. The proud resisted; the humble exalted

D. Life likened to a vapor, 4:11-17

E. End of the rich, 5:1-6

A. Patience, 5:7-12

B. Prayer, 5:13-20

The Structure of the Book of Revelation

A. Introduction, 1

B. The people on the earth, 2, 3   (the seven churches)

I.

C. In heaven, 4   (the throne, the book and the Lamb)

D. On earth, 6:1-7:   (the six seals and 144,000)

II.

C. In heaven, 7:9-8:6   (the great multitude and the seventh seal)

D. On earth, 8:7-11:14   (the six trumpets and the mighty angel)

III.

C. In heaven, 11-15-19   (the seventh trumpet)

D. On earth, 11:19   (the earthquake, thunderings, hail)

IV.

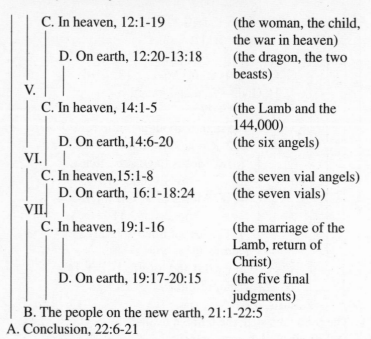

C. In heaven, 12:1-19	(the woman, the child, the war in heaven)
D. On earth, 12:20-13:18	(the dragon, the two beasts)
V.	
C. In heaven, 14:1-5	(the Lamb and the 144,000)
D. On earth,14:6-20	(the six angels)
VI.	
C. In heaven,15:1-8	(the seven vial angels)
D. On earth, 16:1-18:24	(the seven vials)
VII.	
C. In heaven, 19:1-16	(the marriage of the Lamb, return of Christ)
D. On earth, 19:17-20:15	(the five final judgments)

B. The people on the new earth, 21:1-22:5

A. Conclusion, 22:6-21

Notice in this outline/chart that there are corresponding introduction and conclusion; corresponding peoples, first on earth, and then on the new earth; scene shifts from heaven to earth, seven of each making seven alternating pairs. Revelation contains the word "seven" 54 times; there are at least 21 sets of sevens, some more obvious than others; and the whole book can be observed through the alternating heaven/earth sequence which number seven.

3

The Astounding Fulfilled Prophecies of the Bible

Edward E. Hindson

Jesus Christ is the source of Bible prophecy and the subject of the prophetic Scriptures. The most dramatic prophecies in all the Bible point to the coming Messiah — the Savior who would both suffer and reign. These ancient prophecies were so precisely fulfilled in Jesus' life and ministry that there can be no serious doubt that they point to only one person who has ever lived — Jesus of Nazareth.

After His resurrection, Jesus told His disciples, "that all things must be fulfilled, which were written in the law of Moses, and in the prophets, and in the psalms concerning me" (Luke 24:44). Christ himself then taught the disciples which Old Testament Scriptures predicted His life and ministry. Luke 24:45 says, "Then opened he their understanding, that they might understand the scriptures."

The New Testament writers were instructed by the Lord himself regarding biblical prophecies and their fulfillment. The threefold designation: law, prophets, and psalms refers to the three major divisions of the Hebrew Bible. Jesus was specifically stating that the entire Old Testament (law, prophets, psalms) was predicting His life, ministry, death, and resurrection. Therefore, the preaching of the early Christian disciples was filled with references to Old Testament prophecies and their fulfillment in the person of Jesus Christ.

Examples of prediction and fulfillment used in the Book of Acts include:

1:20   Judas' replacement (Ps. 69:25)
2:16-21   Outpouring of the Holy Spirit (Joel 2:28-32)

2:25-27	Jesus' resurrection (Ps. 16:8-11)
2:29-30	Christ would sit on David's throne (Ps. 132:11)
2:34-36	Christ exalted as Lord (Ps. 110:1)
3:22-23	Jesus is the Prophet Moses predicted (Deut. 18:15-19)
4:11	Jesus is the cornerstone of salvation (Ps. 118)
4:25-26	Rejection of Christ by Jews and Gentiles (Ps. 2)
8:27-35	Jesus is the Lamb of God (Isa. 53)
13:46-49	Christ is a Light to the Gentiles (Isa. 49:6)

During His earthly ministry, Jesus was recognized as a "prophet" of God (Matt. 21:11; Luke 7:16) and a "teacher" from God (John 3:2). Jesus even referred to himself as a "prophet" (Matt. 13:57; Luke 13:33). The early preaching of the apostles also emphasized the prophetic nature of Christ's ministry (Acts 3:24-26, 7:37). Matthew's gospel alone makes 65 references to Old Testament Scriptures, emphasizing their fulfillment in Christ.

Dr. Hobart Freeman has observed that, "messianic prophecy, in a real sense, may be regarded as the New Testament in the Old. Messianic prophecy is that which predicts the fulfillment of redemption and the establishment of the Kingdom of God through the Messiah." Freeman points out that the Hebrew term "messiah" comes from the word *mashiach*, meaning to "anoint" for consecration and service. In Psalm 2, the Messiah ("Anointed One") is pictured as both the King of Israel and God's Son. This passage confirms the association of Jesus in the New Testament with the Messiah in the Old Testament. The fact that Jesus is called the Christ (Greek, *christos*, "anointed") is the New Testament equivalent of the Hebrew *meshiach*. He is Jesus the Christ — the Messiah.

The Prophet and the Prophetic Ministry

The prophetical histories are followed in the Hebrew canon by the prophetical books of prediction. The two form a unit in the middle portion of the threefold canon, under the common term "prophets." They are distinguished as the "former prophets" and "latter prophets." Dr. Leon Wood states: "The manner of speaking by the prophets may be best characterized as preaching." Their messages also included symbolic actions (2 Kings 13:17-19), object lessons (Jer. 1:11-14), and written sermons (Jer. 36:4).

The Hebrew prophets were men of God who preached God's Word and also predicted the future. Their preaching had its roots in history since they preached to the people of their own generation. But their messages were also focused on the future and revealed events that were yet to come. In this regard the message of the prophets is supernatural, not natural. H.L. Ellison writes: "It is derived neither from observation nor intellectual thought, but from admission to the council chamber of God, from knowing God and speaking with Him."

The revelation of God to the prophet is a process by which God "reveals His secrets" to the prophet (Amos 3:7). The term "reveal" (Hebrew, *galah*) means to "uncover," as in "uncovering the ear" (1 Sam. 9:15). Thus, when God "uncovers" the prophet's ear, He reveals what has been previously hidden (2 Sam. 7:27), so that the prophet "perceives" what the Lord has said (Jer. 23:18).

It is obvious, therefore, that the "Spirit of God" is necessary for prophetic inspiration (Isa. 30:1). Thus, it was by the Spirit that the Word of the Lord was communicated to the prophet and by the Spirit that the Word was mediated to the people. This communion with God was indispensable to the prophetic consciousness as a medium of revelation, so that under the guidance of the Holy Spirit prophecy can sometimes be quite startling in the individuality and definiteness of its prediction of even remote events. So we see the full picture of prophecy as both a forthtelling of God's messages and a foretelling of God's actions. Through this means God continued to energize the prophet to speak for Him. Isaiah was such a man, addressing himself to his own times as he brought God's direction to the kings of Judah and also a man seeing far into the future of God's plans for His people.

The Messiah in Prophecy

The high aspirations of the Old Testament writers and their ascriptions of God-like characteristics to a coming Prince, the Messiah, the son of David, compel the reader to see one who is more than a mere man. He was called both the son of David and the son of God. Dr. Girdlestone has pointed out that there is no definite statement that all these references in the Old Testament are to be fulfilled in one person, but such is the natural conclusion at which the recipients of the Old Testament arrived. Yet with the development of this messianic expectation came the frustrating close of the Old Testament canon, yet awaiting the reality of these hopes embodied in that one man.

The New Testament based its entire apologetic on the fact that Jesus was the Messiah of the Old Testament and that these were definite predictions which were conclusively fulfilled in this life. Jesus himself was always aware of the "limitations" prophecy made on Him, since it "must be fulfilled." He subjected himself completely to the course that they had, under God's direction, prescribed to Him and considered the details of His life and death as something that must take place because it is written in the Word of God. At the same time, He saw himself as the culminating point to which the whole of prophecy pointed.

The purpose of messianic prophecy was to make the Messiah known after He had fulfilled the event foretold. It served as a preparatory device to signal His arrival. How that "fulfillment" is recognized has been the source of ominous discussion. A. Alexander, author of *The Earlier Prophecies of Isaiah*, warns that although a double-sense of fulfillment is not impossible, it is unreasonable to assume it when any other explanation is admissible. He maintains that it is unlikely that both a common, natural event and a supernatural one would be couched in the same passage.

We must be careful not to look for a fulfillment where none is intended or needed to complete the thought of the passage. Prophetic fulfillment is the consummation of a given prediction in history. The New Testament provides the best guideline to determine whether or not a certain event is fulfilled. It tells us where the prophets spoke of Christ. The indication we are given by the New Testament is that the Old Testament messianic references are a whole that refer totally to one person — Jesus of Nazareth.

Predictive Nature of Messianic Prophecy

It is difficult to consider the concept of messianic prophecy without assuming some type of "prediction" involved. In this discussion the word predict has been used in the ordinary sense of "foretell." The use of the Greek prefix "pro" indicates both "for" and "before." The prophet tells "for" God, and he tells "before" events will happen. This usage is certified by the parallel synonymy given to "foretell" and "foresee" in the New Testament. Peter, in Acts 2:30, speaks of David as a "prophet" because of his "foreseeing" (*proidon*) the resurrection of Christ. It would be ridiculous to insist that this be translated "forthseeing." We can see, then, that the prophets were not always restricted to a "local" or immediate fulfillment.

Dr. Robert Culver gives two essential characteristics of predictive prophecy: it must predict the future as only God could know it and bring it to pass, and it must contain a degree of obscurity. This quality of obscurity necessitates a direct fulfillment. It is only when the prophecy has become history that one may reflect upon it to realize that it has been fulfilled. Seen dimly at first, the intent of the prophecy becomes clear with its fulfillment. The New Testament recognizes the value of predictive prophecy and its fulfillment in using it as apologetical evidence to prove the supernaturalness and credibility of Christianity.

Notice the following list of messianic predictions and fulfillments in the Book of Isaiah alone:

1. Virgin-born Immanuel (Isa. 7:14-16; Matt. 1:23)
2. Great light in Galilee (Isa. 9:1-2; Luke 1:79)
3. One who conquers death (Isa. 25:8; 1 Cor. 15:54)
4. One who resurrects the dead (Isa. 26:19; Eph. 5:14)
5. One Whose forerunner prepares the way (Isa. 40:3; John 1:23)
6. Servant of the Lord (Isa. 42:1-4; Matt. 12:18)
7. The light to the Gentiles (Isa. 49:6; Luke 2:32)
8. Suffering servant who atones for our sins (Isa. 52:13-53:12; Rom. 10:16; 1 Pet. 2:24-25; Rev. 5:6)
9. Preacher of the gospel (Isa. 61:1-2; Luke 4:18)
10. Coming King (Isa. 66:15-18; 2 Thess. 1:7-8)

Central Message of the Old

Willis Beecher pointed out in the Stone Lectures at Princeton Theological Seminary, that the messianic prophecies are not merely a "scarlet thread" that runs indiscernibly throughout the Old Testament, but that they are "everywhere the principal thing, that which underlies all the history, all the poetry, all the prophetic preaching, all the national worship, all the sayings of wisdom." The whole Old Testament is the record of God's promises and the New Testament is the record of their fulfillment.

After healing the lame man, the Apostle Peter addressed the crowd who had witnessed the miracle and told them he had done this in the name and power of Jesus Christ "which God before had showed by the mouth of all his prophets" (Acts 3:18). Then, Peter called upon them to, "Repent . . . and be converted, that your sins may be blotted out" (Acts 3:19).

Dr. Edward J. Young observes: "According to Peter, the prophets spoke of the sufferings of Christ. These prophecies have been fulfilled, he reasons, and since they have been fulfilled, men should repent of their sins. Here in Israel was a phenomenon which could find no equal or parallel anywhere else in all the world. Here were men, raised up of God. . . . Here God did intervene in human history in a peculiar way."

When the early Christians began to preach, they declared that Jesus of Nazareth was the promised Messiah of the Old Testament prophecies. Dr. Culver observes: "The New Testament record reports that they never failed to support these remarkable claims with proof that the claims were true." They insisted that Jesus was the Christ on the basis of three essential arguments:

1. His resurrection
2. Their eyewitness account
3. Fulfillment of Old Testament prophecy

Within weeks of the resurrection, the early Christians were proclaiming the events in Jesus' life as fulfillments of specific prophecies. In the first Christian sermon, Peter announced: "This is that which was spoken by the prophet Joel. . . . David speaketh concerning him . . . [that] he would raise up Christ to sit on his throne; he seeing this before spake of the resurrection of Christ" (Acts 2:16-30).

This is the new Testament proof of the truthfulness of Christianity. The same approach is taken repeatedly in the New Testament. In following this line of proof the apostles were doing what had been done by God's prophets for centuries. They were pointing to the fulfillment of prophecy as the ultimate proof of the truthfulness of God's Word. In so doing, they were urging their listeners to believe the whole message of the gospel of Jesus Christ.

Old Testament Prophecies Fulfilled in the Life of Christ

The Old Testament is filled with prophecies about the human race, the nation of Israel, and future events in general. But the most important prophecies are those that point to the coming of Christ. These are not merely isolated "proof texts." The whole of the Old Testament points the way to a coming future Messiah.

The laws of the Old Testament established the divine principle of righteousness. The history of Israel shows how God was preparing His people for the coming of the Messiah and how desperately they needed a Savior. The institutions of Old Testament religion (temple, priests, sacrifices) pointed to a coming One who would fulfill the reality of these symbols. The Psalms were not only expressions of worship and praise, but prophecies of the coming Messiah. The prophetical books were collections of the sermons of the prophets and their predictions of the coming Messiah and the Messianic Age. Many of these predictions were recognized by the Jews even before the time of Jesus as being Messianic in nature. Here are ten examples:

Genesis 3:15: "And I [God] will put enmity between thee and the woman, and between thy seed and her seed; it shall bruise thy head, and thou shalt bruise his heel." This is a prophecy that some member of the human race — not an angel nor spirit — would be the agent by whom deliverance would come from the awful defeat Satan inflicted on us when he successfully enticed Adam and Eve to disobey the Lord. Jesus our Lord was that man. The two nativity stories (early chapters of Matthew and Luke), the four biographies (four Gospels), and the emphatic truth of Jesus' human nature are the report of how this aspect of the prophecy was fulfilled.

Genesis 12:1-3: "Now the Lord had said unto Abram . . . I will make of thee a great nation . . . thou shalt be a blessing . . . and in thee shall all families of the earth be blessed." At this point the Bible moves from a report of universal events and focuses on Jewish history. These verses are the first of many prophecies that the redemption of the human race would be through a people known as Hebrews, Israelites, or Jews. The New Testament distinctly points out how our Savior was truly Jewish and publicly known as such (John 4:9). The superscription on the cross even proclaimed Him as King of the Jews (Matt. 27:37).

Genesis 49:10: "The scepter [symbol of an ancient ruler's authority] shall not depart from Judah, nor a lawgiver from between his feet, until Shiloh come; and unto him shall the gathering of the people be." The translation can be greatly improved, as commentaries declare, but in all feasible translations this verse turns out to be a prediction that the man of Israel who would ultimately be their Messiah (i.e., "anointed" king) would be of the tribe of Judah among the 12 tribes. This led to the divine choice of David from one of the families of Judah and to the birth of Jesus into his royal line (Matt. 1:1,6-20; Luke 3:31). The doctrinal portions of the New Testament emphasize the importance of our Lord's relation to the house of David (Rom. 1:3; 2 Tim. 2:8). Christ as revelator to John identified himself as "the offspring of David" (Rev. 22:16).

"And when thy days be fulfilled . . . I will set up thy seed after thee . . . and I will establish the throne of his kingdom forever . . . my mercy shall not depart away from him . . . and thine house and thy kingdom shall be established for ever before thee: thy throne shall be established for ever" (2 Sam. 7:12-16).

When Jesus was about to be born, the angel Gabriel announced the fulfillment of this prophecy of David's dynasty in Him. "Thou . . . shalt call his name JESUS. He shall be great, and shall be called the Son of the Highest: and the Lord God shall give unto him the throne of his father David: and he shall reign over the house of Jacob for ever; and of his kingdom there shall be no end" (Luke 1:31-33). Jesus is to have no successor. The risen Christ alone is the proper living claimant to David's throne.

Psalm 16:8-11: "Thou wilt not leave my soul in hell; neither wilt thou suffer thine Holy One to see corruption." This is a prophecy for the resurrection of Jesus. It is so important that Peter used it in his first Christian sermon as the main scriptural proof of the truth of Christianity. It was so convincing that three thousand Jewish converts were made. The passage is quoted in full together with Peter's inspired interpretation of it in Acts 2:25-36. There are many other prophecies of Christ in the Psalms. In Psalm 2:7, He is the Son of God. In Psalm 22, He is the crucified Savior whose hands and feet are pierced (v. 16), whose clothes are parted (v. 18) and who cries: "My God, My God, why hast thou forsaken me" (v. 1). In Psalm 24, He is the King of glory who triumphantly enters Jerusalem. In Psalm 110, He is a priest after the order of Melchizedek. In Psalm 117:22, He is the stone the builders rejected.

Isaiah 7:14 and Isaiah 9:6-7: "Therefore the Lord himself shall give you a sign; Behold, a virgin shall conceive, and bear a son, and shall call his name Immanuel [i.e., God with us]. . . . For unto us a child is born, unto us a son is given: and the government shall be upon his shoulder: and his name shall be called Wonderful, Counselor, The mighty God, The everlasting Father, The Prince of Peace. Of the increase of his government and peace there shall be no end, upon the throne of David, and upon his kingdom, to order it, and to establish it with judgment and with justice from henceforth even for ever. The zeal of the Lord of hosts will perform this."

Here we have the opening and closing words of a single prophetic oracle. The majority of scholars, both liberal and conservative, agree on this. Too often expositors have sought to explain one portion of the prophecy without the other. In context, it is most difficult to prove that the virgin's Son has any connection at all with Mary's Babe unless one continues on to the final verses of the prophecy just quoted. Then we understand that a virgin would bear a human baby whose character would be divine. Matthew 1:21-23 quotes the fulfillment of this prophecy in the virgin birth of Jesus.

Micah 5:2: "But thou, Bethlehem Ephratah, though thou be little among the thousands of Judah, yet out of thee shall he come forth unto me that is to be ruler in Israel; whose goings forth have been from of old, from everlasting."

It was very unlikely that a woman living in Nazareth would give birth to a child in Bethlehem, several days' traveling time to the south. Yet according to this seven-centuries-old prophecy, that was where Mary's child should be born. It took an imperial decree from Rome that every citizen in the empire should be properly enrolled in his ancestral locality to bring it about, but so it was (Luke 2:1-6). In accordance with Micah's prediction, as Matthew 2:1-6 informs us, Jewish scholars of the day expected Messiah to be born in Bethlehem.

Isaiah 42:1-7: Too lengthy to quote, this reads like a poetic history of the earthly life of Jesus, or perhaps it is a summary statement of His holy character. An obedient slave of God, who would please God perfectly, who would live a quiet life of gentle ministry to others in constant loyalty to justice and truth, was to teach the whole world God's truth, establishing even Gentiles in a divine covenant of salvation. The morally blind and spiritually darkened were to be the special beneficiaries of His tender love and care. The whole gospel story together with the expansion of the Church — not to exclude the second advent of Christ— is the record of the remarkable fulfillment of this prediction.

Isaiah 52:13-53:12: There is not one word in these 15 verses that is not directly predictive of Christ. They apply to Him and to no others. Those who have sought to convince unbelievers throughout the Christian centuries have relied on these verses more than all other texts of prophecy put together.

The story of the background of Jesus' rejection by His own people is laid out with bold strokes in Isaiah 53:1: "Who has believed what we have heard? And to whom has the arm of the Lord been revealed?" This means Jesus was to be rejected by people who "heard" enough so that they should have believed Him, especially since His deeds of divine power authenticated Him as sent of God. When the generation who had the words of the prophetic Scriptures before them knew of the message of the angels at His birth, heard the sermons of John the Baptist, the 70, the 12 apostles, Jesus, and who had even heard the demons addressing Him as the Christ — when these people rejected the Savior, they were fulfilling their own Scriptures. Paul, on a certain occasion, commented on this: "They that dwell at Jerusalem, and their rulers, because they knew him not, nor yet the voices of the prophets which are read every Sabbath day, they have fulfilled them in condemning him" (Acts 13:27).

"He is despised and rejected of men; a man of sorrows, and acquainted with grief: and we hid as it were our faces from him; he was despised, and we esteemed him not" (Isa. 53:3). "He was oppressed, and he was afflicted, yet he opened not his mouth: he is brought as a lamb to the slaughter, and as a sheep before her shearers is dumb, so he openeth not his mouth" (Isa. 53:7). This is exceedingly minute in its specifications. The servant would be harassed and mistreated by His persecutors, but He would submit to them without protest. At His trials, Jesus upstaged His accusers with such moral integrity that He outshined them all — the Sadducees, Pilate, Herod, soldiers, and guards. Even the thieves were amazed at Him (Luke 23:39-42). And the disciples never forgot it (1 Pet. 2:21-25).

Isaiah 53:9: "And he made his grave with the wicked, and with the rich in his death." This incredible prophecy points to Christ's crucifixion between two thieves as a common criminal. Yet, after His death, He was buried in a rich man's tomb. The bodies of executed criminals were generally thrown to the dogs in the city dump, but Matthew 27:57-60 tells us of the amazing fulfillment of this prophecy by the interaction of the rich man, Joseph of Arimathea.

There are about three hundred distinct prophecies of Christ in the Old Testament. They are like pieces of a puzzle. Each presents a distinct element of the Savior's life and ministry, but the whole picture they portray can only be seen after their fulfillment. They remained obscure until Jesus came and put them all in clear relation to one another. The chances of all these prophecies being fulfilled in the life of one man is one chance in 84 followed by 131 zeroes.

These prophecies of Christ are overwhelming evidence of the divine origin of Scripture, the Messiahship of Jesus and the truth of Christianity. When viewed as a whole, the collective impact of these prophecies and their fulfillment in the gospels cannot be easily dismissed. Dr. Culver states: "Any one of these alone might be explained away to the satisfaction of antagonistic people, but taken together their force is devastating to unbelief."

John's Gospel ends by reminding us that the "world could not contain" the books that should be written about Jesus Christ (John 21:25). But John himself, Jesus' personal disciple, states: "But these are written that ye might believe that Jesus is the Christ, the Son of God; and that believing ye might have life through his name" (John 20:31).

While biblical prophecies and their literal fulfillment may fascinate our curiosity and challenge our minds, they are ultimately intended to bring us to a personal point of decision and faith as well. If the Bible predicted these things would happen and they actually did happen, then we must take Jesus' claims seriously. If He alone fulfilled these prophecies, then He alone is the Savior — the Son of God. If not, He is a liar or a lunatic. But if so, then He is Lord of lords and King of kings. And if He is — He deserves our faith, our lives, and our complete devotion.

Hallelujah! What a Savior!

4

The Miraculous Preservation of the Jews, People of the Bible

David Allen Lewis

Far more than eschatological considerations are at stake in the return of the Jewish people to the land of Israel. God's integrity is at stake. His sovereignty has been challenged. How will He respond?

The return of the Jews to the land of Israel is holy in the eyes of the Lord, a thing not to be taken lightly. It is holy because without its accomplishment the name of God is slandered. His ability to perform His Word is brought into question. "Can a woman forget her sucking child, that she should not have compassion on the son of her womb? yea, they may forget, yet will I not forget thee. Behold, I have graven thee upon the palms of my hands" (Isa. 49:15-16).

The Christian might even ask, "If God cannot keep His promise to Abraham, how can we be sure He will keep His new covenant promise to the believer?"

The re-establishment of the nation of Israel has a very high priority on God's agenda of dealings with the nations. Strong nations rise and fall because of their reaction to this premise. It is best for nations not to attempt blocking the progress of the revealed plan of God regarding Israel.

God made a covenant with Abraham (Gen. 12,15) in which He promised Abraham that his chosen seed would inhabit the land forever. It is a unilateral, unconditional covenant. Its fulfillment depends only upon the integrity of Jehovah God.

How Is God's Name Profaned?

When Israel is not in the land the name of God is profaned in the eyes of the Gentiles. God seems unable to keep His Word. His sovereignty is threatened. His reputation is impugned. His holiness is brought into question. We must consider the holiness of the Almighty in relation to His promise. It has nothing to do with the holiness of Israel or the lack thereof. This concept is based on God's own evaluation of His situation, not upon our philosophical ponderings.

The promise is stated in many ways, always without equivocation or wavering. The heathen may rage. Israel may fail, but God will never fail to keep his promise. He will honor the promise. The descendants of Jacob —Israel will inhabit the land.

> Thus saith the Lord, which giveth the sun for a light by day, and the ordinances of the moon and of the stars for a light by night, which divideth the sea when the waves thereof roar; The Lord of hosts is his name: If those ordinances depart from before me, saith the Lord, then the seed of Israel also shall cease from being a nation before me for ever. Thus saith the Lord; If heaven above can be measured, and the foundations of the earth searched out beneath, I will also cast off all the seed of Israel for all that they have done, saith the Lord (Jer. 31:35-37).

The Macrocosm — the Broad View

Let us take a look at the promise in the macrocosm. We peer through the wide-angle lens to get the broad picture. God spoke through the prophets. Their testimony is uniform, that wherever the Jews are driven in dispersion among the nations, God will bring them back to the land. This is to preserve His own integrity and personal testimony to the world. The word of the Almighty is not to be viewed casually. This is serious.

> Behold, the days come, saith the Lord, that the plowman shall overtake the reaper, and the treader of grapes him that soweth seed; and the mountains shall drop sweet wine, and all the hills shall melt. And I will bring again the captivity of my people of Israel, and they shall build the waste cities, and inhabit them; and they shall plant vineyards, and

drink the wine thereof; they shall also make gardens, and eat the fruit of them. And I will plant them upon their land, and they shall no more be pulled up out of their land which I have given them, saith the Lord thy God (Amos 9:13-15).

Dr. Arnold Olson, president emeritus of the Evangelical Free Church of America quoted Kuyper, Lightfoot, and Tolstoy, commenting on the fate of the Jews:

> Dr. Abraham Kuyper, while Prime Minister of the Netherlands, visited Palestine in 1905. Noting that Baron de Rothschild had assisted a few Jewish settlers from Russia who were going to redeem the land, he commented, "The Jews have come on a vain mission. Here, in this land where the voice of God has been once heard, man's voice will never be heard again. Only God can check the blight of the inrushing desert. Only a miracle can save the Holy Land!"[1]
>
> Bishop Lightfoot wrote decades ago, "You may deny if you will every successful miracle in the Bible, but this miracle — the preservation of Israel — is more convincing than all."
>
> It was [historian] Leo Tolstoy, who wrote long before there was any thought that the dream of a homeland for the Jew would come true, "The Jew is the emblem of eternity. He whom neither slaughter nor torture could destroy; he whom neither fire nor sword, nor inquisition was able to wipe off the face of the earth; he who was the first to produce the oracles of God; he who has been for so long a time the guardian of prophecy, and who has transmitted it to the rest of the world — his nation cannot be destroyed. The Jew is as everlasting as eternity itself."[2]

> Fear not: for I am with thee: I will bring thy seed from the east, and gather thee from the west; I will say to the north, Give up; and to the south, Keep not back: bring my sons from far, and my daughters from the ends of the earth. . . . I, even I, am the Lord; and beside me there is no saviour. . . . Remember ye not the former things, neither consider the things of old. Behold, I will do a new thing; now it shall spring forth; shall ye not know it? I will even make a way in the wilderness, and rivers in the desert (Isa. 43:5-19).

The Microcosm – Focusing on the Details

Let us now look at some of the details of God's promise to Israel. We will see the promise in microcosm. In addition to general promises to preserve the Jews as a people and to bring them back to the land, the Bible is filled with hundreds of details relating to the grand plan. Now we look through the lens of the microscope to examine the minutiae of the prophetic word.

Resurrection of a Language

The Hebrew language has many unique aspects, but foremost in our attention is its restoration. Never in the history of mankind has a dead language been restored to common usage. Hebrew language was "dead," used only by scholars and rabbis, much like dead Latin is used by the Roman Church. Isaiah predicted a loss of the Hebrew language and Zephaniah saw it restored.

"Woe to Ariel [Jerusalem]. . . . Yet I will distress Ariel, and there shall be heaviness and sorrow. . . . And thou shalt be brought down, and shalt speak out of the ground, and thy speech shall be low out of the dust, and thy voice shall be, as of one that hath a familiar spirit, out of the ground, and thy speech shall whisper out of the dust" (Isa. 29:1-4). Indeed the Hebrew language was reduced to a mere whisper.

"For then will I turn to the people a pure language, that they may all call upon the name of the Lord, to serve him with one consent" (Zeph. 3:9).

In the latter part of the 19th century Eliezar Ben Yehuda undertook a revival of the Hebrew language. This amazing story is told and carefully documented by Robert Saint John in his book *Tongue of the Prophets.*[3]

> Thus saith the Lord of hosts, the God of Israel; As yet they shall use this speech in the land of Judah and in the cities thereof, when I shall bring again their captivity; The Lord bless thee, O habitation of justice, and mountain of holiness (Jer. 31:23).

Return of the Ethiopians

Thousands of Ethiopian Jews have been rescued by airlifts Operation Moses and Operation Solomon. "From beyond the rivers of Ethiopia my suppliants, even the daughter of my dispersed, shall bring mine offering" (Zeph. 3:10).

To see the Jewish people coming from all nations and diverse cultures, yet preserving and treasuring their Jewish identity brings to mind the words of Isaiah: "And I will preserve thee, and give thee for a covenant of the people, to establish the earth, to cause to inherit the desolate heritages" (Isa. 49:8).

Like the Russian Jews, the Ethiopians were persecuted and in virtual bondage and ostracism. They were called "falashas," a derogatory term meaning "stranger." They lived in primitive poverty, most of their rights stripped from them. Isaiah continues: "That thou mayest say to the prisoners, Go forth; to them that are in darkness, Shew yourselves. They shall feed in the ways, and their pastures shall be in all high places" (Isa. 49:9).

Tom Sawicki says:

> The dramatic rescue of Ethiopian Jewry in 1991's Operation Solomon is to be immortalized in *The Guinness Book of World Records.*
>
> The 1995 edition includes an entry headed "1,088 people in one aircraft. The record," notes a detailed, four paragraph item, "was set on May 24, 1991, when 1,086 Ethiopian Jews were evacuated to Israel in one plane. . . . Two babies were born en route, bringing the total who landed in Israel to 1,088."
>
> In all, over 14,000 Jews were flown to Israel in 36 hours. *Guinness* notes: "On the record-breaking flight, some of the rows of ten seats had as many as 18 people jammed into them."
>
> The entry was suggested to Guinness by Arnon Mantver, director general of the Jewish Agency's immigration and absorption department.[4]

Where Did I Get These Children?

With Jews having different appearances, even black Ethiopians coming to Israel, the need for land and housing is apparent. One can hear the questions birthed by Isaiah being asked today:

> For thy waste and thy desolate places, and the land of thy destruction, shall even now be too narrow by reason of the inhabitants, and they that swallowed thee up shall be far away:
>
> The children which thou shalt have, after thou hast lost the other, shall say again in thine ears, *The place is too*

strait for me: give place to me that I may dwell.

Then shalt thou say in thine heart, *Who hath begotten me these, seeing I have lost my children, and am desolate, a captive, and removing to and fro? and who hath brought up these? Behold, I was left alone; these, where had they been?* (Isa. 49:19-21; emphasis added).

Out of the North — the Russian Jews

In the 1970s and throughout the 1980s, many of us in the Church began to agitate for the release of the Soviet Jews. Of course, Jewish people were at the forefront of this struggle. Were we trying to fulfill prophecy? Of course we were. "Faith without works is dead" (James 2:20). God frequently uses human instrumentality to bring His purposes to pass. How shortsighted are those who merely examine the purposes of God and never find the blessing of being in partnership with God. "For we are laborers together with God: ye are God's husbandry, ye are God's building. . . . Every man's work shall be made manifest: for the day shall declare it" (1 Cor. 3:9-13).

My own awareness of the plight of the Russian Jews was aroused when, in 1970, I read the book *Three Million More?* by Gunther Lawrence. After detailing the climate of growing anti-Semitism in the Soviet Union, Gunther challenged us with the words, "Yet, protest appears to be the only present effective course of action."

Leonid Vladimirov, the Russian-Jewish author of *The Russians*, wrote: "I am absolutely positive that the effectiveness of the world protest movement about the plight of Soviet Jewry is great. It is actually now the only restricting force affecting the Kremlin's wild anti-Semites. So far as the future of the Soviet Jews is concerned, I know only one thing that will never occur, and this is assimilation."[5]

Protest we did but, along with other awakened Christians, added intercessory prayer, the Mordecai Outcry, the Esther Fast, the Jehoshaphat Victory March, letter writing to refusniks,[6] and pleading the cause of the Russian Jews to our own political and church leaders.

The vision was clear. Jeremiah even declared a day when the return of the northern Jews would be so great that it would overshadow the Exodus out of Egypt under the leadership of Moses. That was hard to imagine!

Therefore, behold, the days come, saith the Lord, that they shall no more say, The Lord liveth, which brought up the children of Israel out of the land of Egypt; But, The

Lord liveth, which brought up and which led the seed of the house of Israel out of the north country, and from all countries whither I had driven them; and they shall dwell in their own land (Jer. 23:7-8).

An interesting chapter on the prophetic aspect of the return of the Russian Jews to Israel can be read in my book *Prophecy 2000*.[7]

Roses — Fruit — Trees

As we continue our journey in the microcosm, we note that one of Israel's major exports is roses. And guess what country imports tulips from Israel in certain seasons of the year? Right, the Netherlands. "The wilderness and the solitary place shall be glad for them; and the desert shall rejoice, and blossom as the rose" (Isa. 35:1). It has come to pass. Today you can travel through Israel and view vast fields that were formerly wilderness and desert areas, now growing the finest of roses.

Formerly barren hillsides and swampy lowlands now flourish with fruit-bearing trees. "He shall cause them that come of Jacob to take root: Israel shall blossom and bud, and fill the face of the world with fruit" (Isa. 27:6).

A large percentage of Israel's vegetable and fruit harvest is now exported to foreign markets. One can stand at the Allenby bridge, spanning the Jordan river, and see truckloads of unmarked fruit going into the Hashemite Kingdom of Jordan for distribution throughout Arab nations.

Behold the trees on the hills of *eretz* (Hebrew for "the land of") Israel! During the last century, scores of books written by travelers in Turkish-ruled Palestine described the desolation of the land, the erosion of topsoil, and the scarcity of trees. A British author, George Sandys, counted the trees and numbered them at less than one thousand in the whole land. Surely this reflects the fulfillment of Isaiah's warning to ancient Israel: "And the rest of the trees of his forest shall be few, that a child may write them" (Isa. 10:19). For a description of the harsh wilderness Israel had become, read the chapters on Palestine in Mark Twain's *Innocents Abroad*.[8]

But the prophet also foresaw a day when the land would be green once again, and the hills would be covered with forests as in happier times. "I will plant in the wilderness the cedar, the shittah tree, and the myrtle, and the oil tree; I will set in the desert the fir tree, and the pine, and the box tree together: That they may see, and know, and consider, and understand together, that the hand of the Lord hath done this, and the Holy One of Israel hath created it" (Isa. 41:19-20).

Through the efforts of the Jewish National Fund, millions of trees have been planted in Israel. Today there are over 350 million fully grown, mature trees on the hills of the Holy Land. About half of them are forest and half fruit trees. We have planted over five thousand trees in our Christian's United For Israel Forest at the Golani Junction, high above the Sea of Galilee.

My good friend Ya'akov Kirschen, cartoonist of *Dry Bones* fame has produced a cartoon-style book *Trees . . . The Green Testament.* Kirschen has tried to impress me with the notion that he is a totally secular man. I told a *Wall Street Journal* reporter who interviewed me about the book, "Kirschen has a wellspring of faith deep inside him, waiting to gush forth and find expression. He has written a very biblical book."

Trees starts with the Bible account of Adam, Eve, and the Garden of Eden; carries one through centuries of prophecy and fulfillment; and ends with a quotation of Amos 9:9-15. Kirschen is also deeply distressed with the advances of neo-paganism, the New Age movement, and considers his book to be a partial answer to them. I highly recommend that every Christian and Jewish person obtain and read this delightful, entertaining and informative 192-page book![9]

The Walls of Jerusalem

Greater Jerusalem contains an ancient walled city, but is not a walled city. After the times of Jesus, for century after long century, Jerusalem was a small town. Sometimes its population waned and reports show a population inside the walls of as low as four thousand wretched inhabitants. The number of its dwellers never swelled to over twenty thousand. Living conditions were miserable in the old walled city. There was nothing outside the walls. Robber bands roamed the area and no one wanted to be outside the walls at night. You will read the full account of this amazing prophecy in chapter 6 of my book, *Signs of His Coming.*[10] When a British Jew, Sir Moses Montefiore, began building houses in the mid-1800s outside the walls, no one would live in them until Sir Moses hired a private security police force to protect the people. How unlikely seemed the words of Zechariah spoken two thousand five hundred years earlier: "And said unto him, Run, speak to this young man, saying, Jerusalem shall be inhabited as towns without walls for the multitude of men and cattle therein" (Zech. 2:4).

The Holiness of God at Stake

Now we return our attention to the holiness of God in the light of the Aliyah (the return of the Jews to the land). See how God loves

Israel: "He found him in a desert land, and in the waste howling wilderness; he led him about, he instructed him, he kept him as the apple of his eye" (Deut. 32:10).

"For thus saith the Lord of hosts; After the glory hath he sent me unto the nations which spoiled you: for he that toucheth you toucheth the apple of his eye" (Zech. 2:8).

Israel is chosen by God. "O ye seed of Israel his servant, ye children of Jacob, his chosen ones" (1 Chron. 16:13). "For the Lord hath chosen Jacob unto himself, and Israel for his peculiar treasure" (Ps. 135:4). "But thou, Israel, art my servant, Jacob whom I have chosen, the seed of Abraham my friend" (Isa. 41:8). "Yet now hear, O Jacob my servant; and Israel, whom I have chosen" (Isa. 44:1).

Has Israel Failed? — The Diaspora

Has Israel failed God? Yes, as has all mankind, but in Israel's case it is more serious. Other nations may pass out of existence, but not Israel. Should the veracity of God be brought to question? "God forbid: yea, let God be true, but every man a liar" (Rom. 3:4).

"I scattered them among the heathen, and they were dispersed through the countries: according to their way and according to their doings I judged them" (Ezek. 36:19). But that is not the end for Israel. Because of His promise to Abraham, God must act to preserve Israel. No nation in the world has absolute promise of survival except Israel.

God's Character

The regathering is a thing holy to God. We may confidently speak of the holiness of the Aliyah. The very sovereignty of God and His character are at stake. His honesty is at stake. It is for His own sake that God brings Israel back to the land and preserves her through all troubles and trials.

"And when they entered unto the heathen, whither they went, they profaned my holy name, when they said to them, These are the people of the Lord, and are gone forth out of his land" (Ezek. 36:20).

God's Name Slandered

How was the holy name of God profaned? By Israel not being in the land. In Ezekiel 36:20 we see how the heathen scorn God.

The heathen could mock God for His seeming inability to keep His word. "But I had pity for mine holy name, which the house of Israel had profaned among the heathen, whither they went. Therefore say unto the house of Israel, Thus saith the Lord God; I do not this for your sakes, O house of Israel, but for mine holy name's sake, which ye have profaned among the heathen, whither ye went. And I will sanctify my great name, which was profaned among the heathen, which ye have profaned in the midst of them; and the heathen shall know that I am the Lord, saith the Lord God, when I shall be sanctified in you before their eyes" (Ezek. 36:21-23).

There is no implication that the Jews were any more profane than any other people. The name of God was profaned by Israel being scattered. How will God rectify this unacceptable situation? By regathering and restoring the Jews to their land. "For I will take you from among the heathen, and gather you out of all countries, and will bring you into your own land" (Ezek. 36:24). This land covenant relationship has nothing to do with individual redemption, but rather with national destiny.

The Day of Israel's Sanctification

As you read further in this chapter of Ezekiel you will find that following the national, physical restoration of Israel, in a future Messianic age God will cleanse Israel from all sin (Ezek. 36:25-27). They will continue to "dwell in the land that I gave to your fathers; and ye shall be my people, and I will be your God (Ezek. 36:28, also vs. 33-35).

"Then the heathen that are left round about you shall know that I the Lord build the ruined places, and plant that that was desolate: I the Lord have spoken it, and I will do it" (Ezek. 36:36).

For the Sake of God

The concept of the holiness of God's action in regathering Israel is expressed in the often repeated phrase, "For mine own sake." "I, even I, am he that blotteth out thy transgressions for mine own sake, and will not remember thy sins" (Isa. 43:25). "For my name's sake will I defer mine anger, and for my praise will I refrain for thee, that I cut thee not off" (Isa. 48:9). "For mine own sake, even for mine own sake, will I do it: for how should my name be polluted? and I will not give my glory unto another" (Isa. 48:11).

For His own sake! God loves Israel. He loves all mankind, but it is for His own sake that He must preserve the Jewish people and establish them in their own land. Listen to the voice of Jeremiah as he prays, "Do not abhor us, for thy name's sake, do not disgrace the throne of thy glory: remember, break not thy covenant with us" (Jer. 14:21). God assures, "I wrought for my name's sake, that it should not be polluted before the heathen, in whose sight I brought them out" (Ezek. 20:14). Daniel understood the importance of the return: "O Lord, hear; O Lord, forgive; O Lord, hearken and do; defer not, for thine own sake, O my

God: for thy city and thy people are called by thy name" (Dan. 9:19).

"For Zion's sake will I not hold my peace, and for Jerusalem's sake I will not rest, until the righteousness thereof go forth as brightness, and the salvation thereof as a lamp that burneth. . . . And they shall call them, The holy people, The redeemed of the Lord: and thou shalt be called, Sought out, A city not forsaken" (Isa. 62:1-12). These are prophecies yet to be fulfilled! What a glorious future for Israel.

Bible! Bible! Bible!

A professor in an evangelical seminary said, "Last night my dog got hold of our Bible and ate the Book of Revelation. I wish that dogs would eat the Book of Revelation right out of every Bible!" Another "intellectual" said to me, "Bible, Bible, Bible! Is that all you can talk about?" Yes, that is about right. Nothing gives more reliable information than the Bible. The Bible is never adjusted to fit circumstances of the moment. All phenomena must line up with the Word of God.

Please do not grow weary with reading Scripture. The solid foundation of all our research and teaching is the Bible itself. Surveys show that when an author includes chapter and verse references in an article, without printing out the text, readers seldom find the time to look up the passages. It's a busy world. That is why I am having the following references printed out in full for your convenience. Here are more glorious promises for you to examine. Please read them all. The emphasis is on God's determination to preserve His own reputation and holiness in the eyes of all mankind. Note how many passages include the words, "for mine own sake." *This is not an isolated concept.*

Multiple Witness

"For I will defend this city, to save it, for mine own sake, and for my servant David's sake" (2 Kings 19:34; Isa. 37:35).

"And I will add unto thy days fifteen years; and I will deliver thee and this city out of the hand of the king of Assyria; and I will defend this city for mine own sake, and for my servant David's sake" (2 Kings 20:6).

"For Jacob my servant's sake, and Israel mine elect, I have even called thee by thy name: I have surnamed thee, though thou hast not known me" (Isa. 45:4).

"But I wrought for my name's sake, that it should not be polluted before the heathen, among whom they were, in whose sight I made myself known unto them, in bringing them forth out of the land of Egypt" (Ezek. 20:9).

"But I wrought for my name's sake, that it should not be polluted before the heathen, in whose sight I brought them out" (Ezek. 20:14).

"Nevertheless I withdrew mine hand, and wrought for my name's sake, that it should not be polluted in the sight of the heathen, in whose sight I brought them forth" (Ezek. 20:22).

"And ye shall know that I am the Lord, when I have wrought with you for my name's sake, not according to your wicked ways, nor according to your corrupt doings, O ye house of Israel, saith the Lord God" (Ezek. 20:44).

"In those days the house of Judah shall walk with the house of Israel, and they shall come together out of the land of the north to the land that I have given for an inheritance unto your fathers" (Jer. 3:18).

"And I will gather the remnant of my flock out of all countries whither I have driven them, and will bring them again to their folds; and they shall be fruitful and increase. . . . Behold, the days come, saith the Lord, that I will raise unto David a righteous Branch, and a King shall reign and prosper, and shall execute judgment and justice in the earth. In his days Judah shall be saved, and Israel shall dwell safely: and this is his name whereby he shall be called, THE LORD OUR RIGHTEOUSNESS. . . . But, The Lord liveth, which brought up and which led the seed of the house of Israel out of the north country, and from all countries whither I had driven them; and they shall dwell in their own land. . . . The anger of the Lord shall not return, until he have executed, and till he have performed the thoughts of his heart: in the latter days ye shall consider it perfectly. . . . Am I a God at hand, saith the Lord, and not a God afar off?" (Jer. 23:3-23).

"Thus saith the Lord, The people which were left of the sword found grace in the wilderness; even Israel, when I went to cause him to rest. The Lord hath appeared of old unto me, saying, Yea, I have loved thee with an everlasting love: therefore with lovingkindness have I drawn thee. Again I will build thee, and thou shalt be built, O virgin of Israel: thou shalt again be adorned with thy tabrets, and shalt go forth in the dances of them that make merry. Thou shalt yet plant vines upon the mountains of Samaria: the planters shall plant, and shall eat them as common things. For there shall be a day, that the watchmen upon the mount Ephraim shall cry, Arise ye, and let us go up to Zion unto the Lord our God. For thus saith the Lord; Sing with gladness for Jacob, and shout among the chief of the nations: publish ye, praise ye, and say, O Lord, save thy people, the remnant of Israel. Behold, I will bring them from the north country, and gather them from the coasts of the earth, and with them the blind and the lame, the woman with child and her that travaileth with child together: a great company shall return thither. They shall come with weeping, and with supplications will I lead them: I will cause them to walk by the rivers of waters in a straight way, wherein they shall not stumble: for I am a father to Israel, and Ephraim is my firstborn.

"Hear the word of the Lord, O ye nations, and declare it in the isles afar off, and say, He that scattered Israel will gather him, and keep him, as a shepherd doth his flock. For the Lord hath redeemed Jacob, and ransomed him from the hand of him that was stronger than he. Therefore they shall come and sing in the height of Zion, and shall flow together to the goodness of the Lord, for wheat, and for wine, and for oil, and for the young of the flock and of the herd: and their soul shall be as a watered garden; and they shall not sorrow any more at all. Then shall the virgin rejoice in the dance, both young men and old together: for I will turn their mourning into joy, and will comfort them, and make them rejoice from their sorrow" (Jer. 31:2-13).

"O Lord, according to all thy righteousness, I beseech thee, let thine anger and thy fury be turned away from thy city Jerusalem, thy holy mountain: because for our sins, and for the iniquities of our fathers, Jerusalem and thy people are become a reproach to all that are about us" (Dan. 9:16).

"Seventy weeks are determined upon thy people and upon thy holy city, to finish the transgression, and to make an end of sins, and to make reconciliation for iniquity, and to bring in everlasting righteousness, and to seal up the vision and prophecy, and to anoint the most Holy" (Dan. 9:24).

"For behold the stone that I have laid before Joshua; upon one stone shall be seven eyes: behold, I will engrave the graving thereof, saith the Lord of hosts, and *I will remove the iniquity of that land in one day*" (Zech. 3:9).

"Thus saith the Lord; I am returned unto Zion, and will dwell in the midst of Jerusalem: and Jerusalem shall be called a city of truth; and the mountain of the Lord of hosts the holy mountain" (Zech. 8:3).

Contemporary Jewish Commentary

Allow me to share a Jewish commentary with you. Here are some wonderful insights. Rabbi Shlomo Riskin, dean of Ohr Tora Institutions and chief Rabbi of Efrat, Israel, has some distinct thoughts on the sanctity of the return of the land itself. He begins an essay titled, *The Land and Its Sanctity* with a quotation from Genesis 15:18-21. This is the passage that describes the ideal and greater boundaries of Israel, perhaps to be realized in the Messianic Age.

Riskin writes, "With all the pandemonium and ferment created by the Palestinian 'peace' agreement which cedes all of Judea, Samaria and Gaza to the Palestinians, it is important to define what is included under the rubric of the 'sanctity of the land' (Kedusha ha'Aretz), and what the ramifications of such an inclusion are."

After citing various opinions he notes that, "Hatam Sofer (in response to Yoreh Deah) . . . [Maimonides] believes that there is an eternal, spiritual sanctity to every inch of the Land within biblical borders, based upon the blessing, responsibility and inherent owning implied in the passage, 'It is the land which the Lord God seeks eternally, the eyes of the Lord your God being directed towards it from the beginning of the year until the end of the year' " (Deut. 11:12).

Referring to the teachings of Maimonides, Rabbi Riskin writes, "The difference is because the lands of ten nations constitute Greater Israel, encompassing boundaries which will be realized only during the Messianic period."

Still referring to Maimonides for authority Riskin says, "Towering above the entire world is Jerusalem, which Maimonides sees as embodying eternal sanctity. He insists that in addition to the ethereal and spiritual aspects of God there is also a spiritual dimension to His being in Jerusalem; the divine presence, the Shekhina, is most manifest. The city of Jerusalem may be conquered, the Holy Temple destroyed, and the people of Israel exiled and dispersed, but in the words of Maimonides: 'Hashekhina lo betela,' the indwelling of God will never be nullified (Laws of Beit Habehira, chapter 6, Law 16)."

After the Jews returned from Babylon in 536 B.C., by the decree of Cyrus the Persian who conquered Babylon and made it part of his vast Persian Empire, the Jewish leader Ezra "unveils a new kind of Jew, one who cried out, 'If I forget thee Jerusalem, may my right hand forget its cunning!' Such continual and historic connection creates a dimension of sanctity beyond the level granted to Joshua's military conquests.

"In the language of Maimonides, Joshua's conquest was 'kibush' and Ezra's was 'hazuka.' Hazuka presumes ownership, not simply because one conquers land, but because one lives on it and works it. . . . Fascinatingly enough, returning confers upon the land a higher degree of sanctity than did the original conquest. From the Maimonides concept a magnificent idea emerges: holiness does not exist in a vacuum. The sanctity of the Land of Israel (except for Jerusalem whose holiness is spiritually Shekhina-oriented) depends not only on geography but upon demography. The common denominator is that Israel must be sanctified by Jews living on and working the land.

"Thus the Jewish settlements of Judea, Samaria, Gaza, and the Golan represent a most profound sanctity. According to most authorities, they are areas to which Jews returned during the Second Commonwealth. Moreover, they were liberated in our own times by the Israeli Defense Force as the result of a war fought in self-defense (Kibush Rubim, Maimonides, Laws of Heave Offerings, chapter 1) and further sanctified by Jewish settlement. They are an integral part of our Jewish homeland, from which it is inconceivable that any Jew — in this post-Holocaust age — can ever be 'transferred.'" The underlying reason for this position is that the Land of Israel has awaited the People of Israel to sanctify it from the time of Abraham's Covenant until today.

Israel's Future Temple

Riskin ventures to comment on the future temple of Israel: "The image of the return is twofold, the Shekhina — the loving, faithful mother — constantly awaits the return of her children to the ancestral home, the place wherein the holy temple will eventually be restored as a house of prayer for all nations.

"At the same time, the Land awaits the return of its nation in order for it to be sanctified. God is waiting for us, and the Land is waiting for us. Hopefully, neither will be disappointed."[11]

There is much to be noted in Rabbi Riskin's essay concerning the holiness of the land in the eyes of God. No other land than Israel and no other city than Jerusalem has been chosen and designated as the *Holy Land* and the *Holy City*. Examine the following proof texts carefully.

Holy Land, Holy City

Canadian church leader A. C. Forrest, severe critic of Zionism, calls Israel *The Unholy Land.* For 15 years, Forrest was the editor of an influential paper, The *United Church Observer,* and wrote a syndicated column for the *Toronto Star* and many other newspapers. He spares no effort to damn Israel and defend the Palestinians. His criticism of Jan Willem Van der Hoeven is sharp: "It is one of the strangest mixtures of premillennialist anti-Communist nonsense I have ever heard. . . . His comments are a travesty of the Gospel.[12]

I have known Jan Willem for years. He is outspoken. Many disagree with some of his interpretation of end-time prophecy. He has many accusers. But I will tell you this — Van der Hoeven loves Jesus with all his heart. He loves the Jewish and the Arab peoples. He is a defender of Zion. He has not compromised the major tenets of orthodox, evangelical Christian theology. The difference between A.C. Forrest and Van Der Hoeven is that Forrest denies that Israel is the Holy Land. Jan Willem Van Der Hoeven believes that it is. Who is right? Let's allow the Bible to be the referee in this dispute.

Israel is the Holy Land: "And the Lord shall inherit Judah his portion in the holy land, and shall choose Jerusalem again" (Zech. 2:12).

The New Testament refers to Jerusalem as the Holy City: "Then the devil taketh him up into the holy city, and setteth him on a pinnacle of the temple" (Matt. 4:5). "And came out of the graves after his resurrection, and went into the holy city, and appeared unto many" (Matt. 27:53). "But the court which is without the temple leave out, and measure it not; for it is given unto the Gentiles: and the holy city shall they tread under foot forty and two months" (Rev. 11:2).

Isaiah speaks of the holy mount in Jerusalem: "And it shall come to pass in that day, that the great trumpet shall be blown, and they shall come which were ready to perish in the land of Assyria, and the outcasts in the land of Egypt, and shall worship the Lord in the holy mount at Jerusalem" (Isa. 27:13).

Not Paris, London, Rome, Brussels, New York, nor any city but Jerusalem is called Holy by the Almighty. "To dwell in Jerusalem the holy city, and nine parts to dwell in other cities" (Neh. 11:1). "All the Levites in the holy city were two hundred fourscore and four" (Neh. 11:18). "There is a river, the streams whereof shall make glad the city of God, the holy place of the tabernacles of the most High" (Ps. 46:4).

Zion, Jerusalem, the Holy City! "Awake, awake; put on thy strength, O Zion; put on thy beautiful garments, O Jerusalem, the holy city: for henceforth there shall no more come into thee the uncircumcised and the unclean" (Isa. 52:1). "And they shall call thee, The city of the Lord, The Zion of the Holy One of Israel" (Isa. 60:14). "For I will defend this city to save it for mine own sake, and for my servant David's sake" (Isa. 37:35).

Chosen People

The chosen people: "For thou art an holy people unto the Lord thy God: the Lord thy God hath chosen thee to be a special people unto himself, above all people that are upon the face of the earth" (Deut. 7:6).

Chosen — peculiar: "For thou art an holy people unto the Lord thy God, and the Lord hath chosen thee to be a peculiar people unto himself, above all the nations that are upon the earth" (Deut. 14:2). "Thou art an holy people unto the Lord thy God" (Deut. 14:21).

"And to make thee high above all nations which he hath made, in praise, and in name, and in honour; and that thou mayest be an holy people unto the Lord thy God, as he hath spoken" (Deut. 26:19). "And they shall call them, The holy people, The redeemed of the Lord: and thou shalt be called, Sought out, A city not forsaken" (Isa. 62:12).

Yes, Israel will survive! God has too much at stake to let His great enterprise fail now.

Chapter 4 Footnotes

1 Howard Fast, *The Jews — Story of a People* (New York: Dial Press, 1968), p. 366.

2 Arnold Olson, *Inside Jerusalem — City of Destiny* (Glendale, CA: Gospel Light/ Regal Books, 1968), p. 28-29.

3 Robert St. John, *Tongue of the Prophets* (N. Hollywood, CA: Wilshire Book Company, 1952).

4 Tom Sawicki, *The Jerusalem Report*, February 24, 1994, p. 6.

5 Gunther Lawrence, *Three Million More?* (Garden City, NY: Doubleday, 1970).

6 Refusniks were Jewish people in the former USSR who applied for an exit visa and were refused. They became targets of persecution because of this. Many were imprisoned in psycho prisons and slave labor camps. By writing carefully crafted letters to these people, Christians participated in building a wall of protection about many of them. The KGB monitored all foreign mail. We wrote letters as if we knew the recipient well. This caused the KGB to think that this Jewish person had friends in the West. Being conscious of world opinion, they were less likely to persecute the letter receiver. Some of those who used our letter writing kits have actually been to Israel and have met some of those they aided in this fashion. Some have sought us out. I remember a family bringing a lovely cake to a lady in our tour group whom they credited with their deliverance from Russia. It was a night of celebration!

7 David Allen Lewis, *Prophecy 2000* (Green Forest, AR: New Leaf Press, 1993), 6th edition, p. 404-420. This chapter gives more biblical prophetic reference to the return of the Russian Jews.

8 Samuel Langhorn Clemens (Mark Twain), *Innocents Abroad*, Vol. 2 (New York: Harper and Brothers, 1869/1897/1899), p. 212-388. Note: Many editions of Twain's works have been produced, some in one volume. Simply look for the chapters on Palestine. In my set they are listed as chapters 18 - 24. Chapter 18 ends the Syrian travels and begins in northern Israel at Mt. Hermon and Caesarea Philipi (Banias).

9 Ya'akov Kirschen, *Trees* (New York: Vital Media Enterprises, 1993).

10 David Allen Lewis, *Signs of His Coming* (Green Forest, AR: New Leaf Press, 1997).

11 Shlomo Riskin, *The Jewish Press*, October 23, 1993. Isaiah 49:3: "And said unto me, Thou [art] my servant, O Israel, in whom I will be glorified."

12 A.C. Forrest, *Unholy Land* (Toronto: McClelland and Stewart, Ltd., 1971), p. 141.

Russian Jews arriving to live in the land of Israel.

5

The Fascinating Archaeological Evidence for the Bible

Clifford A. Wilson

We do not use the statement, "Archaeology proves the Bible." In fact, such a claim would be putting archaeology above the Bible. What happens when seemingly assured results of archaeology are shown to be wrong after all? Archaeology is the support, not the main foundation. Very often archaeology does endorse particular Bible happenings. Some would say that in this way it "proves the Bible," but such a statement should be taken with reservation.

Archaeologists are scholars, usually academics, who may have little interest in the Bible, except as an occasional source book. There is, however, a substantial number of scholarly archaeologists who are committed Christians whose research has been of inestimable value in supporting the Scripture.

There are many thousands of facts in the Bible which are not capable of verification because the evidence has long since been lost. However, it is remarkable that where confirmation is possible and has come to light, *the Bible stands investigation in ways that are unique in all literature*. Its superiority to attack, its capacity to withstand criticism, its amazing facility to be proved right after all, are all staggering by any standards of scholarship. Seemingly assured results "disproving" the Bible have a habit of backfiring. Over and over again the Bible has been vindicated. That is true from Genesis to Revelation. The patriarchal background from Genesis has been endorsed. The writings of

Moses do date to his times, and the record of the conquest of Canaan under Joshua has many indications of eyewitness recording.

David's psalms were clearly products of his time (1000 B.C.), and the records about Solomon should no longer be written off as "legendary." He was a literary giant, a commercial magnate, and a powerful ruler who gave Israel their "golden age."

The Assyrian period (900-620 B.C.) has given dramatic confirmation to Bible records, with palace after palace excavated over the last 150 years, and constantly adds to our understanding of the background to Old Testament kings, prophets, peoples, and incidents.

The exile in Babylon (6th century B.C.) is endorsed at various points, and the Cyrus Decree (2 Chron. 36:22-23) makes it clear that captured peoples could indeed return to their own lands and worship according to their own beliefs. Ezra-Nehemiah are accurate reflections of that post-exilic period (5th century B.C.).

Likewise, the New Testament documents have been consistently demonstrated as factual, eyewitness records. Kings, rulers, and officials are named unerringly; titles are used casually but with remarkable accuracy; geographic boundaries are highlighted; and customs are correctly touched on. It is indeed true that "truth has sprung out of the earth" (Ps. 85:11).

Archaeology as It Relates to the Biblical Record

Our understanding of essential biblical doctrine has never changed because of archaeological findings. It should be acknowledged, however, that at times it has been necessary to look again to see just what the Bible is actually saying. There have been times when new light has been thrown on words used in Scripture in both Old and New Testaments. We have seen that the titles of officials of Israel's neighbors are now better understood from the records in clay, on papyrus, and on stone.

An Ancient Book . . .

The Old Testament is an ancient book, not a modern record, and its style is that of the East and not the West. At times it must be interpreted in the symbolic and figurative style of the Jew of ancient times and not according to the "scientific precision" of our modern materialistic age.

The Bible uses "the language of phenomena" — so it will refer to the sun rising. In actual fact, scientifically speaking, it is the earth that "rises." However, though the Bible is not a textbook of science, it is yet wonderfully true that where the Bible touches on science, it is astonishingly accurate. A good example is in that remarkable comment from nearly 2,000 years ago when the apostle Peter referred to the elements melting with fervent heat, as a nuclear explosion (2 Pet. 3:10). It has long ago been pointed out that this contains a hidden indication of Peter's own presentation of then unknown scientific principles. No doubt, he himself did not fully understand the implications of what he wrote!

The more this new science of archaeology touches the records of the Bible, the more we are convinced it is a unique record. At many points it is greatly superior to other writings left by neighboring peoples. Again, we have not said "archaeology proves the Bible," and we do not suggest it. To do so would be quite wrong, even though such a statement is often made by those introducing a lecturer on biblical archaeology. *The Bible itself is the absolute: archaeology is not.* Archaeologists at times acknowledge that new findings have led to the revision of their views that were previously regarded as established. "Proof" of the Bible is not dependent on archaeology or any other scientific evidence. The Bible has the capacity to defend itself and to give its positive message to those who seek God through its pages.

Nevertheless, archaeology has done a great deal to restore confidence in the Bible as the revealed Word of God. It has thrown a great deal of light on previously obscure passages, and has helped us to understand customs, culture, and background in many ways that seemed most unlikely to our fathers in a previous generation. Archaeology is highly relevant for the understanding of the Bible today. There are hundreds of thousands of artifacts related to Bible history available for study.

The Value of Archaeology for the Bible Student

Archaeology has done a great deal to cause many scholars to take the Bible much more seriously. It has touched the history and culture of Israel and her neighbors at many points and has often surprised researchers by the implicit accuracy of its statements.

We shall summarize by briefly considering five important ways in which archaeology has been of great value for Bible students. If it can be shown (as it can) that the Bible writers lived and gave their message against the backgrounds claimed for them, it becomes clear that their amazing prophetic messages are also genuine, written long before the events they prophesied.

What then are those five important ways in which archaeology has been of special value for the Bible student?

1. *Archaeology confirms Bible history*. It often shows that Bible

people and incidents are correctly referred to. An example relates to Sargon, named in Isaiah 20:1. Critics said, "There was no such king." Then his palace was found at Khorsabad, and there was a description of the very battle referred to by Isaiah.

Another illustration is that the death of the Assyrian King Sennacherib is recorded in Isaiah 37 and also in the annals of Sennacherib's son Esarhaddon, whom Isaiah says succeeded Sennacherib.

2. *Archaeology provides local color, indicating that the background for the times and occasions described is authentic.* Laws and customs, gods and religious practices are shown to be associated with times and places mentioned in the Bible. Rachel's stealing her father's clay gods illustrates the correct understanding of customs: she and Leah asked, "Is there yet any portion of inheritance for us in our father's house? (Gen. 31:14). She knew the teraphim (clay gods) were associated with the title deeds to possessions and property in Jacob's time.

3. *Archaeology provides additional facts which help the Bible student understand times and circumstances better than he otherwise could.* Bible writers tell us the names of such Assyrian kings as Sennacherib and Esarhaddon; we now know a great deal more about these rulers from records recovered in their palaces.

4. *Archaeology has proved of tremendous value in Bible translations,* for the meanings of words and phrases are often illuminated when found in other contexts. An example comes from 2 Kings 18:17 where three Assyrian leadership titles are used correctly. They are *tartan* (commander-in-chief), *rabshakeh* (chief of the princes), and *rabsaris* (chief eunuch). They are not the actual names of these individuals, but their official titles. The meanings of these words were unknown at the time of the production of the King James Version of the Bible. The excavation of Assyrian palaces has thrown a great deal of light on their meaning. The fact that these titles are correctly used in the Old Testament is another strong argument for eyewitness recording. Who could know the titles of the enemy without some form of contact?

5. *Archaeology has demonstrated the accuracy of many prophecies,* such as those against Nineveh, Babylon, and Tyre. It is also highly relevant that Isaiah (and others) pointed so accurately to the Messiah. Prophecy has been vindicated by fulfillments, and so have their prophecies about Jesus.

This spiritual application is surely one of the most important aspects of biblical archaeology, reminding us that "Holy men of God spoke as they were moved by the Holy Spirit" (2 Pet. 1:21).

Archaeology has done much to demonstrate that "the Bible was right after all." Its early records of creation, Eden, the flood, long-living men, and the dispersal of the nations are not mere legends after all. Other ancient stone and clay tablets recording the same events have been recovered, but they are often distorted and corrupted.

The Bible record is immensely superior and quite credible, provided one also believes in the true God who intervenes in the affairs of men. *Those early Bible records can no longer be written off as myth or legend.*

Out of hundreds of discoveries from the last two centuries, a few are next selected and keyed to succeeding biblical eras.

"Forever, O Lord, Thy Word is settled in heaven" (Ps. 119:89).

Archaeological Facts, Artifacts, and Discoveries

It is a biblical principle that matters of testimony should be established at the mouths of two or three witnesses. According to Hebrew law, no person could be found guilty of an offense without properly attested evidence from witnesses. We now select evidences according to that biblical principle of "two or three witnesses." In every area of the Bible the evidence has been forthcoming: God has vindicated His Word: His Book is a genuine writing, with prophecies and revelation that must be taken seriously.

In the following outline we suggest certain divisions of the Word of God. Then we list three evidences from archaeology to show that the witness is sufficient to cause the case to be accepted for each section: God's Word is indeed truth. The evidences are derived from stone tablets, clay tablets, papyrus scrolls, ruins of ancient buildings, pieces of pottery, military equipment, statues of gods and animals, coins, metal remains, and other artifacts unearthed in excavations and studied over the last 180 years.

The names in these listings are derived from the places from which various archaeological artifacts were unearthed, the names found in various archaeological "digs," and events and persons who are mentioned in inscriptions carved in clay or stone from 2000 B.C. to the time of Christ. They all are supportive of the factual history of the Bible.

Section of the Bible

A. GENESIS CHAPTERS 1-11. The seed-plot of the Bible and introduction to Abraham and great doctrines such as God the Creator, friend, revealer, judge, restorer and sustainer. The actual history and summary of beginnings (creation to flood).

Three Major Events

1. *Enuma Elish* — Babylonian creation record, and also the Ebla creation tablet (found in Syria in recent years). The Bible record is clearly superior and the original.

2. *Epic of Gilgamesh* includes the Babylonian flood story. Again, the Bible record is greatly superior and is the original.

3. *Long Living Kings at Kish* (Sumerian-present Iraq/Syria/Arabia) supposedly lived from 10,000-64,000 years, but recent research has shown that the numbering system was misread and the years are in the hundreds, consistent with the life spans in Genesis 5, pre-flood.

Section of the Bible

B. GENESIS CHAPTERS 11-36. Patriarchal records with special reference to Abraham, the father of the Hebrews (2000-1800 B.C.).

Three Major Events

1. *Abraham's home city of Ur* excavated by Dr. Leonard Wooley with surprising evidence of near-luxury. Another "Ur" is mentioned in the Ebla tablets (circa 2100 B.C.), showing use of the name.

2. *The Destruction of Sodom and Gomorrah.* All five cities of the plain (Gen. 19) are listed in the same order in the Elba tablets preceding the era of Abraham. Some scholars place them on the Jordan side of the Dead Sea; others believe they are beneath the southern part of the Dead Sea.

3. *Abraham's negotiations with the Hittites* (Gen. 23) include Hittite words and follow the known forms of such Hittite transactions. Nineteenth century skeptics claimed there had never been a kingdom of the Hittites, but discoveries in the late 19th and early 20th centuries revealed that a vast Hittite empire flourished for centuries in what is now Turkey.

Section of the Bible

C. GENESIS CHAPTERS 37-50. Especially Joseph in Egypt (circa 1800 B.C.).

Three Major Events

1. Known *Egyptian titles* such as "*Captain of the Guard*" (Gen. 39:1), "*overseer*" (Gen. 39:4), "*chief of the butlers*" and "*chief of the bakers*" (Gen. 40:2), "*Father to the Pharaoh*" (actually "*Father to the Gods*" which to Joseph was blasphemous as he could not accept that Pharaoh was a manifestation of Ra, the Sun God — Joseph Hebraised the title and so did not dishonor the Lord), "*Lord of Pharaoh's House*"

(the palace), and *"Ruler of all Egypt"* (Gen. 45:8).

2. *Joseph's installation as Vizier (Chief Minister)* is very similar to other recorded ancient ceremonies, and his new name is known — "Zaphnath-Paaneah" is "Head of the Sacred College" (Gen. 41:41-45). Other Egyptianisms and local color are plentiful throughout the record — e.g., the first Bible reference to the horse (Gen. 47:17), embalming (Gen. 50:2, 26), and burial practices (Gen. 50:3).

3. *The Dead Sea Scrolls* make Genesis 46:27 to read 75, not 70 (persons who came to Egypt from Canaan under Joseph's administration), and showing that Stephen's figure was also right (Acts 7:14). The wives of Jacob's sons would boost the 70 persons to 75.

Section of the Bible

D. EXODUS TO DEUTERONOMY. The other four books of the Pentateuch, written by Moses, and probably at times in consultation with Aaron (priestly) and Joshua (military).

Three Major Events

1. *The Law of Moses* — genuinely written against his background, and greatly superior to other codes of law such as those of Hammurabi and Eshnunna. Covenant forms are endorsed as a unity, and from the middle of second millennium B.C. (the time of Moses).

2. *The ten plagues*, as judgments against the leading gods of Egypt (Exod. 12:12).

3. *Ethical concepts not too early for Moses*, despite earlier hyper-criticism that such ideas could not have been recorded in 1000 B.C. (Ebla tablets pre-date Moses and, for example, include penalties against rape.)

Section of the Bible

E. JOSHUA TO SAUL. The conquest, the judges, and the early kingdom (1400-1000 B.C.)

Three Major Events

1. *Deities* such as Baal, Asherah, and Dagan are properly identified, with right people at the right time in history, as artifacts indicate.

2. *City-states are identified* — e.g., Hazor as "the head of those kingdoms" (Josh. 11:10). The excavation of Hazor corroborated its great size.

3. *Saul's head and armor put in two temples at Beth-Shan.* Both Philistine and Canaanite temples were found — the Bible record was endorsed when such endorsement seemed unlikely. (1 Sam. 31:9-10 and 1 Chron. 10:10).

Section of the Bible

F. DAVID TO SOLOMON. The kingdom is established (1000-900 B.C.)

Three Major Events

1. *Gezer calendar.* A record of seasons on a schoolboy's text is in old Hebrew script and shows agricultural practices in Solomon's time as Scripture indicates.

2. *Establishment* (because of Ugarit library) *of date of Davidic psalms* — they should be dated to David's time, not long after his reign as liberals have said. The psalms, some said, are all no earlier than 700 B.C. His prophecies, such as Psalm 22, are evidence of divine inspiration.

3. *Solomonic cities such as Hazor, Megiddo, and Gezer* (1 Kings 9:15) have been excavated. Solomon even used blueprints for some duplicated buildings.

Section of the Bible

G. THE ASSYRIAN PERIOD, the "Reign of Terror" not long after Solomon's death (900-630 B.C.).

Three Major Events

1. Isaiah 20:1 — *Sargon's palace was recovered at Khorsabad* despite earlier hyper-critical argument that there was no such king; the battle against the Philistine city of Ashdod is described in Sargon's records; and "tartan" meant "commander-in-chief."

2. *The death of Sennacherib* is recorded at Isaiah 37:38 and 2 Kings 19:37, and is confirmed from the records of Sennacherib's son Esarhaddon (later augmented by Esarhaddon's son Ashur-bani-pal).

3. Various details about *Nineveh* and the *Jonah story* point to its historicity. The symbol of Nineveh was a pregnant woman with a fish in her womb. "Greater Nineveh" comprised a number of administrative cities such as Nineveh, Kouyunjik, Khorsabad, and Nimrod; Adad-Nirari III (possibly the king of Jonah's time) introduced remarkable reforms.

Section of the Bible

H. THE BABYLONIANS AND NEBUCHADNEZZAR (606-550 B.C.)

Three Major Events

1. *Daniel knew that Nebuchadnezzar built Babylon* (Dan. 4:30). This was unknown to modern historians (if they did not consult Scripture) until confirmed by the German Professor Koldewey who excavated at Babylon early in this century.

2. *The date of Nebuchadnezzar's capture of Jerusalem* (the night of 15/16 March, 597 B.C.) is known from "The Babylonian Chronicle."

3. *Prophecies against Babylon* (e.g. Jeremiah chapters 51 and 52) have been literally fulfilled. Nebuchadnezzar wrote that the walls of Babylon would be a perpetual memorial to his name: Jeremiah said, "The broad walls of Babylon shall be utterly broken" (Jer. 51:58). Jeremiah, inspired of God, has been proved right.

Section of the Bible

I. CYRUS: THE MEDES AND PERSIANS TAKE OVER from the Babylonians, and allow the Hebrews to return to their own land. (6th century B.C.).

Three Major Events

1. *Cyrus captured Babylon from Belshazzar* who was *co-regent* with his absent father, *Nabonidus*. This mention of Belshazzar as king seemed to be an error, but was an accurate statement of the prevailing situation. His father *Nabonidus appointed Belshazzar as co-regent*, and also retained the title of king for himself. Hence Daniel would become third (not second) in the kingdom (Dan. 5:29).

2. *Cyrus' name was given prophetically* (Isa. 44:28, 45:1). It was he who issued the famous Cyrus Decree, allowing captive peoples to return to their own lands. (See 2 Chron. 36:22-23 and Ezra 1:1-4.) God was in control of His people's history, even using a Gentile king to bring His purposes to pass. This policy is substantiated in ancient records.

3. *Some Jews remained in Babylonia*, as shown in the *Book of Esther*. The type of "unchanging" laws of the Medes and Persians shown therein is endorsed from Aramaic documents recovered from Egypt.

Section of the Bible

J. EZRA AND NEHEMIAH, AND THE RE-SETTLEMENT in the land after the exile in Babylon. (5th century B.C.)

Three Major Events

1. *Elephantine Papyrii* (Egypt) *and Dead Sea Scroll*. Targums of Job (etc.) show that Aramaic was in use as Ezra indicates (despite

hyper-critical arguments against this).

2. *Sanballat, the governor of Samaria* (Neh. 4:1; 6:2), was claimed by many to be much later than Nehemiah. We now know of several Sanballats, and the letters even refer to Johanan (Neh. 12:12-13). Geshem the Arab (Neh. 6:2) is also known from an inscription by his son. Ezra-Nehemiah are accurate records of an actual historical situation.

3. *The letters regarding Sanballat* (above) *clear up a dating point regarding Nehemiah.* His time was with Artaxerxes I who ruled from 465 to 423 B.C. (and not Artaxexes II). This illustrates the preciseness with which Old Testament dating is very often established by modern research, and especially from archaeological data.

Section of the Bible
K. THE DEAD SEA SCROLLS AND THE INTER-TESTAMENTAL PERIOD (1st-4th centuries B.C.)

Three Major Events

1. *The Jews were searching for a Messiah or Messiahs.* — The king, the great high priest, the high priest after the order of Melchizedec, the prophet like Moses, and possibly "the pierced Messiah," are described in the Dead Sea Scrolls.

2. *The scrolls have given us copies of much of the Old Testament* — fragments of every Old Testament book except Esther have been found, in Hebrew, about 1,000 years earlier than previous extant Hebrew copies. The Isaiah Scroll: the whole book is virtually word for word identical to much more recent papyrus copies.

3. Considerable light was thrown on *New Testament backgrounds*, and on the Jewish nature of John's Gospel: contrasts such as "light and darkness" are common to John and the "War Scroll." Also, Hebrew was still a living language and not just a priestly language, as skeptics thought.

New Discoveries Being Made

As research continues, the preponderance of the discoveries confirm the reasonable historicity of the peoples, places, and events described in the Bible. Nothing has ever come to light which disproves the biblical record. In instances where the artifacts and inscriptions thus far unearthed offer no supporting evidence as yet, new discoveries may present fresh facts to back up Scripture. For instance, the historicity of David has been challenged, but in recent years the expression "the House of David" has been found on an ancient tablet (circa 850 B.C.).

The Bible was right, after all.

6

The Amazing Ezekiel Stones

David Allen Lewis

Just suppose that somewhere in the Holy Land there is a manuscript of one of the books of the Bible that is so ancient there could be no older copy of that book, simply because it is the original — from the hand of the prophet himself. There are researchers in Israel who believe that they have found the original Book of Ezekiel! It is engraved on stone tablets. Is this possible? Here is much of the evidence.

If this theory can be proven and brought to public light it will be the most astounding archaeological discovery of all time. *It could either authenticate the text of our modern Bible, or tend to discredit it.* Up until this generation there has been no hint that the actual, original text of one of the books of the Bible might still be in existence. Until now the oldest known manuscript has been one of the Dead Sea Scrolls, dating to about 250 B.C. (B.C.E.). This would be a manuscript prepared 350 years after the original document. Actually, our Bible is based on copies of copies of copies of the original, unless there is one exception. This is the story of the stones.

I have spent long hours, over a period of decades, with the scholars who have worked with this project. Almost all our discussions are recorded on cassette tapes. Their case seems convincing, but not all will agree. Read the story of the amazing Ezekiel stones and see what you think.

Intrigue

The atmosphere of Jerusalem seems to be filled with mystery and intrigue. Some of the strangest stories that I have ever heard have come to me from sensible, well-established people in the land of Israel.

Many years ago, I met a man named Shlomo Rosenbaum (pseudonym used at his request, for security reasons). He began to tell me unusual things and shared with me information about strange archaeological artifacts.

Finally he told me that in a secret, highly secured room on the west side of Jerusalem there were 64 marble and 4 basalt tablets, each about 14 inches square. Written upon these stone tablets was the Book of Ezekiel in the original Hebrew language. The tiny letters are in bas-relief form (raised letters). No one knows how this feat was accomplished. No one has been able to duplicate this manner of writing in stone. It has been tried. To say the least, I was intrigued by what this might mean. How old are these stones? Where did they come from? Who found them? How did they arrive in the land of Israel? Are they genuine or just an elaborate hoax? I asked many other questions of my friend Shlomo. Slowly in visit after visit, he eked out information to me.

As time passed, there came a day when Shlomo showed me pictures of the mystical Ezekiel stones. Now I can report that I have many slide pictures and many color print pictures which I took myself, on location. Here is the account of an intrigue of epic proportions.

On the Trail of Grave Robbers

The stones were taken by grave robbers out of the tomb of Ezekiel, which is very near the site of ancient Babylon in the modern day country of Iraq. The grave of Ezekiel is known to be very ancient. It is well marked. We have photos and line drawings of it. This is where Ezekiel, along with the Hebrew exiles, spent the period known as the Babylonian Captivity of the Jews, and there wrote his book of prophecy.

My First View of the Stones

After some years had gone by, Shlomo decided to let me come along to see and to photograph the Ezekiel stones. To my amazement, they were unlike any stones with words upon them that I had ever seen. When you look at a gravestone, or a monument of any kind, you expect to see the words etched *into* the stone. However, the Ezekiel stones are totally different. The letters on the Ezekiel tiles leap out from the stone or stand away from the stone in bas-relief fashion. As far as I have been able to discover so far, there is no other example of any extensive ancient writing in existence that uses this style of stone carving. One can find both ancient and modern monuments which feature words displayed in a large, raised letter style, but there is nothing like the Ezekiel stones. As a matter of fact, Shlomo says that it is a mystery to the researchers working on the Ezekiel project as to how this unique feature was accomplished.

It should be noted that the Bible refers to another prophet who was commanded by God to write the words of his vision on tables of stone. Habakkuk bears witness: "I will stand upon my watch, and set me upon the tower, and will watch to see what he will say unto me, and what I shall answer when I am reproved. And the Lord answered me, and said, *Write the vision, and make it plain upon tables* [Hebrew tables of stone] that he may run that readeth it. For the vision is yet for an appointed time, but at the end it shall speak, and not lie: though it tarry, wait for it; because it will surely come, it will not tarry" (Hab. 2:1-3).

Ezekiel's Tomb — El Keffil

There is substantial evidence that the tomb of Ezekiel can be seen to this day in the village of El Keffil.

A band of desert brigands had found the stones in the ancient tomb of the prophet Ezekiel in the village of El Keffil, very near the ruins of the ancient city of Babylon, in the country known today as Iraq. We think that took place almost one hundred years ago (circa A.D. 1900-1910). The Ezekiel stones were carried by the grave robbers to Syria, where they passed into the possession of a pharmacist who practiced medicine. The chieftain of the robber band had become very ill. He told the pharmacist that if he could cure his sickness, he would give him a great archaeological treasure. Little did he realize what a treasure it is.

Illustration (circa 1850) of Ezekiel's romb at El Keffil, in Iraq.

The Pharmacist's Widow

The pharmacist treated the chieftan successfully, accomplishing a cure. The grateful desert dweller kept his promise and handed the mystery stones over to the pharmacist. The pharmacist died, never knowing the true nature, nor the value of the treasure he had in his possession. After his death the stones became the sole property of his grieving widow, a wealthy Christian Arab lady living in the Syrian city of Damascus. She told a religious authority about the stones. He was eager to see them. Upon examination, he said that these stones have the Book of Ezekiel written on them in Hebrew and that he thought they were something very important. He also told her that someday the Ezekiel tablets should become the possession of the Jewish people. At that time the nation of Israel had not yet come into existence as a modern state.

Enter Davida Hacohen

In the 1940s, before the war between the Arabs and Israel (1948), a Jewish man by the name of Davida HaCohen heard about the stones. He was able to travel to Damascus, Syria. When he finally saw the stones, he was totally amazed and tried to purchase them; however, his attempts were rebuffed. He was able to offer a large sum of money for the stones, but the late pharmacist's wife and the clergyman (both negotiated with him) finally decided to refuse his offer, regardless of how much money he was willing to pay. Davida HaCohen was not a rich man, but he had confided in some wealthy Jewish person(s), and they agreed to back him financially to acquire the stones and bring them to the Holy Land.

War, Orphans, and Gold

When the Arab-Israel war broke out in May of 1948, after Israel declared her independence, a messenger came secretly from Syria to meet with Davida HaCohen, bearing the news that the pharmacist's wife and the Bishop wanted him to purchase the stones for the last sum of money mentioned, with two extra provisions. There were 250 Arab orphan children in an orphanage in Haifa. HaCohen had to provide them safe transportation to Beirut, Lebanon, where their Syrian agents would pick them up and carry them to safety in Damascus. The second condition was that the final, large sum of money to be paid for the Ezekiel tablets had to be paid in gold coins or .999 fine gold bullion bars.

There are more details, but without compromising the security of certain living individuals who were involved, I must be very careful to avoid writing about a few fine points of which I am sworn to secrecy.

I cannot, for example, go into a detailed explanation of how the gold bullion was obtained and transported for the purchase of the Ezekiel stones. Nor am I free at this time to give a full explanation as to how the children were transported out of the war zone and into Beirut, Lebanon. A fierce war was raging in the Holy Land when these delicate operations took place.

Itzhak Ben Zvi

The gold transfer took place near the location of Kibbutz Gesher Haziv which is not far from the beautiful grotto caves of Rosh Hanikra. Had *all* the details of this transaction become known, it could have caused a national scandal and the fall of the infant Ben Gurion government. Nothing was done illegally or unethically or immorally. The problem was that HaCohen could never explain why he, an Israeli, handed over an enormous amount of pure gold bullion and gold coins to suspicious looking Syrians at the Israel-Lebanon border near Gesher Haziv! What was in the heavy boxes (the stones) which changed hands to HaCohen? Full disclosure of this information to the border guards would have endangered the very lives of all involved then and even some persons living today.

Damascus would have been enraged had they learned of such a great treasure leaving Syria and ending up in possession of the newly born nation of Israel with whom they were waging war at that very time.

To the Israeli border guards it looked like a clandestine smuggling operation. They wanted to arrest everybody involved, on the spot. Only a hastily placed phone call made by HaCohen to an official in the new government of Israel (who knew what Davida HaCohen was up to) stayed action on the part of the border guards.

The guards were given strict orders not to interfere. With no further explanation given to the guards, if they had leaked this information, it would have implicated the Ben Gurion government in what looked to the guards like the commission of a crime. Only their respect for the government official, who intervened by a phone call, stopped the guards from pursuing the matter further. Had they spoken out it would have implicated the government in the complex situation.

There was strong opposition to the socialist party of David Ben Gurion, mounted by the conservative political faction led by Menechem Begin. Had the Likud found out about the gold for stones exchange (thought to be an illegal smuggling operation) it could have caused a scandal big enough to destroy the Mapai Labor (Socialist) government.

All Quiet on the Mideast Front
Relative to the Mystery Stones

The border guards kept quiet. There were no serious information leaks. Silence about the stones prevailed in eretz Israel. Secrecy was tight. In 1948 the Jews were concentrating on the war. Survival of the fledgling state hung in the balance.

I met with Menechem Begin 15 times after he was elected Prime Minister of Israel in 1977. I even did some TV shows with him. I never mentioned the existence of the stones to him and I truly believe he was unaware of their existence. This demonstrates how closely the secret of the very existence of the stones was kept. It compounds the mystery.

Davida HaCohen took possession of the Ezekiel stones in 1948. He later gave them to his friend, Mr. Itzhak Ben-Zvi, who became the second president of the state of Israel. Ben-Zvi kept the stones stored in his home. A friend advised him that this great national treasure should be kept in a security vault. This was never done. They continued to lay under Ben-Zvi's stairway, wrapped in old newspapers. Waiting.

Eventually, my friend Shlomo gained permission to examine the stones. He was amazed at some of the things that he discovered, evidence that led him to conclude that the stones were very possibly the original Book of Ezekiel.

The Stones Find a Home

Shlomo obtained funds from a Jewish sponsor to build the small secure room where the stones are currently standing on a rack available for study by scientists, archeologists, historians, and linguists. For this reason he has had continued access to them, even though he has no official position with the foundation that now has a legitimate claim to ownership of the stone treasure.

Actually, it seems that Shlomo and I know more about certain aspects of the story of the stones than those in possession of them. Or, on the other hand, probably they have not told us all they know.

To date, few outside researchers have shown any great interest.

How could this be? The answer lies in the fact that the historical society that has possession of the stones does not want the concept of their originality to become commonly known. Why is this true? The society that has the stones has certain concerns, as explained to me by both Shlomo Rosenbaum and Baruch Ben David (who works for the foundation.)

I will offer four reasons why I believe this situation exists.

First, there is the problem of security, engendering a fear of robbery. Think of the almost immeasurable value of the stones, should their originality be proven.

Second, the foundation holds the view that such probing into the nature of the marble Book of Ezekiel would be a distraction from their primary work, which is to research and document the *modern* history of Israel.

Third, I personally think that the stones are an embarrassment to those in possession of them. This very staid, dignified foundation probably fears that too much publicity could give them a sensationalist image that would be intolerable. Every tourist visiting Israel would be clamoring to see the stones. This "circus" atmosphere would be abhorrent to them. There is a final factor:

Fourth, perhaps the very presence of the stones on their elite campus is potentially embarrassing, *but on the other hand they do not want to lose possession of the Ezekiel tiles.* There is a concern that if the Israel government Department of Antiquities becomes persuaded of even the *possibility* of originality they could seize them and declare them to be a national treasure. Probably they would be added to the collection of the Shrine of the Book where the famous Dead Sea Scrolls are housed, including the complete Book of Isaiah.

The Shape of the Alphabet

Baruch and Shlomo both informed me there is a cover story which discourages outside scholars from becoming too interested. This cover story attributes the stones to the work of an unknown artisan who lived in the 11th century A.D. (CE). This is based on the idea that the form of the Hebrew letters are a "modern" style of letters not used in the time of Ezekiel.

Shlomo says, however, that he has seen documents scientifically dated to about 600 B.C., written on Egyptian papyrus, prepared by Jews living in Egypt during the lifetime of Ezekiel. Shlomo could contend that the style of lettering on the stones very well may have been in use 1,600 years before the 11th century A.D., and that may explain their use on these ancient stones, if indeed they were prepared in the time of the prophet Ezekiel.

He suggests that this particular style of lettering could have fallen into disuse, only to be revived before or during, the 11th century A.D. Anyone looking at the stones could easily date them to the 11th century *if he was unaware of the possible earlier existence of the letter style on the stones.* If this is accurate, then the style of lettering alone does not positively date the Ezekiel stones. Furthermore, this is the only factor that critics could point to that *might* suggest the 11th century date. On the other hand, several other pieces of evidence lead one to conclude the strong possibility of the originality and antiquity of the Ezekiel stones.

Even the more cautious Baruch does not deny that the cover story is exactly that — a cover story. He showed me a letter written to the foundation giving an assessment that the stones should be dated to the 11th century. This letter, written by an American scholar, is no doubt an honest opinion. The writer's evaluation, however, is based solely on the shape of the letters on the stones.

One must not think that the letters are that much different from older and newer styles. It is like the difference between various of our English type faces in common use today, for example:

This typeface is known as New York.

This typeface is known as Zapf Chancery.

This typeface is known as Geneva Bold.

This typeface is known as Optima.

Notice that while there is a different appearance for each of these typefaces, all of them are easily identified for their similarity. The words all come out the same!

How I Got on the Trail of the Stones

Many years ago I took one of my 60 trips to Israel. My wife, Ramona, and I had brought a tour group with us to the Holy Land. One evening I arranged for a prominent physics professor, Dr. Asher Kaufman from Hebrew University, to speak to our group in a conference room in the West Holy Land Hotel in Beit Vegan, a neighborhood in Jerusalem. The famous Model of Herodian Jerusalem is part of the hotel complex. Michael Avi-Ona designed and built the large outdoor model of the Holy City as it was in Christ's time. His daughter Yael Avi-Ona lives today in Jerusalem and is one of Israel's truly great artists. We have met with her and her artist husband on a few occasions. Dr. Kaufman was to speak on the true location of Israel's historical temples.

First Meeting with Shlomo

That evening in the West Holy Land Hotel I noticed that our speaker, Professor Asher Kaufman, had (I assumed) brought a guest with him. Shlomo was wearing a military uniform. Later I would be informed by Kaufman that he was only casually acquainted with Shlomo. Earlier in the day Professor Kaufman had a chance meeting with Shlomo. During their brief encounter Asher told him that he was to speak that very evening to a group of American Christians on the subject of the temple of Israel. Shlomo said quietly, but urgently, "I must accompany you!"

After the evening lecture, Shlomo came to me and said, "I must speak to you privately."

"All right," I said, "let's go over in the corner of the room. There are some chairs over there."

"No, I must talk to you alone."

We went upstairs to a secluded corner in the hotel's main lobby.

For several minutes neither of us spoke. It was a relaxed moment, without tension. Finally Shlomo said, "I am searching for something."

"I know," I responded, without knowing why.

Silenced reigned for a few minutes. Then he said, "I cannot tell you what I want to tell you."

"I am good at reading between the lines."

"But I can't even give you the lines to read between."

We sat looking at each other for just a few moments longer, when it dawned on me. . . . I knew (or guessed) what he was looking for, *and Shlomo knew that I knew!* It was in my mind, "This man searches for the lost ark of the covenant!" I was partly correct. There is so much more.

Rising to his feet Shlomo said, "I will meet with you again." He turned and slowly walked into Jerusalem's night.

No mention was made of the Ezekiel stones. I didn't have a clue. Little did I realize the quest I would ultimately be involved in — a quest for the holy ark and the Ezekiel stones.

A Concert, a Young Lady, a Strange Dream

We never use dreams or visions to determine biblical interpretation or doctrine. I want to make that clear. But the Bible speaks of the Holy Spirit speaking to us by means of dreams and visions. I think this is to encourage us or confirm something of His will in our lives.

After we returned to Springfield, Ramona and I, along with our daughter Sandy and her friend Cindy Dunn, went to a Carmen concert at Evangel College. As we stood waiting in the long line I was approached by an attractive young lady who identified herself as an Evangel College student. I was not acquainted with her.

She said, "Dr. Lewis, I dreamed about you a few nights ago. You were in Jerusalem. I saw you in a large room. You were sitting with a mysterious man in uniform. Neither of you said much, but I knew you both had an interest in the ark of the covenant. That is something I had never thought much about. Then I was looking at a mountain or large hill — the holy ark is hidden under that hill. The reason I know you, Dr. Lewis, is because I saw you on television and also I heard you speak at a church here in Springfield." Let me make it clear, that at this point of time I had told no one of my conversation with Shlomo, not even my wife.

I did not ask the young lady for her name. To my recollection, I have not seen her since.

Some time later I told Shlomo about this unusual incident. We agreed that we did not know what to make of it, except that her dream was accurate. It may mean nothing, or it could have been a personal confirmation for me. This dream neither adds nor detracts from our ongoing research.

More Conversations with Shlomo

Six months later Ramona and I were back in Jerusalem. I phoned Professor Asher Kaufman to get Shlomo's phone number. (We were going to Israel every six months or so at that time.)

We met again and had a rambling but non-revealing conversation. We discussed Asher's interest in the true location of Israel's past temples. Nothing was said about the ark of the covenant. Shlomo did say that he was aware of the existence of an archaeological treasure. He was speaking, as I would later learn, of the Ezekiel stones, of which I was still totally ignorant.

A sense of trust was growing between us, but neither of us was pushing an agenda. I sensed a deep pool of knowledge lay between us, waters Shlomo was swimming in. I had not yet wet my feet. We arranged for an evening meeting later that week.

We met in the old Diplomat Hotel. The hotel had given me the use of their huge multi-roomed presidential suite. There we were in the large "living room" which had several couches, overstuffed chairs and a couple of conference tables. Ramona and our daughter Sandy sat reading. A gentleman from Tel Aviv, a dear family friend, was there reading the daily newspaper. Finally Shlomo entered by way of the private security elevator.

Shortly after Shlomo and I sat down, he said "I must speak to you privately." Hearing this, Ramona went to our room and Sandy went to hers. Our friend Avigdor sat reading his newspaper oblivious to our conversation. Shlomo repeated his need for privacy.

So I said, "Avi, he wants to talk to me alone."

Lowering his paper, Avi said, "So let him talk," and went back to reading his *Jerusalem Post.*

I repeated what I had just said, "Avi, he really wants to talk to me alone." He looked up again, saw that Ramona and Sandy had left, shrugged his shoulders, and went to his own room in the suite.

As our conversation commenced, I thought, *Perhaps tonight we will discuss the location of the holy ark of the covenant.* Little did I know that the ark would be peripheral to our dialogue. That subject would only come up later.

Instead, Shlomo began to weave a mystical tale about 64 marble and 4 basalt tablets with a portion of the Bible inscribed upon them. Then I was told of coded secret messages, intricately woven into the plain text on the stones, telling where to find certain treasures of ancient Israel. Then he said, "It is the Book of Ezekiel." I had no idea that he believed that the stone tablets could be the original document from the hand of the prophet.

Finally, just before leaving Shlomo said quietly, "I have pictures of them, would you like to see them?" I nodded. He said, "Sometime I will show the photographs to you, perhaps next time."

Next time!

There were many "next times." I saw the photographs, Ramona and Sandy were taken into full confidence and sat in on each ensuing discussion. Then Avigdor, our friend, guide, arranger, nudger, a real mensch, and so much more, was added to the circle of confidence.

Then came the exciting day when Shlomo informed me that he had arranged with Baruch Ben David for me to actually see the stones. I stood before them trembling in awe. Possibly the greatest treasure found in our times was before my eyes. Not a treasure of gold or silver. No, far more than that — THIS IS THE WORD OF THE LIVING GOD.

Read, Study, Declare!

It would be wise to begin earnestly studying the book of the prophet Ezekiel. His message is already powerful! Finding the stones does not change that. The stones do not enhance the authority of this prophecy, but what will happen on the day when someone in the foundation publishes a scholarly paper on *"Possible Evidence For the Originality of the Marble and Basalt Stone Book of Ezekiel."*

Serious researchers will want a closer look. Debate will rage. Tabloids will scream their headlines. *Biblical Archaeological Review* will publish articles, pro and con. Old-line denominational seminaries will have their cages rattled. Tired old faithless modernistic doctrines will be challenged. Tielhard de Chardin will "turn over in his grave." "Higher" critics will scratch their old gray heads. And wonder. But many will believe!

Perhaps the Israeli government Department of Antiquities will get involved. Can the foundation be challenged as to legal ownership? Would the Israel government have a right to declare the stones a national treasure? Court cases. Rumors will fly. The foundation will be offered vast sums of money for the stones. Thieves will itch all over. Plots are hatched. Attempts made. Security will have to be intensified.

Stephen Spielberg can produce his crowning Hollywood achievement. What an epic story! People will sit in theaters in absolute awe. The gross take at the box office will rise above all others.

I think that the prophecy of Ezekiel will be the most-read portion of Holy Scripture. People will read with all kinds of motives — good and holy motives, ulterior motives, weird motives, and downright evil motives.

Saints Alive

A Baptist pastor, Ben Saint, told me that the 38th and 39th chapters of Ezekiel were the most powerful witnessing tool he possessed. Just think of a time when the whole world will be focused on the Book of Ezekiel. People will be reading about:

Visions of God: Ezek. 1:1, 8:3, 40:2.

Wheels within wheels and the cherubim of God.

Return of Israel to the land, which is proof of God's sovereignty, to the nations: chapters 36-37.

Invasion of Israel from the far north: chapters 38-39

Israel's miraculous preservation and deliverance: chapters 38-39.

Israel's future temple: chapters 40-48.

God's visible kingdom will be established on earth.

Jerusalem is new world capital.

The new name of the Holy City becomes Yehovah shammah {yeh-ho-vaw' shawm'-maw} — "The Lord Is There." (Read the last verse of the Book of Ezekiel.)

Messiah reigns over the glorious (millennial) kingdom of God on earth.

Resurrected King David is co-regent with Hamashiach.

And so much more.

Never before will there have been such attention devoted to a specific book of the Bible. May God grant us the wisdom, zeal, and anointing to seize on this potential opportunity to bear witness to God and the gospel.

Baruch Ben David emphasized the need for secrecy. "We do not want a tourist concession here."

The last time I called the foundation, asking for Baruch Ben David, the receptionist said, "He is no longer here."

In March 1998 I interviewed Shlomo Rosenbaum in Jerusalem. For two and a half hours we sat with the tape recorder sitting on the table between us. I asked his permission to tell the whole story. He freely said that I could publish *most* of the story but that I must not use his name.

Cafe With the Round Window

My friends and I frequented the *old* Alno for lunches and coffee times. Until it changed ownership it was one of my favorite eating places in Jerusalem. How often I would say, "Meet me at the Alno, #15 Ben Yehuda Street. You can't miss it. It's the only one with a large round window in front." Alas, new owners took it over, replacing the warm Old World atmosphere with a modern plastic look, not to my liking.

One day I sat in the *old* Alno with Shlomo and Avi, having a hearty soup, cheese-egg sandwich, and cappuccino for lunch. We talked about many things, but for sure our conversation always got around to *the stones*.

Our Tour Group Allowed Inside

Off the cuff, I asked Shlomo if he thought he could ever arrange with Baruch for me to bring one of my tour groups to see the stones. I was pleasantly surprised to hear him say, "Yes, when do you want to bring them?"

As my very next party of tourists stood in silent awe looking at the stones, Shlomo lectured, telling my fascinated group of Christian pilgrims why he believed that this was very likely the original Book of Ezekiel, not a copy of it, but direct from the hands of the prophet, or at the least prepared under Ezekiel's hand by one of his students.

Hidden Messages

If Shlomo and his associates are ever able to prove their theory concerning the originality of the stones, it will be one of the greatest, if not *the* greatest archaeological discovery of all time. Remember that our Bibles today are based on copies of copies of copies. No original manuscript of any book of the Bible is in existence as far as we know, unless it is the Ezekiel stones.

I must tell you that there are hidden messages that I am not at liberty to fully disclose at this time, within the stones themselves, and by the manner in which the letters are arranged on the stones. I have carefully guarded the confidentiality that Shlomo has requested of me throughout the years. What I am telling you now is as much as he has given me permission to release. A lot more research needs to be done, and that is not currently taking place.

I think that later on we will be able to give you the complete story of the Ezekiel stones, and truly the world is going to be amazed at some of the things that will be revealed at that time. When asked by one of my friends accompanying me on a tour group a few months ago, whether or not they didn't want more people to come and see the stones, one of the associate directors of the institution where they are stored said in shocked horror, "No, please don't send any other groups, we do not receive tour groups."

My friend asked, "Why are we here today?"

He said, "The only reason that you are here is due to our friendship with Dr. Lewis, but please do not send us any tour groups. We are not prepared to receive them and we do not wish to talk quite so openly as we have today." That always puzzled me. Each of my groups (except one) from then on saw and photographed and videotaped the stones, and were allowed to tape record lectures by both Shlomo and Baruch.

It was my opinion that the researchers, Shlomo, and his friends decided to talk to me and in a sense use our tour groups as a means of leaking information to the general public so that they can watch public reaction to their story. *But now I am not so sure of that.*

Certainly, when (if ever) Shlomo and his associates decide to publish their findings and theories concerning the Ezekiel stones, it is going to rock the world.

Do you remember when the Dead Sea Scrolls, including the Book of Isaiah, were found in the 1940s? I know that you have heard about it. The oldest possible date that can be placed on the scroll of Isaiah is about 200-250 years B.C. That means that the Isaiah scroll is a copy that was produced about four to five hundred years after the original was written. So important was the finding of the Dead Sea Scrolls that there is hardly a month that goes by, even today, that there is not an article in some scientific or general publication, or a book published about the amazing Dead Sea Scrolls. And they are just copies.

Just imagine if the marble and basalt tablets are declared to be the very original Book of Ezekiel. It is going to be the greatest find of all time unless the ark of the covenant should be discovered in the meantime, before the proof of Shlomo and his associates is offered publicly and to the scientific world and archaeological world in general.

Two Temples in Israel's Future

Ezekiel reveals information about the fourth temple — the millennial temple, which will be built under the auspices of Messiah himself.

Some Jewish scholars themselves speak of the possibility of two future temples. Christian scholars who study both the Old and New Testaments see a third temple, built upon Mount Moriah, which will be desecrated by the man of great evil (Antichrist). A concept of the Antichrist is also found in traditional writings of Jewish scholars. He is called anti-messiah or "the golem." The third temple will be of short duration. The final temple, which will be built in the Millennium under the auspices of the Messiah himself, is described in chapters 40 to 48 of Ezekiel. Depending upon whether one accepts the short or the long cubit measurement, that temple will be either 750 feet by 750 feet or a thousand by a thousand feet in size.

The Ezekiel stones hold hidden clues about the location of temple treasures such as the lost ark of the covenant. When the *Bible Codes* researchers (Moshe Katz, Elayahu Rips, Michael Drosnin, etc.) become aware of the stones, they will search for the hidden messages and find information beyond compare!

Ark of the Covenant

The finding of the lost ark (if it still exists on this earth) would almost demand the building of the next temple! It can simply be stated that the search for the ark continues in at least four locations that I know of. I once co-authored a book with Doug Wead (president of Canyonville Bible Academy) and Hal Donaldson (editor of the *Pentecostal Evangel)* titled *Where is the Lost Ark?* (Bethany). In that book we explored 14 ideas about where the ark might be hidden. There is no biblical record of the disposition or location of the Holy ark after the destruction of the first temple by the Babylonians about 600 B.C. It may yet be found. I have my own theory as to its possible location.

How exciting it was to hear of the find of even a replica of the ark in Israel a few years ago. Hollywood jumped into the act with the production of the movie *Raiders of the Lost Ark,* which was shown throughout the USA and the world.

The first time that Mrs. Lewis and I met Rabbi Matiyahu Dan Hacohen, the founder of the School of the Levites, it was on a cold, rainy February day. After Rabbi Hacohen had assembled a small model of the temple and explained his vision for the school and for the rebuilding of the temple, he began to talk to us about some of the excavations under the Temple Mountain. He told of how he was working late at night with Rabbi Getz and some rabbinical scholars. Let me explain at this point that when you stand at the Western or Wailing Wall in Jerusalem, you are actually standing approximately 57 feet above the level of Christ's time (Herodian Period). Jerusalem has been destroyed and rebuilt about 20 times. Each time the city was destroyed, the rubble was pushed into the valley. Thus, the level of the Tyropean Valley gradually built up over the centuries.

Matiyahu Dan Hacohen told of how they were excavating along the lower level of the Western Wall of the Temple Mountain. At one point during the night, they came to a doorway in the Western Wall. Passing through this doorway, the crew entered a fairly long tunnel. At the end of the tunnel, Rabbi Hacohen said, "I saw the golden ark that once stood in the Holy Place of the Temple of the Almighty."

It was covered over with old, dried animal skins of some kind. However, one gold, gleaming end of the ark was visible. He could see the loops or rounds of gold through which the poles of acacia wood could be thrust so that the ark could be properly carried by four dedicated Levites. Matiyahu Dan Hacohen and his friends rushed out to the home of Chief Rabbi Shlomo Goren. They awakened the rabbi and excitedly told him that they had discovered the Holy ark of the covenant! Goren said, "We are ready for this event. We have already prepared the poles of acacia wood and have Levites who can be standing by in the morning to carry out the ark in triumph."

At the earliest dawning of the day, Hacohen, Goren, and the others went to the tunnel. To their shocked amazement they found that during the night the Moslems had erected a wooden form and poured a concrete wall, sealing off the tunnel that would give access to the ark of the covenant. I asked, "Why didn't you break through the concrete? It would have been so easy to do."

He replied, "I begged Goren to give us permission to break through the wall, but Rabbi Goren replied, 'Every time we do anything around the Temple Mountain, it creates big problems for Israel with the Arabs, the United Nations, and the United States. It seems to make everybody upset, so we will not break through. We know where the holy object is and when we receive the word from the Almighty, we will go in and recover it. Don't worry, the Moslems revere the ark as much as we do and they would be afraid to touch it.' "

In the years following, I talked to Rabbi Matiyahu Dan Hacohen on a number of occasions about this previous discussion and each time I talked to him, he was more and more reluctant to have the subject brought up. Finally, in the presence of several people, he simply refused to talk about it at all. I suppose he got in trouble with his colleagues for talking to me and my tour group about their sighting of the ark of the covenant. I would like to point out, however, that we have a tape recording of his original discussion with our tour group on the very first occasion that he talked about the ark. It is our custom on our tours to record everything that every guide and every speaker has to say about any subject, so we have good records of everything that has been said. In addition to that, I have a colored slide showing Rabbi Matiyahu Dan Hacohen holding a map and pointing to the tunnel as he is saying, "This is where I saw the golden ark of the Lord." Only time will tell what he and his friends actually saw. Did they really see the ark, or was it a replica? Until it is actually taken out and verified, we will have to keep the whole question on hold.

My good friend Grant Jeffrey, author of many best-selling books, firmly believes that the ark of the covenant is in Ethiopia. Tom Crotser from Winfield, Kansas, believes that he has seen the ark under Mount Nebo in the country of Jordan. Mister Blaser from Colorado is convinced that the ark is hidden in a cave in Ein Gedi on the shores of the Dead Sea. There is a group of American Christian archeologists who believe that the ark is hidden between Gordon's Calvary and the Garden Tomb. A digging project was in progress while we were there a few years ago. We joined in the search. I took some artifacts that we dug out from near Calvary to Mr. Barakat of Bethlehem, an antiquities expert, for evaluation and dating. We found coins and pottery shards dating all the way back to the Roman period and the time of Christ.

Thus we find that there are many theories as to where the ark might be located. The last biblical reference that we have for the ark is just before the first Temple of Solomon was destroyed by the Babylonians about 576 B.C. Whatever happened to the ark is not a matter of sure record. The Apocrypha does speak of Jeremiah and his friend, Baruch the scribe, hiding the ark. There is further speculation that Jeremiah and Baruch probably hid a replica or two to fool those enemies of God who would try to find the ark and destroy it.

There are several projects going on right now in Israel and other places making attempts to find the ark of the covenant. In Revelation 11, John says that he saw the Holy ark in heaven. Some have concluded that the ark is no longer on earth. However, this would not be true inasmuch as the earthly tabernacle and temple, and the articles of furniture therein, were manufactured after a heavenly pattern. A heavenly temple and a heavenly ark exist, according to the writings of the Book of Hebrews. What John saw in Revelation 11:19 was the heavenly ark, not any ark that had ever been on earth. That is my opinion.

We cannot prove to you that the ark of God is still in existence, but I will offer you my opinion that it is in existence and that it will be found. The Bible says in Jeremiah that the day will come when the children of Israel will no longer inquire after the ark of the covenant. That day has not yet arrived, for the inquiry after the ark of the covenant is intense and interest in its recovery is increasing. Many Jewish leaders, especially those who are religiously conservative, believe that finding the ark would be the one thing above all else that would literally force Israel to start rebuilding the temple. Rabbi Hacohen said, "If we find the ark, it will force us to build the temple. After all, the first temple was built to house the ark of the covenant. If we find the ark, what would we do with it? We couldn't store it in the prime minister's basement. It would demand the rebuilding of the temple. However, if we find the ark or not, we are going to build the temple of the Almighty, Baruch Ha Shem (blessed be His name), on the Har Habayit, the Temple Mountain."

For the Record

A prominent Christian author called me and asked a lot of questions regarding my views concerning the ark of the covenant, the future temple, and of my conversations with Matiyahu Dan Hacohen. He did not tell me that he was writing a book about the temple. He then went to Israel and talked to Rabbi Hacohen, who told him that he never had such a conversation with me, and in fact that he did not even know me. But we have photographic and tape-recorded records to prove what we say.

We also have photos of Rev. Jess Gibson handing a check for $500.00 to Rabbi Hacohen. He was with my tour group, visiting in Yeshiva Aterit Cohanim, a seminary for Levites and Cohanim.

From another tour we have a similar photograph of Rev. Tommy Nichols (father of Sherry Herschend, of the Herschend family Silver Dollar City empire). The picture of Tommy Nichols shows him putting a good-sized donation right in Mati Dan Hacohen's hand. Recently we went to Point Lookout, Missouri, to hear General Norman Schwarzkopf speak at the College of the Ozarks. After his lecture, Sherry came over and talked to us, recalling our Holy Land trip, especially our visit to Yeshiva Aterit Cohanim and the lecture given to our group by Matiyahu Dan Hacohen.

Many other donations were given by various members of our tour groups for the work of Yeshiva Aterit Cohanim.

I regret that this very capable author did not come to me for clarification before he talked to M. Dan Hacohen. He wrote in his book that Rabbi Getz, the Wailing Wall Rabbi, said that I was a liar when asked about my conversation with Hacohen.

Fortunately we have all of our conversations with Rabbi Hacohen on audio tapes. I even have a picture of my wife, Ramona, standing by Hacohen with the ubiquitous tape recorder, taping one of the lectures he gave to one of our tour groups.

A Great Mystery

When Shlomo told me about clues "coded" in the stone texts that allowed him to know about the location of some temple treasures, and even of a strange concept of a "hidden" temple, he spoke rather enigmatically. "As you stand on the Abu Tor observatory, and look toward the mountain, that is where the buried temple is located." This led me to the wrong conclusion, that he meant it was buried in the Valley of Gehenna.

I wrongly assumed that when he said, "the mountain," he was referring to the Temple Mountain, Mount Moriah, which is seen clearly from the Abu Tor overlook. In more recent conversations I asked him what he exactly referred to as "the mountain." Did he mean Mount Moriah?

"No I meant the Mount of Olives," was Shlomo's reply. Both mountains, parallel to each other, stand before us in plain view from the Abu Tor Overlook. Olivet stands to your right and Moriah to the left. Between them lies the Valley of the Brook Kidron, also known as the Valley Jehosaphat. Gehenna valley is further to the left of Moriah and joins the Kidron as they both amble to the south.

Secrets of the Holy City

When I am in Jerusalem, some people come and visit me very quietly by night. They share secrets that are so bizarre that they are hard to believe. We stumbled upon something of this nature a few years ago. First of all, I was talking one day to one of the gentlemen who heads up one of the temple organizations, and as you know, there are several of them. He said that there is a group of people who are sinking a shaft, a bore hole on the eastern slope of the Mount of Olives. My informant said that there is a theory that the temple of Ezekiel was built long ago and buried under massive amounts of dirt and rubble.

Doura Europas

In discussing this idea Shlomo once told me, "If you can discover the secrets of Doura Europas you will comprehend one of the deepest mysteries of the hidden messages coded into the text of the Ezekiel stones." There were times when I had not the foggiest notion of what Shlomo was talking about, and he will not be pressured for answers. Eventually, however, everything falls into place.

Doura Europas (Dura Europa) is an archaeological tell located in Syria. It is the remains of a very ancient city, originally built in the days of the prophets Ezekiel and Daniel. It existed in the days of Nebuchadnezzar, ruler of the mighty Babylonian Empire. Daniel spent time there. On the walls of an ancient Jewish house of worship at Dura Europa one can see mosaic tile frescos depicting various biblical scenes including the prophecies made by Ezekiel in his book. Photographs of Doura Europas are displayed in *Encyclopedia Judaica,* Vol. 6, p. 275-298. You will find a few websites on the Internet with studies about and photographs of Doura Europas.

I asked Shlomo what I should look for in my research of Doura Europas. He cryptically replied, "Look for a building on the eastern side of the Mount of Olives." I have seen a photograph of one of the Doura Europas frescos depicting the temple. One picture of a temple in the artwork of Doura Europas can be seen in *Encyclopedia Judaica,* as mentioned above.

Hard to Believe!

I frankly expect that some will find the idea of a buried temple hard to believe. I am only sharing these intriguing concepts with you because the information came to me, independently, from three different sources in Israel; also because Shlomo says it is tied in to the coded message of the stones. It is offered here only as a curiosity. We will watch and wait to see if there is any substance to the claims that have been made.

One night, a gentleman who came to me very quietly and secretly, was talking to me about matters concerning the temple. I shall protect his identity here by calling him Jacob. I related to him that the gentleman previously mentioned, and yet another person, had come to me with this idea that the temple of Ezekiel (the millennial temple?), was already in existence and buried in the valley between Abu Tor and the Mount. This scholarly gentleman, Jacob, had previously said that he believed that the "spirit" of the Roman Caesar Hadrian was alive in the world today. From his Jewish point of view, there would be a revival of the Roman Empire, which would bring a lot of trouble to Israel. He spoke of a man *like* the Roman Emperor Hadrian, one of the most evil of the Caesars, who would rule a revived Roman Empire.

I told him that many Christians have a similar point of view. Here is part of the discussion that took place between the two of us (from a tape recording):

Lewis: "There is an idea that has been presented to me since I came to Israel this time. There are some people who theorize that a temple is buried between the Abu Tor Observatory and the Temple Mountain [actually not the Temple Mount, rather it is alleged to be on the east side of the Mount of Olives], a temple constructed after the model in Ezekiel 40-48. It was built and then buried there. There is a theory that there will be two temples in the future: one will be constructed on the Temple Mountain and will be defiled like the second temple was profaned by Antiochus Epiphanes during the Maccabean period, 165 years before Christ lived here.

I continued, "During a time of great trouble for the whole world, a man of great evil, the man who will rule the new Roman Empire will, like a Caesar, declare himself to be God. Then the defiled temple will be replaced by the true fourth and final (Ezekiel) temple. So there will be two temples in the future. I hear the rabbis arguing about whether to build a temple now or whether to wait for the Messiah to come and build the temple."

Jacob: "Ah, yes, there are two theories. Yes, but what we are looking for is the one that has already been there."

Lewis: "These people I am talking about, they have dug a shaft. . . ."

Jacob: "That's what we did. That's what we did."

Lewis: "And, they work at night."

Jacob: "That's what we did, because it's very dangerous."

Lewis: "Jacob, they believe there is a building underground."

Jacob: "And I believe it too, and the place we are going — we are not looking for a hidden cellar. It is not a cellar. It's a marvelous building and we have the proofs there."

Lewis: "So, maybe you are looking for the same thing?"

Jacob: "Yes. Now the entrance we are entering, you see, Ezekiel mentions a wheel within a wheel. So, what do we have there, what did we find there as we dig our tunnel? Against the wall, a wheel within a wheel."

Lewis: "You mean where you started digging?"

Jacob: "Yes. The stone is carved, wheel within the wheel. Wheel within the wheel. It goes like this [here he draws a "picture" with his hands, in the air]. What else could you want?"

Lewis: "You mean when you started digging it was like a design?"

Jacob: "Yes, there was a shaft [filled in with reconstituted rock]. There was a design [wheel in the wheel]. It is still there, on both sides — the wheel within a wheel. Then there is a lion. There is a large lion that faces the entrance, not us. It is beautifully carved. We got where we got, but that's it. So there must be something there. And it fits with the measurements."

Lewis: "These designs don't happen by accident."

Jacob: "No, no, it cannot. It cannot. And they are painted also — in red. And we found many things."

For many hours we discussed things pertinent to the discoveries of great treasures in the Holy Land. This secret informant whom we call Jacob has been coming to me for years with information that up until now has always proven to be accurate. I will admit that the idea of an underground temple is one of the strangest things that I have ever heard.

Ezekiel's description of the temple of the Messianic Era and the city of Jerusalem of that time describes great topographical changes. Jerusalem itself will become a great plain. Is it possible that the Ezekiel Temple, the Messianic Temple, is already in existence? I cannot say for sure, but I do know that the people who came to me before I talked to Jacob said that bore hole had been dug (not Jacob's project) and that some massive underground structure had been detected. What shall we say of these mysteries? Only time will tell.

This we know for sure: there is great interest in Israel in the rebuilding of the temple, the finding of the lost ark of the covenant, and the restoration of the priesthood. The high level of interest — in spite of contradictory stories and searches in places that look almost like rivalry between archaeological groups — should not discourage us from believing that the temple will be rebuilt. Indeed, the temple will be rebuilt, not because of all these activities, but because it has been so prophesied in the Word of God. These activities are simply an indication that we are living very near the close of this age and the fulfillment of incredible prophecies.

Textual Reasons that Argue for Originality

Shlomo has explained to us about textual reasons indicating the originality of the stones. Actually, this was the first clue that led him in his search for the meaning of the stones. I am not a Hebrew reader, so my disadvantage is that while I have good photos of each of the stones, I do not know how to locate some of the passages Shlomo is referring to. This is further complicated by the fact that the entire text of the Book of Ezekiel, as on the stones, has no spaces between the letters, and also there are no vowels (an old style in Hebrew writing). Perhaps this will all fall into place before the second edition of this book is printed. Please bear with and pray for us in this ongoing research. There is so much yet to be done.

One of the textual clues is found in Ezekiel 1:2. Here is how the verse reads on the stones: "In the fifth day of the month, which was the fifth year of Jehoiachin's captivity. . . ."

Here is the verse in the King James Version: "In the fifth day of the month, which was the fifth year of *King* Jehoiachin's captivity. . . ." (same as the Masoretic text). The word "king" does not appear on the stone tablets.

Could it be that a scribe, copying the passage hundreds of years later, might have added the word *king* to clarify who Ezekiel was referring to, presuming that hundreds of years after the original writing, the average reader might not know who Jehoiachin was?

For example, I might write, "And in 1999, Bill Clinton was in deep trouble because of the Kenneth Starr investigation." It is conceivable that if my writing were copied 1,000 years from now that the copyist of that future time might write, "And in 1998, *President* Bill Clinton. . . ." Everyone today knows who Bill Clinton is, but a few hundred years from now, probably only history buffs will remember him. The addition of the word *president* would establish his identity for far future readers. This editorial addition would in no way destroy the original meaning of the passage.

Shlomo Rosenbaum also discovered a passage on the stones that reads, "And I say. . . ." This is Ezekiel writing in the first person. In the Masoretic (later Hebrew) text we find "And he said. . . ." Thus, another scribal change indicates the originality of the stones.

The Prophets Protest Their Calling

It seems that most, if not all, of the prophets felt their prophetic calling was an odious burden, not a thing to be desired. Think of Jeremiah, "I will not speak." Jonah refused to go to Ninevah. Isaiah cried out, "Woe is me." Amos complained that he had no desire to prophesy in the big city, preferring a bucolic, country life.

It seems that only the prophet Ezekiel refrains from complaining about his calling.

On the Ezekiel stones there is a Hebrew word that Shlomo translates, "He [God] cursed me." This could complete the register of protesting prophets. A very similar word in more recent Hebrew manuscripts replaces the word on the stones giving a different meaning. With this, Professor Stanley M. Horton, a great Hebrew scholar, agrees.

The only difference between the word on the stones and the later Hebrew manuscripts is the transposition of two adjacent letters in the word, but that slight change does away with the sense, "He *cursed* me," as it appears on the stones. Could this indicate an error on the part of the (later) scribe who copied the document?

Dr. Stanley Horton of Evangel University Writes

It is not likely that Ezekiel himself chiseled his book on stones. Jeremiah dictated his prophecies to his scribe Baruch, who wrote them with pen and ink on a scroll (Jer. 36:18). When Jehudi read the scroll to the king, the king cut it up and threw it into the fire. That they burned easily shows the scroll was papyrus rather than leather. Ezekiel was in Babylonia where they stamped cuneiform into clay tablets. However, clay tablets would not be suitable for Hebrew lettering. So it is probable that Ezekiel wrote on papyrus as Jeremiah did. Later, someone copied his prophecies on the Ezekiel stones, probably wanting them preserved in a form that would be even more permanent than clay tablets.

Our current Hebrew Bibles use what is called the Masoretic (traditional) text. The oldest dated copy is the Leningrad manuscript coming from A.D. 1008.

One of the Jewish scholars who is working with the Ezekiel stones believes they are copied from a very early manuscript, perhaps the original. He pointed out textual evidence for this. For example:

(1) In Ezekiel 2:2 after the spirit stood Ezekiel on his feet, we read in the Masoretic text, "Eshma eth middabber eli" — "And I heard with God speaking to me." The Ezekiel stones have "el God" instead of eli "to me." Also, since vowels were not included in the Ezekiel stones, "th mddbbr" is better taken as reflexive, "I heard God talking to himself." This makes more sense and is undoubtedly an earlier reading than the Masoretic text.

(2) Jeremiah, like most prophets, protested his calling. In the

Masoretic text, Ezekiel does not. However, in Ezekiel 2:3, the Ezekiel stones transpose two letters in the first word so that "He said (wy'mr) to me" becomes "He cursed (wym'r) me." This fits with what follows where God tells Ezekiel He is sending him to a rebellious nation. It is also easy to see how a scribe might transpose letters accidentally when copying. I do that all too often when I am typing. It would be easier as well since m'r is not the common word for curse (through the corresponding noun was common), while 'mr is a common word for "said."

(3) In Ezekiel 2:5, the Masoretic text has, "They will know that a prophet *was* (hayah) among them." The Ezekiel stones leave out "hayah" without any space where it could have been. This makes it read "They will know that a prophet *is* among them," which fits the context better.

These are all minor things that do not change the meaning of the prophecies. But they do give strong indication that the Ezekiel stones are at the very least earlier than the best Masoretic text we have."

Dr. Stanley M. Horton wrote the previous paragraphs especially for this book. He is considered to be one of the truly great Hebrew scholars of our time.

A Hot Discussion on a Cold Winter's Day

Shlomo had been startled when he first found secret messages imbedded in the text on the Ezekiel stones, giving the location of temple treasures. There are many people searching in many places for relics from the first and second temples.

It was a cold, rainy day in the Old City of Jerusalem. Tom Brimmer, Leonard Salvig, and I sat huddled around a rough old conference table along with Stanley Goldfoot and Rabbi Baruch ben Yosef, as we engaged in a heated discussion on the building of Israel's future temple. The miserable room was small, damp, and cold, but so engrossing was our topic of discussion that it seemed to warm us like a crackling fire in the hearth.

Four or five others were there at the table or standing around the small room. I do not know the identity of the latter few. One of these was a screaming, loudmouthed, bellicose person who, in principle, seemed to disagree with everyone present.

Leonard Salvig had brought up the subject of the true original location of Israel's past temples, holding out for Professor Dr. Asher Kaufman's theory that the temple stood about one hundred yards north of the Moslem shrine, the Dome of the Rock, on the Temple Mount. Rabbi Loudmouth vehemently protested, "No, the temple stood where the Dome of the Rock stands today!" This agrees with the theory of

Leen Ritmeyer's most recent research. There was also discussion of
Tuvia Sagev's theory that the first and second temples indeed stood on
Mount Moriah, but that it was south of the location of the Dome, where
today the Moslem's Fountain of Ablution can be seen.

The Bore Hole

I asked whether anyone had heard that there might be a buried
temple, or some huge, hidden building under the eastern slope of Mount
Olivet. I was greeted with loud, skeptical comments. To my amaze-
ment, Stanley Goldfoot spoke up saying, "Hold on! Before you hoot
Dr. Lewis out of the room, let me tell you something very interesting.
There has been a secret bore hole dug on the far side of the Mount of
Olives, and I can confirm that some kind of building is there."

One must not confuse the bore hole project with "Jacob's" dig for
the same thing. Jacob's was a much bigger project and vastly more
productive.

Recently, Brian Westoby told me about a conversation he had
about three years ago with Baruch Ben David, who has been the "keeper
of the stones" at the foundation where the Ezekiel stones are in hiding.
Brian claims that Baruch knows about the bore hole project, and the
finding of some huge underground buried structure. Now I am won-
dering if, in fact, the foundation was a sponsor of, or involved in the
bore hole search.

We Get the Run-around

In February 1998, I was in Jerusalem on my 60th visit to Israel,
and we had with us a most delightful group of tourists. I could not find
Baruch. The foundation associate director, whom I had spoken with on
the phone, was bent on stopping us from seeing the stones. Prior to
this, Baruch had always been our contact person, and he is normally a
very agreeable man.

One day Avigdor, my wife, Ramona, and I went to the foundation
to see what we could do or find out on location. They talked to an
official person in the building where the stones are securely housed.
Same party line. The answer is "no."

In the meantime, since the campus is only minimally handicapped
accessible, I sat outside waiting in my wheelchair. I asked everyone
who passed by, "Are you connected to the foundation?"

Finally a gentleman said, "Yes, I am a department secretary here.
How can I help you?"

"My name is David Lewis. I have brought several groups to
see the Ezekiel stones. Could you arrange for me to bring some

folks here tomorrow morning at 9 o'clock?"

"Hmm, yes, I will meet you here at that time tomorrow." Then he said, "Baruch is not here for a few days, so you will have to make your own lecture for your people."

"No problem," I responded, and so it happened one more time.

Leonard Salvig Perseveres

In March 1998 my friend Leonard Salvig went to Israel to work on the Asher Kaufman video project, and also to view the Ezekiel stones again. I had taken him to see the stones with one of our tour groups. The people at the foundation gave him a real run-around. One person said, "The stones are not available for viewing." His call to another person brought a blunt refusal: "Do not bother to come back, you will not be allowed inside."

He then asked another person, identified as an associate director of the foundation, for permission to see the Ezekiel stones. She said that if he would come to the special door, she would allow him inside the next morning. When he had stood waiting at the door for some length of time he realized that she was not coming. Salvig then proceeded to walk about the premises, looking here and there. He spotted Baruch Ben David and tried to engage him in conversation, but Baruch said, "I cannot talk to you, and please do not bother Shlomo, he cannot talk to you either, and you can't look at the stones."

I know Leonard Salvig to be a very persistent person. Last week I talked to Leonard and this is what he had to say:

> So I said, "I am not going to listen to him [Baruch]," so I kept going and I found an office, and I said, "I have been given permission by the associate director to see the Ezekiel tablets."
>
> The lady said, "Okay, let me meet you over there at the other side."
>
> So she went and opened the door for me, and I said, "I was here with David Lewis a couple [of] years ago."
>
> She said, "I know."
>
> "How do you *know?* How can you remember me after a couple of years?"
>
> She replied, "Well, I don't remember you, but I do know that David Lewis is the only one we allow to come in here from the outside."

She had rightly assumed that if Leonard had gotten in previously it had to have been with one of my tour groups. Altogether I have taken 12 or 13 groups to see the stones. Both Baruch and Shlomo have told me repeatedly that I am the only one who has taken tourists to see the stones!

Secrets

It amazes me that those who control the Ezekiel stones are so secretive on one hand, but on the other they have *never* forbidden any of our tourists to take photographs, video tapes, or to tape record the detailed lectures given to us. Until now we have been asked not to publicize these facts. Only in 1998 did Shlomo indicate to me that was all right to go ahead and write about the Ezekiel tables of stone!

I hope that the foundation will completely open the doors of research, and assign more top scholars to determine the age and authenticity of this great treasure. The foundation should then publish their findings everywhere. That is my opinion.

It is possible that some minor details in this account are not completely accurate. The reason for this is that some of this information comes from several different sources, which do not always agree with each other on minor details. However, the main elements of this story are accurate. As an example, I will mention that one account says that the stones did not arrive in Israel until 1953. I have used the 1948 date because that is what all other sources have told me. No doubt, as our research continues we'll make minor adjustments to the account and a lot more information will be shared as it comes to light.

LATE EDIT: Even as this book is about to go to press, "new" information has become available just in time to be included here. It relates to the Tomb of Ezekiel being located at El Keffil, and of the "manuscript" being in the tomb. Of special value is the mention of Benjamin of Tudela's travel in Iraq and his description of the tomb of Ezekiel. The following quotation comes from the book *Discoveries in the Ruins of Ninevah and Babylon,* by Austin P. Layard (1853). It pushes the authentication back to the period of A.D. 1159-1173 when Benjamin Ben Jonah of Tudela, Spain, traveled in the region!

Layard wrote:

From the summit of the Birs Nimroud I gazed over a vast marsh, for Babylon is made "a possession for the bittern and pools of water" Isaiah 14:23. In the midst of the swamps could be faintly distinguished the mat huts of the

Kazail, forming villages on the small islands. The green morass was spotted with flocks of the black buffalo. The Arab settlements showed the activity of a hive of bees. Light boats were skimming to and fro over the shallow water, whilst men and women urged onwards their flocks and laden cattle. The booming of the cannons of the Turkish army, directed against the fort of Hawaina, resounded in the distance; and the inhabitants of the marsh were already hurrying with their property to safer retreats in anticipation of the fall of their stronghold.

To the southwest, in the extreme distance, rose the palm trees of *Kifil*, casting their scanty shade over a small dome, the *tomb of Ezekiel*. To this spot annually flock in crowds, as their forefathers have done for centuries, the Jews of Baghdad, Hillah, amid other cities of Chaldaea, the descendants of the captives of Jerusalem, who still linger in the land of their exile. Although tradition alone may place in the neighbourhood of Babylon the tomb of the prophet, yet from a very early period the spot appears to have been sought in pilgrimage by the pious Hebrew.

I visited the edifice some years ago. It is now but a plain building, despoiled of the ornaments and *manuscripts* which it once appears to have contained. The description given by *Benjamin of Tudela* of this place is so curious, that I cannot forbear transcribing it.

The following is cited by Layard from Benjamin of Tudela's *Book of Travels*:

On the banks of the Euphrates stands the *synagogue of the prophet Ezekiel, who rests in peace.* The place of the synagogue is fronted by sixty *towers,* the room between every two of which is also occupied by a synagogue; in the court of the largest stands the ark, and behind it is the *sepulcher of Ezekiel,* the son of Busi, the Cohen. This monument is covered by a large cupola, and the building is very handsome; it was erected by Jeconiah, king of Judah, and the 35,000 Jews who went along with him, when Evil Merodach released him from the prison, which was situated between the river Chaboras and another river. The name of Jeconiah, and of all those who came with him, are inscribed on the wall, the king's name first, that of Ezekiel last.

This place is considered holy unto the present day, and is one of those, to which people resort from remote countries in order to pray, particularly at the season of the new year and atonement day. Great rejoicings take place there about this time, which are attended even by the Prince of the Captivity and the presidents of the Colleges of Baghdad. The assembly is so large, that their temporary abodes cover twenty miles of open ground, and attracts many Arabian merchants, who keep a market or fair.

On the day of atonement, the proper lesson of the day is read from a *very large manuscript Pentateuch of Ezekiel's own hand-writing.*

A lamp burns night and day on the sepulcher of the prophet, and has always been kept burning since the day that he lighted it himself; and the oil and wicks are renewed as often as necessary. A large house belonging to the sanctuary contains a very numerous *collection of books, some of them as ancient as the second, some even coeval with the first temple,* it being customary that who ever dies childless, bequeaths his books to the sanctuary. Even in time of war neither Jew nor Mohammedan ventures to despoil and profanate the sepulcher of Ezekiel.[14]

The following is from pages photocopied of an old book. By examining its page layout and design, we know the book is an encyclopedia of some sort. It was sent to us a few years ago and lay forgotten in a file drawer until this past week. The author cites Benjamin of Tudela, Loftus, and Layard. This quote seems to be from a scholarly source.

He [Ezekiel] is said to have been murdered in Babylon by some Jewish prince (called in the Roman martyrology for vi Id. Apr. "judex populi," Carpzov. *Introd.* 1.c.), whom he had convicted of idolatry; and to have been buried in a *double tomb,* the tomb of Shem and Arphaxad, on the banks of the Euphrates (Epiphan. *De Vit. et Mort. Prophet.*). The tomb, said to have been built by Jehoiachin, was shown a few day's journey from Bagdad (Menasse ben-Israel, *De Resurrec. Mort.* p.23), and was called "the abode of elegance" (habitaculum elegantiae). A lamp was kept there continually burning, and the *autograph copy of the prophe-*

cies was said to be there preserved. This tomb is mentioned by Pietro de la Valle, and fully described in the Itinerary of R. *Benjamin of Tudela* (Hottinger, *Thes. phil.* II, i,3; *Cippi Hebraici,* p. 82). His tomb is still pointed out in the vicinity of Babylon (Layard's *Nineveh and Babylon,* p. 427), at a place called *Keffil*; and Mr. Loftus is inclined to accept the tradition which assigns this as the resting place of the prophet's remains (*Chaldea,* p. 35). The spire is the frustum of an elongated cone, tapering to a blunted top by a succession of steps, and peculiarly ornamented.[15]

There is so much that I do not know, *yet.* I am not willing to say at this point that I am 100 percent sure that this is the original Book of Ezekiel. Or is it the earliest copy, perhaps made by one of Ezekiel's students, under his direction? I think that the least we could say is that this is, in all probability, the earliest biblical manuscript in existence (so far discovered). The research in this and related realms is ongoing.

Until this forum of inquiry reconvenes, whether in another book, in a scholars conference, in one of our publications, (*Jerusalem Courier* or the *Prophecy Watch International),* on radio or TV, please pray that we shall all approach all of the subjects of this book with humility and awe. May God grant an even greater gift of wisdom to each of our authors and to each of you, our dear readers.

"The heavens were opened, and I saw visions of God" (Ezek. 1:1). "Beh Ezrat Hashem!"[16]

Chapter 6 Footnotes

1 Actually, the Hebrew on the stones is virtually identical to the Masoretic text that today's Hebrew Bible is based upon. There are only slight scribal differences, such as the spelling of a word (by no means changing the meaning of the word). We will deal with two or three other changes which are integral to "proving" the originality of these stones. Compare the standard English translation of the Hebrew Bible with the King James version of the Original Covenant (OT) and you will be struck with the fact that they are virtually identical.

2 Photographs of the tomb of Ezekiel are displayed in the small room where the Ezekiel tablets are on display. The tomb of Ezekiel lies below an imposing structure that resembles a synagogue. Now a mineret towers over it. Shown in the photographs are a number of Iraqi Jews in Arab-like clothing. Compare this to the Moslem Mosque Machpelah in Hebron. In the subterranean chambers are found the tombs of Abraham, Isaac, Jacob, and their wives, except for Rachel who died in childbirth on the way to Bethlehem. The mosque is a much later construction.

In addition there are historical references from the 1850s in which authors of that period wrote of traveling to the tomb of Ezekiel. For example, William Kennett

Loftus wrote in his book *Travels and Researches in Chaldea and Susiana, chapter IV. [Loftus. New York. Robert Carter and Brothers. 1857]:*

> The view from the summit of the Birs Nimrud is very extensive. . . . Bordering upon this marsh, a few spots attract the eye and relieve the long level of the horizon. Due south stands the tomb of the prophet Ezekiel, and at the distance of fifty miles, in the mirage of early morning, may be discerned the mosque of the sainted Ali, glistening like a speck of gold as the beams of the rising sun play upon its surface.

> From the Birs Nimrud southwards, a road runs along the raised bank, which here in a measure restrains the marsh within bounds. A succession of large canal courses, now dry, are crossed during a ride of twelve miles to the little town of *Keffil,* which, from its want of luxuriant trees and vegetation, looks dull and sombre in the extreme — a fitting place for the *sepulcher of a captive prophet* in a strange land.

> The town of Keffil is protected by a high wall, and defended at intervals by small towers. An old broken-down mosque, with minaret to match, stooping to its fall — the spire of the prophet *Ezekiel's tomb* and the tops of the houses peeping above — are all that invite further approach. Except when a crowd of pilgrims collect at the annual festival, the exterior of the place is deserted.

> There is no reason to believe that the tradition is unworthy of credence, which assigns to Keffil the honour of *possessing the bones of the prophet Ezekiel.* The continued residence of the Jews in the land where their forefathers were consigned in exile, and the respect with which the tomb has for so many centuries been regarded, not only by the Jews themselves, but by the Mohammedans, ought to be considered a sufficient guarantee for the correctness of the tradition. The Jewish traveller, *Benjamin of Tudela,* [a Spanish Jew] in the middle of the *twelfth century,* tells us, that "the monument was covered by a large cupola, and the building was very handsome. It was erected by Jeconiah, King of Judah, and the 35,000 Jews who accompanied him."

> It is remarkably plain, both externally and internally, containing two vaulted apartments — the roof of the outer one being supported by heavy columns. The sepulcher is cased in a large wooden box of considerable age, which measures ten feet long by four feet high. Its decoration consists of a piece of Englischintz and small red and green flags. The chamber itself is square, the side walls being extremely dirty and greased with oil. The floor is covered with a filthy matting. The vaulted ceiling is very prettily ornamented with scrolls of gold, silver, and bronze. Built into one corner is an ancient Hebrew copy of the Pentateuch. A scanty light is admitted from above, and an ever-burning lamp sheds a solemn gloom into the sanctuary. The flat terrace or roof affords a good view of the marshes extending to the base of the little elevation upon which the town of *Keffil* stands.

> A large proportion of the inhabitants are Jews, a host of whom, surrounding the door of the sanctuary, looked daggers as our large party, booted and spurred from the journey, crossed the sacred threshold.

3 David Ben Gurion had harvested hatred for himself and his party by having his Haganah soldiers fire upon and destroy the Likud owned *Altalena,* a sea-going cargo ship, as she lay, loaded with guns and ammunition, along the shore of Tel

Aviv. Begin and his underground Irgun army planned to use the weapons and munitions on board the *Altalena* to fight both the British overlords and the Arabs.

4 Baruch Ben David is a pseudonym used here for his security.

5 See *Where is The Lost Ark?* by David A. Lewis, Doug Wead, and Hal Donaldson. (Minneapolis, MN: Bethany House, 1982). This out-of-print book explores 14 locations where various researchers and adventurers have sought this ancient object. We came to no conclusion in the book. I argued for a different title. My choice was *Search for the Lost Ark*. I felt that we should not ask a question on the front cover which we knew we could not answer. The publisher's prerogative to choose the title prevailed at the end of the discussion. Now I believe I have found the answer. I believe, along with many reliable people, that it is in a sealed chamber beneath Mount Moriah, the Temple Mount. This theory is partially explained in chapter 5 of *Where is The Lost Ark?* Since 1982 a lot more has been discovered lending credence to this location being the correct one. Some Israelis even claim to have seen it beneath the Har Habayit.

6 Ben Saint is one of the most effective soul winners I have ever met. He explained how he could walk up to a perfect stranger and get a conversation going by referencing events in the news with Ezekiel's Gog and Magog prophecy. His brother, Nate Saint, was one of the five Baptist missionaries martyred by the Auca Indians in South America, I believe in the late 1950s. Read the book *Through Gates of Splendor.* A majority of Aucas are now Christians due to the witness of Nate and his partners. Some of the wives stayed in South America, teaching the gospel to the Aucas. Thousands of Aucas were converted and many of them are preachers and evangelists today.

7 Ezekiel 1:1: "Now it came to pass in the thirtieth year, in the fourth month, in the fifth day of the month, as I was among the captives by the river of Chebar, that the heavens were opened, and I saw *visions of God*."

8 Not UFOs, but rather IFOs (Identified Flying Objects) i.e., the angelic cherubims.

Ezekiel 1:16: "The appearance of the wheels and their work was like unto the color of a beryl: and they four had one likeness: and their appearance and their work was as it were a wheel in the middle of a wheel."

Ezekiel 10:6: "And it came to pass, that when he had commanded the man clothed with linen, saying, Take fire from between the wheels, from between the cherubims; then he went in, and stood beside the wheels."

Ezekiel 10:9: "And when I looked, behold the four wheels by the cherubims, one wheel by one cherub, and another wheel by another cherub: and the appearance of the wheels was as the color of a beryl stone."

Ezekiel 10:1: "And as for their appearances, they four had one likeness, as if a wheel had been in the midst of a wheel."

Ezekiel 10:11: "When they went, they went upon their four sides; they turned not as they went, but to the place whither the head looked they followed it; they turned not as they went."

Ezekiel 10:13: "As for the wheels, it was cried unto them in my hearing, O wheel. . . ."

9 Messiah.

10 Hence the use of pseudonyms for *both* "Baruch" and "Shlomo."

11 We had no idea that he would soon be accused of plotting to capture the Temple Mountain. It was a plan that did not succeed.

12 *Biblical Archaeological Review* (cover story) "Ark of Covenant Once Stood on Bedrock Beneath this Unimposing Cupola." March/April 1983; Vol. IX No. 2., p. 40-61.

13 From a tape-recorded conversation with Leonard Salvig, October 19, 1998. Actually I know of a couple of people who have gotten in to see the stones who were not with one of my groups. One author hired a former employee of the foundation to sneak him in. Another man, Brian, heard me talking about the stones, went to Jerusalem on his own, got acquainted with Baruch, and learned a great deal about the subject. When I talk to Brian, I get the feeling that he knows something about the mystery that has eluded me thus far. I do not think he is deliberately avoiding sharing information. I think it is rather that he may assume that I know more than I do.

14 Austin H. Layard, *Discoveries in the Ruins of Ninevah and Babylon* (London; John Murray, Albemarle Street, 1853), chapter 22, p. 500-502.

15 From an unidentified, photocopied source, as mentioned in the text of this essay.

16 Hebrew: "May it be the will of God."

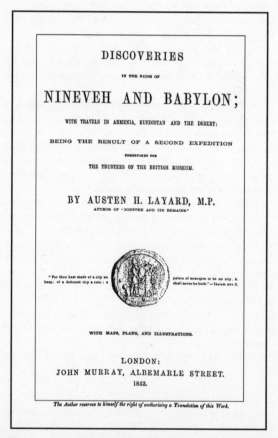

Title page from Layard's *Discoveries in the Ruins of Nineveh and Babylon.*

Jews at the entrance to Ezekiel's tomb, Iraq.

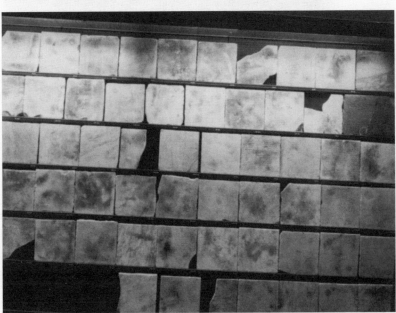

The mysterious Ezekiel stones.

A close-up of the raised lettering.

TRAVELS AND RESEARCHES

IN

CHALDÆA AND SUSIANA;

WITH AN ACCOUNT OF EXCAVATIONS AT

WARKA, THE "ERECH" OF NIMROD,

AND

SHUSH, "SHUSHAN THE PALACE" OF ESTHER,

IN 1849–52,

UNDER THE ORDERS OF

MAJOR-GENERAL SIR W. F. WILLIAMS OF KARS, BART., K.C.B., M.P.,
AND ALSO OF THE ASSYRIAN EXCAVATION FUND IN 1853–4.

BY

WILLIAM KENNETT LOFTUS, F.G.S.

"Why dost thou build the hall, son of the winged days?—Thou lookest from thy tower to-day; yet a few
years, and the blast of the desert comes; it howls in thy empty court."—Ossian.

NEW YORK:
ROBERT CARTER & BROTHERS,
530 BROADWAY.
1857.

Title page from Loftos' *Travels and*
Researches in Chaldaea and Susiana.

7

The Factual Scientific Accuracy of the Bible

Robert W. Faid

I f the Bible is truly the book that Christians claim it to be, there can never be any conflict between the Bible and science — the author of the Bible is also the author of the basic scientific principles which govern every aspect of nature from the origin of the universe, the workings of the atom and everything else in between, from the snowflake to the quasar.

There can be, and always has been, however, conflict between theologians and scientists. This comes about through several routes. Often there is no real dialogue between them, resulting in polarization of their points of view. At other times, the scientist does not know what the Bible actually says. Sometimes it is the theologian himself who does not know what the Bible actually says.

Any time that a conflict exists between scientists and theologians, either the theologian does not have the proper interpretation of the Scriptures, or the scientist does not have his facts straight.

One of the classic battles between theologians and scientists was over Galileo's work on the solar system, which met head-on in 1633. Galileo had published his "Dialogue on the Two Chief Systems of the World," in which he brilliantly expounded and defended the Copernican System which held that the earth revolved around the sun as did all the other planets in the solar system.

The church had invaded the domain of science and was using its own erroneous interpretation of the Book of Genesis as a scientific tome.

Galileo was summoned before the inquisition at Rome and was forced to recant his belief. Legend has it that he muttered to himself as he arose from his knees after withdrawing his theory, "But it does move!"[1]

Today it would be hard to find any theologian who would hold the view that the Bible claims that the earth is the center of the solar system and that it remains stationary while the sun and the planets revolve around it. But not only has the point of view of the theologian changed, the scientist has had his eyes opened also to the truth contained within the pages of the Bible.

It would take more space than is available here to enumerate all of the instances where modern science has confirmed what this book has said for thousands of years. I have chosen a few which were discussed in detail in several of my books.

Dietary Laws in the Bible

God laid out definite rules on what the Hebrews were allowed to eat and what was to be strictly prohibited. These dietary laws were recorded in the 11th chapter of Leviticus. Only certain animals, fish, fowl, and insects were considered "clean" and could be eaten. There was no prohibition on any kind of fruit or vegetables.

However, not all parts of the "clean" animals could be eaten. The Hebrews were not to consume blood from any acceptable meat, and certain organs of these animals were not to be eaten. These dietary laws were later to include the separation of types of food so that meat and dairy products could not be eaten at the same time nor prepared in the same vessels. This was called kosher, from the Hebrew word meaning "fitting" or "proper," and included the slaughter of animals by the humane method of draining of the blood, and washing, salting, and soaking meat to remove all possible traces of blood.

I had always been told that the reason that God forbade the eating of pork was because of the possibility of the Hebrews contracting the parasite which causes trichinosis if the meat is not thoroughly cooked. It is true that many pigs do carry the larvae of *Trichinella spiralis* and that insufficiently cooked pork can transmit this larvae to man, where it reaches maturity in the intestines. The mature worm then gives birth to multitudes of larvae which are carried in the lymph and blood to the muscles where they become encysted. This causes severe pain, swelling, fever, and even prostration in extreme cases.

But trichinosis was not primarily why God did not want the Israelites to be around pigs. There is a much more serious and potentially deadly reason. Pigs are perfect incubators for epidemics caused by viruses. Within the pig, mutations can take place in these viruses, making them deadly to man.

It has been discovered that many epidemics are carried around the world by migratory birds, especially waterfowl. These organisms are not harmful to the birds who carry them in their intestines. And they would not usually be pathogenic to man — unless a mutation occurs — or the genes get crossed with a virus from a human.

A prime example of this is Asian flu. Each year as the birds migrate, they carry the influenza virus from Asia to other parts of the globe. Birds being birds, they litter the ground along the migratory route with their droppings. Humans rarely come in contact with bird excrement — but pigs do. As a pig eats its food from the ground, it also ingests the bird droppings.

Pigs are also exposed to viruses from their keepers. Any virus a man or a bird can catch, a pig can catch, too. Usually, bird viruses do not replicate well in humans and human viruses do not replicate well in birds. But both do very well in pigs.

When both a human virus and a bird virus infect the same cell in the pigs respiratory tract, and both begin to re-arrange the cell's genetic material to duplicate their own, the genes can get crossed between them. A team of Italian and American scientists have been investigating this for 12 years and show that not only can this happen — it does happen. What results is a new and sometimes more virulent strain than either virus had previously been.

Humans transmit a respiratory virus infection by coughing, distributing airborne viruses to those nearby. Astonishingly, pigs also cough. When the bird-human virus is coughed or breathed into the air by the pig, humans are infected with the mutant strain. They then spread this new virus to other humans and the epidemic has begun.[2]

According to virologist Robert Webster, who led the American half of the research team, these findings prove that pigs do indeed act as the mixing vessels for the transfer of avian-carried viruses to man. "Pigs are perfect mixing vessels," says Dr. Webster, "and may well be the source of the next pandemic.

"All subtypes of influenza occur naturally in waterfowl," says Dr. Webster. "They are the ultimate reservoir of influenza. These strains usually are not able to infect people, but some may infect pigs, as can some human flu strains. So if a pig becomes infected with two virus strains — one from waterfowl, one from humans — simultaneously, their genetic information can mix to give a duck-human strain. We can postulate that the human epidemic began when a farmer caught the new virus while tending to his pigs."[3]

I believe that this was the reason that God did not allow the Israelites to keep pigs. It would have taken just one large-scale epidemic to wipe out the relatively small group of Hebrews. It was not that the Lord didn't like pork chops, but strictly for health reasons that He forbade the Israelites to keep pigs.

Other forbidden animals included any that did not have a cloven hoof or did not chew its cud. This meant that the Israelites could eat oxen, cattle, sheep, and goats and could hunt deer and other related species. But forbidden were animals such as the camel, the coney weasels, ferrets, mice, snails, lizards, chameleons, and moles. Most of the forbidden animals were scavengers.

Mice can carry deadly pathogens. Recently the mysterious illness which killed a dozen people in the southwest has been traced to the Hantaan virus, a usually fatal hemorrhagic fever carried by field mice. This virus is diagnosed in over 100,000 cases each year in China alone. It is not a new disease, having been described in ancient Chinese medical text over a thousand years old.[4] Certainly, this was around in biblical times. Mice carry other pathogenic organisms such as Junin, which causes a painful and sometimes fatal type of hemorrhagic fever. It is no wonder God prohibited the eating of mice or other animals which fed on mice.

It is interesting that all of the animals which God allowed the Israelites to eat were those which grazed on grass or ate grain. This minimized the possibility of disease from eating animals which picked up infectious diseases from scavenging on the carcasses of dead animals.

There were also laws concerning seafood. "Whatever hath no fins nor scales in the water, that shall be an abomination to you" (Lev. 11:12). This eliminated eels, frogs, and all shellfish, lobsters, crabs, and shrimp.

Eels and crabs are scavengers, so their inclusion in the list of forbidden seafood is for much the same reason as animal scavengers. Shellfish such as oysters and clams are known to carry pathogens which can cause hepatitis, especially when eaten raw. They also spoil very quickly without proper refrigeration. The Israelites had no means of refrigeration. In fact, the only means of preservation were by salting or drying. Fish are readily preserved in this manner and it is used even today with some species.

The fowl that were prohibited included the eagle, osprey, raven, vultures, owls, nighthawks, cuckoo, cormorant, pelican, swan, heron, and the lapwing. Most of these feed on small animals such as mice and could become carriers of the same organisms for which the mice were forbidden.

When we first look at the dietary laws of the Bible, they seem to be very restrictive. But on closer examination, these laws made extremely good sense. Today we are advised by health professionals that a low-fat, low cholesterol diet is good for us. We are told to exercise and to get sufficient rest. That's exactly what the biblical laws dictated for the Israelites.

Who else but the Creator himself would be able to prescribe the ideal diet for His creation's best health in a time when such scientific facts were completely unknown. And science has confirmed that the Bible was far ahead of the knowledge of that day in what it allowed and what was forbidden.[5]

Why Circumcision Specifically on the Eighth Day?

The practice of circumcision is very ancient. It did not originate with God's command to Abraham to circumcise all male Hebrews as a sign of the covenant. In fact, it was practiced long before by the Egyptians. But in all of the cultures where circumcision is practiced, only Jews perform this on the eighth day of a male child's life — as God commanded that it be done.

Why the eighth day? Did God have a reason to require that this be done *exactly* on the eighth day? The Egyptians circumcised boys between the ages of 6 and 14. This ceremony is depicted in a wall painting in the temple at Karnak, and was practiced at least three thousand years before the time of Christ and at least a thousand years prior to Abraham's covenant with the Lord. Of the other major religions, only Islam requires this of its adherents as a sign of spiritual purification.

The Babylonians and Persians who ruled over the Israelites for several centuries did not practice circumcision, and it became a special sign of the Hebrew devotion to their God which puzzled these people and infuriated the Greeks and Romans who later became their masters. In the second century A.D., the Romans outlawed the practice, but the Jews ignored this and continued it. Circumcision was excluded from Christian requirements after the first Council of Jerusalem, where Paul described the attempt of Jewish Christians to impose it upon Gentile converts. Among Christian churches, only the Abyssinian Church recognized circumcision as a religious rite to be practiced by its adherents.

Abraham was 99 years old when God spoke to him and made a covenant with him and his descendants. "This is my covenant, which ye shall keep, between me and you and thy seed after thee; Every man child among you shall be circumcised. And ye shall circumcise the flesh of the foreskin; and it shall be a token of the covenant betwixt me and you. And he that is eight days old shall be circumcised among you" (Gen. 17:10-12).

God is the one who ordered circumcision to be carried out on precisely the eighth day of the child's life. There was to be no variance in this. If the eighth day fell on the Sabbath, or on a Feast Day, it was still carried out on that day. Why? What was so special about that particular day? Was there a reason that God specified exactly the eighth day for this to be carried out? We could not answer that question until scientists made some fairly recent discoveries in the intricacies of the working of the human body.

When you cut your finger and it bleeds, a marvelous mechanism within your body is set into motion to stem the flow of blood. It is a highly complex process which takes place in several stages and involves many different enzymes and other organic compounds. What happens, and this is a very simplified description, is as follows:

> The injured tissue around the wound and the degenerated blood platelets release a substance called thromboplastin.
>
> The thromboplastin then converts prothrombin, which is produced in the liver, to thrombin, a clotting enzyme.
>
> This enzyme, in turn, converts fibrinogen, which is a soluble substance, to insoluble fibrin.
>
> The fibrin forms an organic mesh, the basis for the clot which begins to seal off the wound and stop the flow of blood.
>
> As the fibrin forms, it contracts and squeezes out the blood serum, forming a firm clot.

This is a *very* simplified description of what occurs. Many other factors are involved. One of these is the role of vitamin K, which is essential in the human body to enable the liver to produce prothrombin. Vitamin K is contained in many foods, including milk. It is the action of the normally present good bacteria in the intestines which release the vitamin K and allow the body to absorb it for use by the liver in the manufacture of prothrombin.

But breast-fed babies do not get this essential ingredient for the normal clotting process. It is not until the child is two to three days old that the bacteria in newborn infants begin to release vitamin K in quantities large enough to assure that bleeding from a cut will not be excessive — or fatal in some cases.

It is not until the eighth day of an infant's life that all of the processes necessary to stem the flow of blood reach an *optimum* level. In fact, research has shown that the eighth day is actually the *most favorable* time to circumcise a male infant, for all of the factors required for blood clotting and healing reach *optimum* conditions on the eighth day of life.

By the eighth day the infant also had time to recover from the trauma of birth. The natural defense against infection would have had time to gain strength. Around the wound the white cells, the body's first line of defense against invading germs, would also have had time to reach an optimum level. In the days of Abraham, sterilization of the circumcision knife was not practiced. It would have certainly been covered with germs.

In Abraham's time, no one knew this. The fact that blood circulates in the human body was not discovered until A.D. 1616 by William Harvey, and germs were not proven to be the cause of infection until much later. But God knew! And modern science has demonstrated that the eighth day of an infant's life is exactly the perfect time for circumcision to take place.[6]

A Scientific Approach

The science of archaeology continues to confirm the Scriptures. David is a case in point. His name meant "beloved," but would you be surprised to hear that some scholars question whether David's name was actually David — at least in his early life? In tablets found at Mari on the Euphrates, the word *Davidum* was found repeatedly in them. In the context in which this word was used, it meant "commander" or "general." It was not a proper name, but a title. Could it be possible that the man we know as David was actually called something else as a child? Later in life when he exhibited great ability as a military leader, was he called the *Davidum*, the commander, and this became his name? Since the tablets found at Mari were written almost a thousand years prior to David's time, is it just a coincidence that the name and the title are so similar?

It does seem rather strange, however, that the name "David" is mentioned in the Bible referring to only one person. It must have been quite an uncommon name in those times. Some skeptical biblical scholars have long doubted that anything in the Bible before the Babylonian exile can be established with any historical accuracy. This included claims by some that David, himself, never existed and that David and his kingdom were a "myth," invented by later writers to build up a false pride in the accomplishment of early Israel.

Now an inscription has been deciphered which was found at Tel Dan in northern Galilee near the headwaters of the Jordan River. What it contains bears witness that David was indeed king of Israel and the kingdom was an important and powerful force in the Middle East at the time the Bible tells us that it was.

In 1993, Avraham Biran and his team of archaeologists from the Nelson Glueck School of Biblical Archaeology, found an inscription in a basalt stone protruding from a wall they had uncovered. In this inscription was the reference to *"the king of the House of David."* The script in which this is written is Old Hebrew, the type of script used before the destruction of the first temple by Nebuchadnezzar in 586 B.C.

This find, together with the deciphering of the Mesha stela, which tells of the victory by the Moabite King Mesha over the Israelites' territory east of the Jordan, should dispel any doubt that the biblical account of David and his kingdom are truly based on historical fact. Again, archaeology has put those who relegate the Bible to "myth" and "fiction" in their place.

The Sign of Salvation in the Lifeblood of All Living Things

In Leviticus 17:14 we are told, "For the life of the flesh is in the blood: and I have given it to you upon the altar to make an atonement for your souls: for it is the blood that maketh an atonement for the soul."

Before Jesus Christ made His ultimate and everlasting sacrifice for us on the cross of Calvary, the blood of animals was required as a sacrifice for the sins of the people. No longer is the blood of lambs or goats or bulls required for the salvation of our souls, for Jesus — the Lamb of God — made one final blood sacrifice for the sins of the world.

"Neither by the blood of goats and calves, but by his own blood he entered in once into the holy place, having obtained eternal redemption for us" (Heb. 9:12).

But did the blood of the sacrificed animals contain some sign of the supreme sacrifice which was to come, when God would offer up the life of His only begotten Son to bring salvation to all who would accept the blood of Jesus as atonement for their sins?

Blood is mentioned frequently in the Bible, appearing a total of 375 times. It is extremely important to us, for we could certainly not live without the blood which flows through our veins and arteries. But to Christians, blood has another, more spiritual, meaning. It was by the blood which Jesus shed for us on the cross that we have the promise of eternal life. And a sign of that promise is contained in the very blood which courses through our bodies, a sign of promise which God placed within us at the moment of our creation.

Let us try to find this special "sign," this mark of the promise which we have been given. To do this we have to examine just what this extraordinary life-giving fluid is that we call blood.

The volume of blood contained in the body of an average man or woman is approximately 1/11th of the weight of the body, from five to six quarts in volume. The heart pumps blood through the vascular system of arteries and veins.

In the lungs, the carbon dioxide which the blood has carried from the cells is released to be exhaled. The blood exchanges carbon dioxide for oxygen which is then carried to the cells of the body. It is this life-giving oxygen that allows the cells to metabolize food to sustain us. It is the red blood cells which are the carriers of both oxygen to the cells and carbon dioxide away from them to be exhaled.

One cubic centimeter of normal blood contains about five million red blood cells. It is a compound called hemoglobin within the red blood cells which allows this extraordinary metabolic process to occur. Without hemoglobin, we could not live. Not only people but the blood of all vertebrate and invertebrate animals depend on this system of oxygen/carbon dioxide transfer to exist. Surely, the Bible is correct when it states that "the life of the flesh is in the blood" (Lev. 17:11).

Blood is responsible for many other necessary functions. The white cells fight bacterial infections throughout the body. Blood carries antibodies which fight other infectious invaders such as viruses. It carries enzymes and proteins from the organs which produce them to where they are needed. Blood platelets are involved in the clotting process to stop bleeding. The blood also plays a major part in regulating our body temperature.

But it is the hemoglobin which contains the "sign" of the redemptive power of blood. Hemoglobin is a compound formed by the protein globulin joined together with an organo-metallic compound —

hematin. The metal portion of hematin is an atom of iron, held within the compound by a porphyrin complex. It is this structure which forms the hidden "sign" of the redemptive power of the blood which flows through our veins. This is clearly shown in Figure 1.

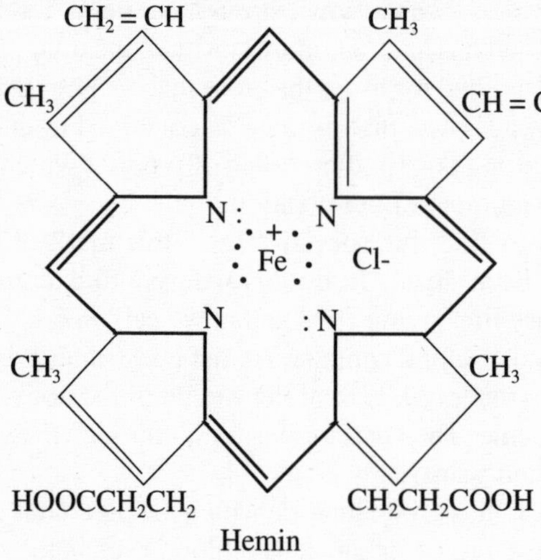

Hemin

Figure 1. The cross in the center of hemoglobin.

It is a cross!

When God created animals and man, He knew that it would be only through the shedding of the blood of Jesus Christ that our redemption would come. He placed the sign of that shed blood, the cross of Calvary, within the very life-blood of His creation.

But this is not the only place where this sign may be found, for the Creator placed it in other living things on earth as a testament to our salvation. Plants do not have blood, but there is a circulation of liquid in the green leaves of plants which carry nutrients from the roots to the growing portions of the plant.

Plants need carbon dioxide to exist and give off the oxygen that animals — and people — need in order to live. Plants do not contain hemoglobin; they depend on chlorophyll and light for photosynthesis.

The chlorophyll molecule is similar to hemoglobin in our blood in that the central portion of its structure is a magnesium complex of porphyrin. As in the center of the molecule of hemoglobin in blood, the center of the structure of chlorophyll also forms a cross. This is illustrated in Figure 2.

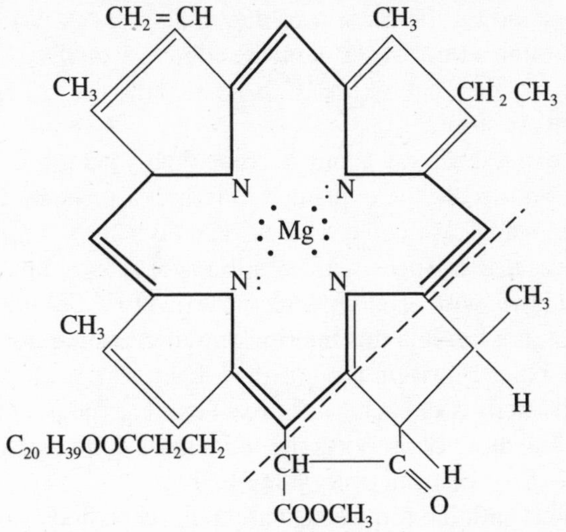

Chlorophyll a

Figure 2. The cross in the center of chlorophyll.

The Bible tells us that "life is in the blood." And the cross, the doorway which the sacrifice of Christ has provided for mankind to achieve eternal life, has been placed by the Creator within the blood of every man and woman on earth as a sign of that promise. It is fitting that secular science has found that sign within all living things.

Theories of Creation

Let us examine the current state of proven facts and the most prominent current theories of the creation of the universe and see for ourselves if the Bible and science are in conflict.

In the beginning God created the heaven and the earth.
And the earth was without form, and void (Gen. 1:1).

It is impossible to comprehend the vastness of the universe. To stand outside on a crisp, clear night and to gaze up at the glory of the heavens is to peer down the corridor of eternity. Our awe is identical to the Psalmist's who wrote, "When I consider thy heavens, the work of thy fingers, the moon and the stars, which thou hast ordained; What is man, that thou art mindful of him? And the son of man, that thou visitest him?" (Ps. 8:4).

What we see as scientists is order — magnificent, timeless order.

And as we stand on the surface of this minute speck of earth matter revolving around a third-rate star on the edge of a small galaxy, can we presume to explain what we see? Can we but guess at its beginning, its limits, and its destiny?

What can science say about this remarkably balanced and orderly universe? Can it really be explained in terms of physical laws which we can understand? We can try. All we can do is try.

This expanse of space with its billions of stars is linked together by physical laws, with each separate mass tied to every other mass by the forces of gravity. It is this interlocking force which holds together the delicate balance within the universe. Each star, each planet, each comet, each asteroid, or each galaxy itself exerts a force on every other body, which is directly proportional to its mass and inversely proportional to the distance from every other body.

This gravitational force constantly pulls each body toward every other body. But the universe is expanding. What causes each galaxy to be speeding away from some central point at a fantastic speed? The law of inertia causes this. A body at rest remains at rest until acted upon by an external force; and conversely, a body in motion remains in motion until some external force acts upon it.

Something, then, gave the tremendous push to the galaxies which are speeding away from a central point. But if this is true, then all of the galaxies must have at one time been located at that central point.

This means that the universe had to have a beginning. It was not always there. Some powerful force had to have acted upon all of the bodies in the universe to send them speeding away at the speed of 25,000 miles per second.

Theory has it that all of the matter in the universe was at one time concentrated at a single point, the central point from which the galaxies are now speeding away. The gravitational force of this mass would have resulted in a density of unimaginable magnitude. Or, since the Einstein equation, $E=mc^2$, states that matter and energy are interchangeable, then the energy concentration at that point would be of unimaginable magnitude.

The explosion of this point, resulting in the expulsion of all of the matter and energy in the universe, was then the beginning of creation.

Does this cause any controversy with the first chapter of Genesis? I can find none. The Bible tells us that in the beginning, God created the heaven and the earth. It does not tell us how.

The heat of the creation explosion caused matter to vaporize. But as this matter cooled, it coalesced, forming the stars and their accompanying planets. Does this contradict the biblical account? Not at all. In fact, the Genesis description of the earth being without form and void is an excellent description of just this happening.

The theory we have been examining is the big bang theory. It has found wide acceptance within the scientific community. But an explosion of the magnitude which we are considering would have resulted in chaos, not the orderly and law-abiding universe which we observe.

Well, say the astrophysicists, the law of gravity worked on the cooling gases, resulting in the orbital motions of the planets around their suns, and the rotation of each solar system within its galaxy. What began in chaos, they explain, was brought into order by the law of gravity.

This sounds good until the second law of thermodynamics is applied to it. This law just won't let that happen. The second law of thermodynamics tells us that an orderly system, if left to itself, will develop into a disorderly system. Things go the wrong way.

There are many other flaws in the big bang theory. The initial explosion would have resulted in at least a temporary random system. There is no evidence of the debris which would have resulted from such a random system, although recent discoveries have found the missing energy from such an event is all around the universe, even in areas of space where no matter can be detected.

If the universe had begun with a "big bang," elements would have been uniformly distributed throughout the universe. Spectroscopic examination of stars and the other planets in our own solar system indicate that the makeup of our earth is quite unique. In contrast with what we observe elsewhere, the earth contains only minute amounts of the rare gases such as neon, argon, and the like, and much greater quantities of oxygen, nitrogen, carbon dioxide, and water.

The big bang theory raises as many questions as it solves. But what about other theories of the origin of the universe?

Fred Hoyle of Cambridge and other astronomers have advanced what they call the steady-state expanding universe theory. These men do not ignore the evidence that the galaxies are rushing away from a central point at great speed, but postulate that at that central point matter is being continuously produced. This theory would have us to believe that all the galaxies will continue to expand away from the central point into infinite space and that the matter which is continuously being produced will condense into still more galaxies which will follow after them, forever, ad infinitum.

This theory runs into considerable opposition from one of the most basic natural laws. Matter can be converted into energy, and energy into matter, but matter can never be produced from nothing. Hoyle later questioned his own theory.

Another theory was advanced by Einstein, that of a finite universe of curved space. This is based on his theory of relativity and postulates space curved in a non-Euclidean form. In this theory, the universe would be both unbounded and of finite volume. But in this theory, as in the others, no attempt is made to explain the origin of matter or the energy required to start it in motion.

The universe had to have a beginning. Our observations indicate that the universe is composed of 98 percent hydrogen. The sun burns hydrogen at the rate of four million tons per second. If the universe had always been in existence, the sun and the billions upon billions of other stars would have long ago burned up all of their hydrogen fuel and the universe would be composed of frozen dead bodies, speeding on their way, unobserved in total and complete blackness.

None of these theories answer all of the questions concerning the origin of the universe. They are, as we have said, only theories. There are no proven answers to the question of how the universe was born.

But neither do any of them contradict the simple statements made in the first chapter of Genesis. Science does not know just how the universe came into being; and God does not tell us.

But doesn't it seem strange that this book of truth was given to us by way of a tribe of simple, wandering shepherds, a nation which had just been freed from centuries of slavery, when in the world at that time some great civilizations were flourishing?

The Egyptians had already built the pyramids, the Chinese had a very sophisticated culture, empires had risen and fallen in Babylon. Yet such great and simple truth came from men who had nothing which could not be carried from place to place on beasts of burden or upon their own backs.

The Bible was not intended to be a scientific book. It is a book concerned with man's relation with his creator. But what God does choose to tell us in the Bible about history, geography, politics, or science is true and accurate. There cannot possibly be any contradiction between science and the Word of God. All science can do is discover and report what God has already accomplished.

In the theories which we examined concerning the birth of the universe, all agree that the galaxies are rushing away from a central point at great speed. This is calculated from the red shift of their light caused by the Doppler effect, or so we believe. But we are really not certain that this red shift is actually caused by the Doppler effect or whether we are observing some other principle which we do not as yet understand.

It could very well be that we are measuring a contaminant, and not the speed of the galaxies at all. So you see that we really do not know very much at all about this universe in which we live.

Science and the Bible

The Bible was not intended to be a scientific text book. It was written so that we would have God's plan in order to live the lives that He intended for us to live. But where the Bible touches on a scientific subject, modern scientists are discovering that it has been far ahead of science in what it says.

This chapter certainly cannot give every example of this which exists, but I hope the reader can see from the few examples given, just how far ahead of the world's scientific knowledge the Bible really is.

Psalm 24:1 tells us, "The earth is the Lord's and the fulness thereof." Something flat cannot have fullness. Only something round can have fullness. But in the day that these words were written, the people of the earth believed that it was flat. Of course, God, the Creator of the earth, would know that it was round.

Job 26:7 tells us more. "He stretcheth out the north over the empty place, and hangeth the earth upon nothing." Who else but God would know, in the age when Job was written, about space — and the emptiness of it?

Who but God could have put forth dietary laws that even today make good sense for health. Who but the Creator, in the days when men had no knowledge of germs and the diseases which they cause, could know to forbid the eating of the foods which were most likely to carry them.

No one on earth could even guess that on the eighth day of a male infant's life, all of the natural forces would be at the optimum level for that child to be circumcised.

Who else but God would have been aware of bird-carried viruses being mutated in the intestines of pigs to make them pathogenetic to human beings?

The sign of His Son has been found within all of His living creation. And after man has wondered and theorized for so long about the origin of the human race, modern genetics has shown that the answer was right before our eyes — in the first chapter of the first book of God's book — the Holy Bible — which is far ahead of the limited and somewhat questionable knowledge that we call science.

Chapter 7 Footnotes

1 Robert W. Faid, *A Scientific Approach to Christianity* (Green Forest, AR: New Leaf Press, 1990), p. 81.

2 "Breakthroughs in Medicine," *Discover Magazine*, June 1993.

3 Stephen S. Morse and Robert D. Brown, "The Enemy Within," *Modern Maturity*, June/July 1993.

4 Ibid.

5 Robert W. Faid, *A Scientific Approach to More Biblical Mysteries* (Green Forest, AR: New Leaf Press, 1995), chapter 10.

6 Robert W. Faid, *A Scientific Approach to Biblical Mysteries* (Green Forest, AR: New Leaf Press, 1993).

8

The Unique Historical Distinctives of the Bible

Frank Harber

The Bible is the revelation of God to man. It is the record of God's dealings with man which serves as a divine compass to navigate men to eternal life. We know about God by reading about him in the Scriptures. The Bible never tries to prove the existence of God. It starts with the basic premise that God is real. The Bible purports itself to be the divine message of that God. If the Bible were not true, it would be certain that its God could not be real.

There are many religions of the world, each of which claims that its god is "real." Many religions also have scriptures which claim to have the same authority as the Bible. Other scriptures include the *Book of Mormon* of the Church of Latter Day Saints; the *Koran* of Islam; the *Eddas* of the Scandinavians; the *Tripitokas* of the Buddhists; the *Zendavesta* of the Persians; the *Analects* of Confucianism; the *Kojiki* and *Nihongi* of Shintoism; and the *Divine Principle* of the Unification Church (the Moonies). The Bible emphatically proclaims that all other gods are false and that there is only one true God (Ps. 96:4-5).

So how can we be so sure the Bible is written by the true God? After all, was not the Bible just written by a group of men? How can one know for sure that the Bible is true and can be trusted? Many say, "What does it matter if I believe the Bible; I believe in God, isn't that enough?" If you believe in God and you don't believe in the Bible, is your god really the God of the Bible? Of course not! If your god is not the God of the Bible, how do you know that your god could be real? You do not.

Belief in the Bible is no small matter. The stakes are eternal. Thus, for someone to declare that the Bible is not true is of grave consequence. Many attempts have been made to prove that the Bible is false, but these attempts have miserably failed. The evidence that the Bible is true is overwhelming.

The fact is the Bible is different and distinct from any other book ever written or collection of books ever compiled. Its distinguishing special features and characteristic qualities set it apart from any other publication, sacred or secular.

In the following pages, ten major distinctives, well established in the history of its existence and circulation, are offered as evidence that the Bible is true. While this list is not exhaustive, it contains more than enough information to demonstrate the unique historical accuracy and truth of the Bible.

The Distinctive of Fulfilled Prophecy

The Old Testament contains well over 2,000 predictive prophecies, which are very distinctive, specific, and detailed. A powerful evidence for the divine origin of the Scriptures is the fact of fulfilled prophecy. Isaiah reports that God has said, "Remember the former things of old: for I am God, and there is none else; I am God and there is none like me, DECLARING THE END FROM THE BEGINNING, AND FROM ANCIENT TIMES THE THINGS THAT ARE NOT YET DONE . . ." (Isa. 49:9-10).

The ability to predict the future is the unanswerable argument whether or not one is from God or merely a pretender. In Old Testament times, a prophet of God had to be one hundred percent accurate. Would-be prophets in ancient times whose predictions failed to come to pass were to be rejected . . . "thou shalt not be afraid of him" (Deut. 18:21-22). Under the law, such false prophets risked the death penalty if their predictions failed or even if they came to pass if they were teaching a false and idolatrous religion.

Only in the Bible does one find predictive prophecy. This important verification is noticeably absent from all other major religions such as Islam, Buddhism, Zoroastrianism, or in the writings of Confucius and Lao-tse. Other self-proclaimed prophets such as Nostradamus, Mother Shipton, Edgar Cayce, and Jean Dixon have delivered prophecies of which almost all have failed. The few which could be deemed as true are for the most part nebulous, general, and capable of multiple meanings.

Religions such as Jehovah's Witnesses and Mormonism are laden with many false prophecies and errors which create serious doubt as to their credibility. But the Bible has never failed in any single aspect of predictive prophecy.

The Bible also predicted the fall of great cities and civilizations. All such prophecies have occurred. The chart on the following page lists just a few examples of such prophecies.

In addition to the many prophecies of the Gentile nations, the Bible has much to say about the Jewish people. Deuteronomy 28 tells how they would be removed from their land if they were disobedient to God. God predicted that because of their disobedience, they would be scattered across the earth in unfamiliar lands (Lev. 26). The nation of Israel did indeed fall into idolatry and was removed from her homeland and later returned. They were removed a second time in A.D. 70 when the Romans destroyed Jerusalem as predicted by Jesus Christ (Luke 19:43-44; Matt. 24:2).

The Bible also predicted that though they would be scattered, they would one day return to their homeland (Ezek. 36; Amos 9). For years people said this would be impossible, yet in 1948 the Jews returned to their homeland from all parts of the earth.

Many other prophecies about the first coming of Jesus the Messiah were fulfilled in meticulous detail. This is covered extensively in another chapter in this book.

It is sufficient to say here that God has validated His Word through predictive prophecy so that you might know the Bible is true. No other religious book can authenticate itself like the Bible. This is a major and irrefutable distinctive of the Scriptures.

The Distinctive of Divine Inspiration

The Bible guarantees its own truthfulness by deriving its origination from the inspiration of God. The term "inspiration" comes from 2 Timothy 3:16 which says that "All Scripture is given by inspiration of God." The word translated as inspiration means "God-breathed." The Greek word for inspiration is *theopneustos,* which comes from the words "God" and "breath."

Consequently, the biblical writers were not inspired in the same way a great composer writes a song. Biblical writers were instructed by God to communicate that which they had received from God (2 Pet. 1:21). God chose to deliver His divine message through men. In doing so, God did not merely dictate His message word for word but used the personality and style of individuals to communicate His message.

God did not use men as tape recorders making the Scriptures some

SELECTED PROPHECIES

Civilization	Prophecy Location	Judgment	Fulfillment
Tyre	Ezek. 26:7-21	Destruction, never rebuilt	by Nebuchadnezar in 585-573 B.C. and Alexander the Great in 332 B.C.
Zidon	Ezek. 28:22-23	Blood flow in streets; destruction but no extinction	By Persians in 351 B.C.
Thebes, Egypt	Ezek. 30:14-16	Broken up and destroyed	Lies in ruins
Edom	Ezek. 35 Isaiah 18	Perpetual desolation, extinction	Disappeared after the fall of Jerusalem Jerusalem in A.D. 70.
Gaza, Philistia	Zeph. 2:4	Abandoned, baldness	Totally disappeared, buried under sand dunes
Bethel	Jer. 47:5	Brought to Amos 3:14-15	The original Bethel nothing disappeared
Babylon	Isa. 13:19-22	Destroyed, uninhabitable	Final destruction in A.D. 4
Nineveh	Nah. 1-3 Zeph. 2:13	Destroyed and desolated	Disappeared in 6th century B.C.
Samaria	Mic. 1:6	Destroyed, foundation ucovered, would become vineyard	By Sargon, 722 B.C.; Alexander, 331 B.C.; and John Hyrcanus, 120 B.C.
Capernaum	Matt. 11:23	Go down to hades	Disappeared after A.D. 800

kind of mechanical dictation. God did not place each writer in an unconscious trance, but used the personality of each writer to deliver His message. This may be readily observed in a careful reading of Luke's Book of Acts. Because Luke was a physician, he used medical terms which gave further insights into his message.

The New Testament writers recognized the authority of their message. Paul writes in 1 Corinthians 14:37, "If any man think himself to be a prophet or spiritual, let him acknowledge that the things which I write to you are the commandments of the Lord." Peter, in writing about the writings of Paul, puts them in the category of being "the Scriptures" (2 Pet. 3:15-16).

Some people teach that only some of the Bible is inspired, thus teaching that the Bible is not the Word of God, but that it only *contains* the Word of God. This is inconsistent with 2 Timothy 3:16 which says, "All Scripture is given by inspiration of God." Theologians refer to the entire Bible being inspired as "plenary verbal" inspiration of the Bible. Plenary means "all" and verbal means "word." Plenary verbal inspiration asserts that every word is God breathed, nothing is missing, and nothing is uninspired.

God's process of inspiration and supervision guarantees us that the message of the Scriptures is what God intended the writers to write. Therefore, when we read the Bible, we are reading the Word of God, and because we are reading the Word of God, we know that the Bible is true.

The Distinctive of Biblical Inerrancy

Because the Bible is the Word of God and God cannot lie (Isa. 55:10 - 11; John 17:17; Titus 1:2; Heb. 4:12), the Scriptures are totally trustworthy and are free from any mixture of error. Jesus said to the Father "Your word is truth" (John 17:17). God's word is described as "the word of truth" (2 Cor. 6:7; Col. 1:5; 2 Tim. 2:15; James 1:18). Inerrancy is not a theory about the Bible; it is the teaching of Scripture itself.

Some assert that only parts of the Bible are true. If this is so, how do we know that any of it is the truth? The truth is found in the fact that the Bible is never wrong. There are no verifiable errors to be found in the Bible. There are many who have claimed to have found supposed errors in the Bible.

In the late 19th century, the Institute of Paris issued 82 errors which it believed could discredit Christianity. Since that time, all 82 difficulties have been cleared away with new discoveries. What most people claim as errors in the Bible are not "errors" but "difficulties." Inconsistencies occur when people do not take time to find out all the facts. In most cases, Bible difficulties can be cleared up with an in-depth study of the problem. Two things should be understood at this point: lack of understanding is not an error nor is an unresolved difficulty an error. Many Bible difficulties have been solved as new historical and archeological discoveries have been made. A difficulty does not constitute an error!

Many fine scholarly and popular books have been written on the doctrine of biblical inerrancy and many others have examined the difficulties in the Bible. My book, *Reasons For Believing*, published by New Leaf Press, provides a great deal more information on this and other kindred subjects.

Regardless of any kind of difficulty found, not one "irreconcilable error" is to be found in the pages of Scripture. This is true of no other compilation of works by different authors on any subject. No other book has ever been subjected to such careful scrutiny and minute examination of every line of text by so many people in all of history.

The Bible can be trusted as truthful and accurate. It has withstood the test of time.

The Distinctive of Accurate Transmission

Because the Bible is an ancient book, some wonder if they are reading the original message of the Bible. The Bible is the most trustworthy document from all of antiquity. In standards of reliability, it stands without any single peer.

The original autographs of the Old Testament were written on papyrus. Papyrus deteriorates at a very rapid rate. Because of this, scribes were employed to copy the books of the Old Testament. These scribes believed the Scriptures to be the Word of God and went to great lengths to eliminate error. They followed strict Jewish traditions which even dictated how many columns and lines could be on a page, counting every line, word, and letter to find any mistakes. Any copy with even one mistake was destroyed. Because of this, the Old Testament has been preserved in its original form.

Prior to 1947, the oldest existing Old Testament copy was the Masoretic Text which is dated about A.D. 900. In 1947 the Dead Sea Scrolls were found at Qumran. Many of the scrolls dated older than the Masoretic Text. The Dead Sea Scrolls read almost identically to the Masoretic Text, both of which are identical to the Hebrew translations in our own Bibles. Only a small percent of variation can be found, all of which can be attributed to variations in spelling.

The reliability of the New Testament is also beyond reproach. More than 24,000 old partial and complete copies of the New Testament are available today. No other document of antiquity can even come close to such large numbers. Homer's *Iliad* is second with a mere 643 existing manuscripts. So sparse are copies of ancient classical works that 20 copies would be a lofty number of manuscripts. In addition to the New Testament manuscripts, there are over 86,000 quotations of the New Testament from the Early Church fathers. So thorough are these quotations that all but 11 verses of the New Testament can be reconstructed from this material, which dates to less than two hundred years after the coming of Jesus.

The New Testament, in comparison to other ancient manuscripts, is virtually free from any corruption. Textual critics have found only 1/2 of 1 percent differs. Thus, 99-1/2 percent of the New Testament has no variation. These variations, for the most part, deal with matters of spelling or word order. Not one single variant has any bearing on a doctrine of faith. In any case, the church has in its possession 100 percent of the New Testament.

Such confidence cannot be attributed to any other piece of classical literature. The accuracy of transmission in the manuscripts of the Bible testifies to their truthfulness.

The Distinctive of Archeological Evidence

Prior to the 19th century, there were many facts contained within the historical narratives which were not verifiable. In other words, there were many people, places, battles, and dates which were only found in the Bible. Severe attacks on the Bible originated in the 19th century which asserted that the writers of the Scriptures resorted to folklore and myth to validate their spiritual teachings. These critics asserted that the people and places recorded in the early parts of Scriptures were mere legend.

Just as these theories of higher criticism seemed on the verge of destroying the integrity of the Scriptures, an explosion of archeological evidence silenced the critics. In the early 19th century, scientists began to dig beneath the surface of the earth. They found ancient cities and civilizations they never knew existed. At a time when the Scriptures were said to be void of historical confirmation, the stones began to cry out otherwise. Another chapter in this book details much of this evidence.

The New Testament was also called into question in the 19th

century. The Book of Acts was thought to be a forgery from the mid-second century, but as the evidence poured in from modern archeological discoveries, Luke was found to be an historian of the highest order. Many places such as the Pool of Bethesda, the Pool of Siloam, Jacob's Well, and Pilate's residence in Jerusalem have been clearly identified.

The Bible is not a fairy tale of make-believe such as *Alice in Wonderland*. The Bible has been verified historically, which demonstrates that it is no forgery. In every instance, without exception, where the Bible has been examined in light of archeological evidence, it is true in what it says.

The Distinctive of Biblical Unity

The Bible towers above all other books as the all-time best seller in history. Over 40 authors combined to write the 66 books found in the Bible. It was written over a span of 1,500+ years, in three languages, and was composed in 13 countries on three continents. The Bible was written by men from all walks of life including kings, peasants, herdsmen, tax collectors, philosophers, statesmen, fishermen, poets, and scholars. It uses various literary forms such as history, poetry, proverbs, preaching, prophecy, parables, allegories, biography, drama, exposition, law, and letters. Yet, in spite of all this diversity, the Bible contains a vast unity. This unity is so unique that the books of the Bible form a unit, such that the Bible is not a mere collection of books, it is just one book.

Only an omniscient, all-controlling, all-directing Architect could construct such a cosmic drama. Every single author in the Bible is in perfect harmony with all the other writers in the areas of doctrine, ethics, faith, and the plan of salvation. One cannot even find a handful of books over a span of 1,500 years which all agree with one another without any conflicts whatsoever. Yet, all 66 books of the Bible are in perfect harmony.

The logical order of the Bible is truly amazing. The Old Testament is the preparation for the coming of Christ. The theme of Christ runs throughout the entire Bible. Just as the British navy's rope has a scarlet thread through it to prevent theft, the Bible contains a crimson aura that surfaces in every book of the Bible. The entire Bible exists to reveal Jesus Christ — He is the sole reason for every event in the Bible. The word "gospel" literally means "God's story." Bible history is actually His-story.

The New Testament is not a separate, later addition to the Old Testament, but the New maintains an indissoluble relationship to the

COMPARISON OF MAJOR WORKS OF ANTIQUITY WITH THE NEW TESTAMENT MANUSCRIPT

Author/ Work	No. of Copies	When Written	Earliest Copy	Time Span
New Testament	24,000+	A.D. 40-100	A.D. 125	25 yrs.
Homer	653	900 B.C.	400 B.C.	500 yrs.
Pliny the Younger (history)	7	A.D. 61-113	A.D. 850	750 yrs.
Suetonius	8	A.D. 75-160	A.D. 950	800 yrs.
Tacitus (minor works)	1	A.D. 100	A.D. 1000	900 yrs.
Caesar	10	100-44 B.C.	A.D. 900	1,000 yrs.
Tacitus (Annals)	20	A.D. 100	A.D. 1100	1,000 yrs.
Aristophanes	10	450-385 B.C.	A.D. 900	1,200 yrs.
Plato (Tetralogies)	7	427-347 B.C.	A.D. 900	1,200 yrs.
Herodotus (history)	8	480-425 B.C.	A.D. 900	1,300 yrs.
Demosthenes	200*	383-322 B.C.	A.D. 1,100	1,300 yrs.
Thucydides (history)	8	460-400 B.C.	A.D. 900	1,300 yrs.
Sophocles	193	496-406 B.C.	A.D. 1000	1,400 yrs.
Aristotle	49+	384-322 B.C.	A.D. 1100	1,400 yrs.
Euripides	9	480-406 B.C.	A.D. 1100	1,500 yrs.
Catullus	3	54 B.C.	A.D. 1550	1,600 yrs.

*All from one copy   +From any one work

Old. They are theological twin pillars which support the same redemptive message. There is nothing in the New Testament which cannot be found in the Old Testament:

> The New is in the Old contained;
>> the Old is by the New explained;
> The New is in the Old concealed;
>> the Old is by the New revealed;
> The New is in the Old foreshown;
>> the Old is in the New full-grown.

The New Testament compliments the Bible in every way. Each Testament serves as a column which holds up the entire structure. The structural unity of the Bible is symmetrically arranged so that it displays perfect agreement and order.

There was no chance of human conspiracy. The first writers had no way of knowing what others would write centuries later. The Bible towers as a great temple with 66 perfectly laid stones, and as with any structure, there must be an architect who provided the design. So complete is the unity of the Bible that no stone dare be taken away or added to its structure (see Rev. 22:19). This type of unity is a miracle of God which serves to alert mankind to the truthfulness of the Bible.

The Distinctive of Christ's Authentication

One of the greatest reasons for believing that the Bible is true is that Jesus believed in the truthfulness of the Scriptures. To reject Scripture is, in essence, to reject Jesus.

In controversies, Jesus simply quoted the Scripture to end the debate (Matt. 4:4-10; John 8:17). Jesus authoritatively answered His critics with questions like "Have you not read?" Jesus even used Scripture to overcome the temptations of Satan (Matt. 4:4).

It is illogical to affirm Jesus as the Son of God but assert that the Scriptures contain errors. If it were true that there are errors in the Bible, there are only four possibilities regarding the statements of Jesus.

First, Jesus was a fraud and lied about the Scriptures. It insults the intelligence of the reader to think for one moment that Jesus was a devious, evil, sinister liar. Jesus loved humanity. The entire life of Jesus was of kindness. The character of a person goes hand in hand with the claims of a person.

Second, Jesus knew there were errors but covered them up to accommodate the beliefs of His day. This is known as the

Archaeological Find	Significance
Mari Tablets	Over 20,000 cuneiform tables which date back to Abraham's time period explain many of the patriarchal traditions of Genesis.
Ebla Tablets	Over 20,000 tables, many containing law similar to the Deuteronomy law code. The previously thought fictitious five cities of the plain in Genesis 14 (Sodom, Gomorrah, Admah, Zeboiim, and Zoar) are identified.
Nuzi Tablets	They detail customs of the 14th and 15th century B.C. parallel to the patriarchal accounts such as maids producing children for barren wives.
Black Stele	Proved that writing and written laws existed three centuries before the Mosaic laws.
Temple Walls of Karnak, Egypt	Signifies a 10th century B.C. reference to Abraham.
Laws of Eshnunna (c. 1950 B.C.) Lipit-Ishtar Code (c. 1860 B.C.) Laws of Hammurabi (c. 1700 B.C.)	Show that the law codes of the Pentateuch were not too sophisticated for that period.
Ras Shamra Tablets	Provide information on Hebrew poetry.
Lachish Letters	Describe Nebuchadnezzar's invasion of Judah and give insight into the time of Jeremiah.
Gedaliah Seal	References Gedaliah is spoken of in 2 Kings 25:22.
Cyrus Cylinder	Authenticates the biblical description of Cyrus' decree to allow the Jews to rebuild the temple in Jerusalem (see 2 Chron. 36:23; Ezra 1:2-4).
Moabite Stone	Gives information about Omri, sixth king of Israel
Black Obelisk of Shalmaneser III	Illustrates how Jehu, king of Israel, had to submit to the Assyrian king.
Taylor Prism	Contains an Assyrian text which details Sennacherib's attack on Jerusalem during the time of Hezekiah, king of Israel.

"Accommodation Theory." This theory holds that Jesus went along with erroneous views in order to present His message to listeners. This theory is not consistent with the gospels which show that Jesus never accepted the mistaken views of His time. Jesus often refuted wrong traditions saying, "You have heard that it was said. . . . But I say to you . . ." (Matt. 5). If Jesus would have taught error as being truth, He would have been guilty of deception.

Third, there were errors in the Bible but Jesus was ignorant of them. If Jesus was mistaken, He certainly was not who He claimed to be and was a fraud. If the errors were in the Bible and Jesus was not aware of them, He could not have been the Son of God as He claimed.

Fourth, the view of Jesus was correct. The Bible is free from errors. Thus, it is illogical for a believer to reject the truthfulness of Scripture. For the Christian, the authority of Christ settles the issue of the truthfulness of the Bible.

The Distinctive of Faithful Integrity

The Bible contains no traces of being a forgery. If the Bible was the invention of human minds, the characters of the Bible would have been cast in a favorable light. Yet, the great victories of the Israelites are never attributed to courage or superior strategy. The weaknesses of men are exposed as the greatness of God is extolled. Even the greatest heroes of God are exposed when they erred in their own judgment. A forged Bible would have tried to cover up all negative elements.

However, the writers of the Bible did not try to cover up the facts. One finds the prominent disciples arguing, struggling with doubts, and giving up hope. The New Testament writers were committed to telling the truth as eyewitnesses. They wrote their writings in the same generation as the actual events. If they did not tell the truth, there were plenty of people around that could refute them. Because most of the New Testament was written between A.D. 40 and 70, there was not enough time for myths about Christ to be told without being refuted.

The New Testament writers had nothing to gain by falsifying information. Even when subjected to persecution and martyrdom, they maintained that what they had preached and taught was truth. No atheist would be willing to die for such an elaborate religious sham. Why would the disciples risk eternal damnation over a religious enterprise from which they would not receive material or financial benefits? Only men of great spiritual integrity would have maintained their position of the Scriptures under such intense life-threatening pressures.

The Distinctive of Historical Canonicity

The question which invariably arises when speaking of the Scriptures is, "How does one know which books in today's Bible are the right ones?" It is important to note at this point that a group of men did not just arbitrarily select a group of books to be used in compiling the Bible. They only officially "recognized" which books had always been upheld as being scriptural.

The processes of formation for the Old Testament and New Testament differed. The Old Testament developed over a period of 1,100 years. When Moses produced the Torah, it was immediately identified as inspired and authoritative. In time, other works were added which were deemed to be authenticated by God. A threefold division arose of Law, Prophets, and Writings. These writings eventually became a completed collection and came to be referred to as "the Scripture(s)." The Christian Church accepted these completed works in their entirety as found in the Hebrew Bible (Matt. 22:29; John 10:35, 19:36; Acts 18:24; Rom. 1:2; 2 Pet. 1:20).

The New Testament developed in a much shorter time span. Because Jesus was the promised Messiah of the Old Testament, His words were considered divine and authoritative. The early Christians produced works which recorded the words of Jesus called "the gospels." The letters of the apostles and Paul were reproduced and circulated along with gospels throughout all the churches (Col. 4:16; 2 Pet. 3:16). These writings begin with the Book of James (circa A.D. 45) and conclude with the Revelation. The collection of these works became known as the "Canon." *Canon* is a Greek term which meant a "list" or "index." The process of canonization was not a formal process by which church leaders all met to decide which books could be included in the canon. Books which were deemed to be inspired by God were immediately treated as authoritative. These works began to be assimilated into a collection of sacred writings.

A crisis in the fourth century caused the church to give a formal statement on which books were canonical. In A.D. 397, a church council was held in Carthage which endorsed the exact 27 books of the New Testament we now regard as canonical. These 27 books were all apostolic in origin, authoritative in spiritual content, and accepted universally among the orthodox churches. These tests were used at the council to eliminate the spurious gospels and epistles written by heretical groups. This process of canonization has ensured that today's Bible contains only the books which were attested as being inspired by God.

The Distinctive of Absolute Preservation

The Bible has been the most persecuted book in all of history. For two thousand years every possible effort has been made to undermine the authority of the Bible. Attacked by emperors, popes, kings, and scholars, the Bible has endured attacks by intellectual, political, philosophical, scientific, and physical forces.

The earliest attacks came in the form of arguments from Celsus, Porphyry, and Lucien. It was next attacked by the emperors who made it a capital offense to have a Bible. The fiercest opposition came in A.D. 303 from the Roman emperor Diocletian. Every family caught with a Bible was put to death. Every confiscated Bible was burned, and thousands of Christians were slain. So successful was Diocletian's attack that he thought he had brought an end to the Bible. He erected a column and inscribed the words *Extincto nomine Christianorum*, which means "The name of the Christians has been extinguished." His efforts failed. Within just ten years Christianity became the official religion of the Roman Empire.

Great thinkers throughout the centuries have sought to destroy the Bible. The famous French philosopher of the 18th century, Voltaire, attacked the Bible and predicted that within 50 years it would be forgotten. However, 50 years after his death, the Geneva Bible Society used Voltaire's printing press and home to produce Bibles.

Similarly, two centuries ago, Thomas Paine attacked Christianity in his book entitled *The Age of Reason*. Paine believed his arguments were powerful enough to dispose of the Bible permanently. He asserted that within a few years the Bible would be out of print. Two hundred years later Paine and his book have been relegated to antiquity, yet the Bible remains the all-time best seller since its first printed copy.

How would one regard a man who had been hanged, poisoned, drowned, burned, and yet would not die? One would regard this person as superhuman. This is how the Bible should be viewed. It has been burned, persecuted, mocked, and torn to pieces, yet never damaged. The Bible is a superhuman book. If it were the work of men, it would have long since been destroyed.

If the Bible were merely a human book, its survival would be difficult to account for. Books, like humans, have a very short life span. The average book only survives about 20 years. The Bible, with its thousands of ancient manuscripts, towers above any other work which has survived a thousand years. But one need not go back to the ancient past to make comparisons. Today, more has been written about the Bible than any other one thousand books put together. It has now been translated, at least in part, into over 2,200 languages, with 363 languages with the whole Bible.

How remarkable for a book which for centuries was pitted against the most intelligent and powerful forces in the world. During such dark times, only a persecuted and despised minority sought to uphold the Bible. No powerful army ever defended the Bible, but for every Bible destroyed, thousands have appeared. Like the three Hebrew men thrown into the fiery furnace, the Bible could not be burned out of existence. Out of the ashes arose the reproductive seeds of multiplication. Like a mythical Hydra with nine heads, each time one head was cut asunder, two more appeared. Every persecution brought against the Bible has resulted in the multiplication of the Scriptures. Throughout history, many times it seemed as though the Bible had been driven out of existence. Though the death bell rang, the corpse would not stay buried. The hammers of the Bible's critics have long since been worn out on the anvil of the Word of God.

God himself promises the perseverance of his Word: "Heaven and earth will pass away, but My words will by no means pass away" (Matt. 24:35). Isaiah wrote over 2,500 years ago, "The grass withers, the flower fades, but the word of our God stands forever" (Isa. 40:8).

The Bible is at the same time the most loved and most hated book of all time. Why has the Bible generated so much animosity? Precisely for the simple reason that the Bible reveals the guilt of men and holds them accountable for their sins. The problems most people have with the Bible are not its alleged difficulties, but with its teachings on how sinful man is reconciled to a Holy God. Mark Twain spoke of this problem when he commented, "Most people are bothered by those passages in Scripture which they cannot understand. The Scripture which troubles me the most is the Scripture I do understand."

Dr. R.A. Torrey was once confronted by a young man who attacked the Bible. Insightfully, Torrey asked the question, "Is your life right?" The young man abandoned the conversation and quickly excused himself. Like this young man, most people have not rejected Christianity on intellectual grounds but on spiritual grounds. What about you? Have you ever honestly done an in-depth study on the veracity of the Scriptures? To reject the Bible without conclusively demonstrating it to be false is a most unwise decision. The evidence clearly favors the truthfulness of the Bible.

Jesus, archeology, history, prophecy, and transformed Christians all testify to the fact that the Bible is true. The Bible's message is that man is in rebellion against God. The Bible requires man to repent (Luke

13:3) of his sin and commit his life to Jesus Christ as Lord and Savior. Is your life right? If not, you can change that right now. You can at this very moment commit your life to Jesus and become a Christian.

9

The Powerful Worldwide
Impact of the Bible

Jim Combs

Not only is the Bible the most unique book in history, it has had the most profound impact on the culture, the beliefs and the practices of this planet's inhabitants of any single volume in all of history. WHY?

It began 3,500 years ago in written form in Hebrew, penned by kings, shepherds, historians, and prophets, all of whom were Jews, or Israelites as they were called prior to 550 B.C. The Old Testament was written altogether by Jews with the possible exception of Daniel 4, where Nebuchadnezzar is recorded as the author of an ancient state document.

The New Testament, recorded on papyrus scrolls between about A.D. 45 and 100, was likewise of Jewish composition with the single probable exception of Luke, who wrote both a Gospel and the Acts of the Apostles. Many scholars believe he was a Gentile, based in part on Paul's listing of Jewish disciples in Colossians 4:7-11 in which Luke is not named (as is Mark and several others). Luke is listed (Col. 4:10) with another group, including Epaphras and Demas, who are presumed to be Gentiles, but were followers of Paul the Jew, who was "the Apostle to the Gentiles" (Rom. 11:13). This was written in Greek, an international language in the First Century.

From this relatively tiny racial and religious group came the Christians, the "sect of the Nazarenes," which primarily in the post-Resurrection years was a Jewish sect. They expanded their outlook in one generation to reach, in time, the whole Gentile world with the gospel, a goal which Jesus had commanded.

How the Bible Came Down to Us Through the Centuries

Prior to the coming of Jesus and His powerful ministry, the sacred Scriptures were considered by the Jews to be theirs alone, except for a relatively few Gentile converts to Judaism. The death, burial and Resurrection of Jesus changed that, for He began to be recognized as the Savior of the world, who died for the sins of all mankind.

At first, wherever Jesus was preached, first among Jews in the first century by the 12 Jewish Apostles, the Scriptures used were what we call the Old Testament. That consisted of the 22 or 24 (as some counted) books, which contain the same material as the 39 our Bibles have always had. In the Jewish canon the order is different and a number of books are combined, such as all the minor prophets, known as the Twelve.

As the gospel of Jesus, the good news of salvation for the whole world, was preached, the Apostles and a few other "apostolical men" began to write the biographies of Jesus, letters of instruction for godly living, and historical and prophetical material. The New Testament began possibly as early as A.D. 45 with the composition of the Gospel of Mark, according to Dr. Joseph O'Calligan of the Pontifical Biblical Institute in Rome, who has studied a fragment of that gospel found in the Dead Sea Scrolls. By not later than A.D. 100 and the completion of the Apocalypse, all of the Gospels, the historical Book of Acts and the letters of Paul, Peter, John, James, and Jude were completed, comprising 27 books with Revelation crowning and concluding the Bible.

The Hebrew Scriptures had been translated into Greek two centuries before Christ and most Old Testament quotations found in the New Testament are quoted from that version.

As proven by the Dead Sea Scrolls, handwritten copies of the Old Testament on leather and papyrus were meticulously written with extreme accuracy with scarcely any variation, other than spelling or occasional word placement. The oldest Hebrew manuscripts are practically identical with copies made centuries later. No other book has ever been so perfectly preserved by divine providence for all time.

New Testament writings were likewise very carefully copied, but not always with as great exactitude as the Old Testament. However, multiplied thousands of copies of the Bible, or portions of the New Testament or pages have been found which go back to the second century, in some cases, not far removed from the original autographs. There is more evidence for the accuracy of the New Testament and the care which copyists exercised in being exact than there is for any other books which have come down from antiquity. Frank Harbor provides us a wonderful chart demonstrating this fact in his chapter on the unique distinctives of the Bible.

Though originally written in *Koine* (common) Greek, in the second century, some of these books were translated and copied in other languages spoken by various peoples both within and on the fringe of the ruling Roman Empire. Probably the first is known as the Peshitto (which means "common" or "simple") which is in Syriac, a form of Aramaic commonly spoken in Syria and surrounding provinces in the Eastern Mediterranean world. Before A.D. 200 much of the Bible was beginning to appear in Old Latin.

However, in the centuries following the conversion of the emperor Constantine to Christianity (circa A.D. 313) and the consequent popularization of the Christian religion, the Bible was translated into Coptic (old Egyptian), Ethiopic, Armenian, Gothic (Germanic) Georgian (spoken around the Black Sea), Arabic, and Slavonic.

The Latin language, spoken throughout the Western Roman Empire, and the Greek language, used throughout the Eastern Roman Empire, with its capital at Constantinople, were the major languages of civilization for centuries. A great scholar named Jerome translated the Gospels into Latin, then the vernacular of "vulgar" tongue, about A.D. 383; the remaining New Testament slightly later; and the Old Testament from the Hebrew between 390 and 405. The Vulgate became the major Bible of the Western world and continued in use for a thousand years.

Scholars and monks in the Eastern Roman Empire, known by historians as the Byzantine Empire, preserved and copied the Scriptures in Greek, producing thousands of manuscripts for circulation among the churches over a period of a thousand years. A vast body of material survives unto this day. This was known as the "Byzantine" Text, which has been designated the Received Text or Majority Text on which English Bibles, including the King James Version, were based in modern times.

After the fall of the Western Roman Empire (A.D. 476), a long, dark night of illiteracy descended on the Western world. While mainly the clergy, the educated, and the elite were literate, their knowledge of biblical ideas and ideals gradually influenced the barbarian tribes who overran the Empire. However imperfect it may have been, Christian civilization, based on the Bible, survived.

After A.D. 1054 the Greek Orthodox Church and other "Orthodox" communions in Eastern Europe and Western Asia no longer co-operated with the Western or Roman Catholic form of Christianity. But all claimed to base their religion, traditions, and practices on a biblical foundation. In A.D. 988, the teachings of the Bible penetrated further into the vast Asian continent, and what evolved into "Holy Russia" became nominally "Christian."

Thus, the Bible in the first millennium after Christ, through the preaching and teaching of the churches, however imperfect they may have been, nevertheless impacted all of Western civilization and influenced the East.

Though militant Islam sought to conquer the nominal Christian world by force and to convert the millions, neither the Bible nor the flawed Christianity of those centuries were totally supplanted by the Koran and the new Muslim religion coming out of Asia in the 7th through the 12th centuries. Many African and Middle Eastern countries and cultures, however, became Islamic.

Until less than six centuries ago, all copies of the Scriptures, all books and records of all kinds, could only be preserved for posterity in letters and words written by hand. However, a remarkable, defining event would dramatically and vastly enhance the circulation and impact of the sacred Scriptures, exceeding all that had been before.

The Invention of the Printing Press
The Gutenberg Bible

Named after Johannes Gutenberg, who completed and printed it in about 1455, this Bible in Latin was the first complete book (in three volumes), produced with movable metal type and published, in the history of the world. His methodology, based on a concept of printing developed by the Chinese and imported to the West, was shared or copied by several contemporaries, some of whom are occasionally given credit for the actual printing of this first book, the first Bible. Undoubtedly, it was the dream and work of Gutenberg which made it a reality. Publication was in Mainz, Germany.

It is sometimes called the "42 line" Bible. Since Cardinal Mazarin of Paris received an early copy and evidently was involved in its production, the title "Mazarin Bible" is also used.

Experts generally agree that the Bible, though uneconomic in the use of space (it required 3 large volumes), displays a technical efficiency not substantially improved upon before the 19th century.

The original number of copies of this milestone work is unknown, but some 47 are still in existence, 13 in the United States. There is a perfect velum copy in the United States Library of Congress. Almost complete texts may be found at the Huntington Library (California), the New York Public Library, the Harvard and Yale University libraries and several other places.

This first elegant Bible, printed by movable type, would serve as a portent for the massive, worldwide distribution of the sacred volume, eventually in hundreds of languages and billions of copies of part or all of the Word of God. During the last 500 years it has been "the best seller" of this Second Millennium.

Christopher Columbus, Christ-bearer to the World

At the close of the 15th century printed Bibles in Latin began circulating into universities, churches, monasteries, and in the homes of the wealthy. Thousands were printed by various publishing houses, as other books began to roll off the presses all over Europe. Finally, for those who understood Latin, the official language of the Church in the West and understood by the educated everywhere, the Word of God became available for personal study. One man powerfully impacted by his study of the Scriptures was Christopher Columbus, whose voyages began the defining geo-political event of the Second Millennium, the discovery of America.

Secular history has given inadequate recognition to the spiritual motivation that prompted the great "Admiral of the Ocean Seas" to spearhead for many years his dream of opening the Far East to travel, trade, and THE GOSPEL.

His sincere and deep spirituality has been highlighted by Kevin Miller, editor *of Christian History* in a series of articles in 1992. These following quotations from his research reflect the spirituality of Columbus' heart:

> "He (our Lord) has bestowed the marine arts upon me in abundance."
>
> "Who can doubt that this fire was not merely mine, but also the Holy Spirit who encourage me with a radiance of marvellous illumination from His Sacred Scriptures . . . urging me to press forward."
>
> "With a hand that could be felt, the Lord opened my mind to the fact that it would be possible . . . and opened my will to desire to accomplish this project . . . the Lord purposed there should be something miraculous in this matter of the voyage to the Indies."
>
> "I spent six years at your royal court (Ferdinand and

Isabella), disputing the case with so many people of great authority, learned in all the arts. And finally, they concluded that it was all in vain, and they lost interest. In spite of that it later came to pass as Jesus Christ our Saviour had predicted and He had previously announced through the mouths of his holy prophets . . . I have already said that reason, mathematics and maps of the world were of no use to me in the execution of the enterprise of the Indies. What Isaiah said was completely fulfilled."

Possibly he was thinking of Isaiah's prophecies of the word of the Lord going to the ends of the earth and he may have pondered Isaiah 40:22, which speaks of "the circle of the earth."

Let it be emphatically stated that Columbus never set out just to prove that the world was round, as this was an acknowledged probability among the educated people of his day. Various ancient Greek writers had advanced this theory, seeing the curved shadow of the earth on the moon during lunar eclipses. Rather, Columbus wanted to gain access to the wealth of the Orient in order to help fund a new Crusade to the Holy Land, hopefully wresting its control from the Muslims. He also wished to "Christianize" the heathen of the Orient. He wanted to spread the message of the Bible, as he understood it. This was a major motivation. A few years ago his unfinished book entitled *Book of Prophecies* was translated into English. In it he sets forth his conviction that he was a chosen vessel to spread the knowledge of God and Christianity to unreached peoples. Though by no means faultless and not a saint, he nevertheless was deeply religious and loved the Bible. His name means "Christ-bearer."

Perhaps in those years prior to the Reformation, when some were truly trusting Christ as the sole Savior, Christopher Columbus, by divine providence, really was "Christ-bearer" to the new world.

With Columbus and the successor explorers and colonizers of the New World came also the Bible and the clergy to spread the message of Christianity. Of course, these people were not perfect any more than the warring tribes and peoples in the Western Hemisphere were perfect. But Catholic Christianity became the dominant religion of what we now call Latin America, while eventually Protestantism thrived among the majority in North America. While there are major differences in theology, the fact is that the Bible powerfully impacted civilization on both continents, again, however, imperfectly.

In Print!
The Bible in English and Other Languages

Space forbids a full recounting of the translation of the English Bibles from Greek and Hebrew through the last half-millennium. Suffice it to say that the first major translation of the New Testament was from Latin Vulgate in about 1360-80, prepared by John Wycliffe, a Catholic priest sometimes called "the morning star of the Reformation." About 150 handwritten copies were produced by him and his followers.

During the 16th century, printed translations of the Bible in various languages began to circulate. The great reformer, Martin Luther, translated the Bible into German from the Greek and Hebrew texts, preserved by the monks of Eastern and Western Europe (as well as the rabbis of the Jews). Soon the Bible appeared in Spanish, Portuguese, French, Dutch, and other European languages. While circulation was limited with copies held mostly by clergy in many countries, "the Word of God is not bound" (2 Tim. 2:9).

Contemporary with Martin Luther and aided and protected for a time by him in Germany, the English Greek language scholar William Tyndale translated the New Testament from the "Received (Greek) Text," as compiled from various manuscripts by another scholar named Erasmus. This was in 1525. So fluently magnificent and so accurate in translation was his masterful work that some 90 percent of his phraseology appears in the 1611 King James Version. Those political and religious forces that fought the Reformation succeeded in putting him to death in 1536. His offense was circulating the Word of God in the English tongue.

From 1535 (one year before Tyndale martyrdom) to 1539 several other editions of the English Bible appeared in print. These bore the names of Coverdale, Matthew, and Tavener. Of the several revisions and the Bible which were published, two are worthy of special mention. The *Geneva Bible* came off the press in 1560 and was popular for nearly a century. It was the Bible of the Puritans and Pilgrims. Produced in 1568, the *Bishop's Bible* was widely promoted in churches by the Anglican bishops of the times, but was never very popular. Finally, in 1604 King James I gave an endorsement to the Church to produce what has become known as the *Authorized Version*. Some 54 learned men spent several years in careful translation of the Old and New Testaments from the original languages to produce the revered King James Version. Actually, it was the Third Authorized Version endorsed by the Anglican Church, the first being the Geneva Bible and the second the Bishop's Bible.

All drew heavily on the genius of William Tyndale.

The KJV was revised several times in minor ways in the years that followed (1615, 1638, 1762, 1769) with many slight improvements in the way of correcting various misprints and modernizing spelling. A few obsolete words like *sith* and *fet* were retranslated. It was the King James Version primarily which most powerfully impacted English-speaking people in England and America and in the 18th and 19th centuries the British Empire's colonies all over the world.

Among Catholics, the Douay-Rheims Version, a translation of the Latin Vulgate with comparisons from the Greek and Hebrew texts into English made its appearance in print between 1582 and 1610.

America's Beginnings and the Bible's Use

By the beginning of the 17th century the Bible had become the most read book among English-speaking peoples. Its ideas of personal responsibility to God, freedom of conscience, democratic self-government in local churches (among the non-conformists who declined to be a part of state controlled churches), and humanitarian ideas of love, hope, faith, respect, and hundreds of other biblical concepts were increasing in influence, as more people could read the Word of God.

The Mayflower Compact

In 1620 the famous Pilgrims on the sailing ship *Mayflower* arrived at Plymouth Rock in Massachusetts. Seeking religious and personal freedoms, which we now take for granted in America, they composed the Mayflower Compact, which begins as follows:

> In ye name of God. Amen. We whose names are underwritten, the loyal subjects of our dread sovereign Lord, King James, by the grace of God, of Great Britain, France & Ireland king, defender of the faith, &c., having undertaken, for the glory of God, and the advancement of ye Christian faith, and honor our king & country, a voyage to plant ye first colonies in ye northern parts of Virginia, do by these presents solemnly & mutually in ye presence of God, and one another, covenant & combine our selves together into a civil body politic for our better ordering and preservation & furtherance of ye ends aforesaid.

Three years later Governor William Bradford issued the first Thanksgiving Proclamation, which reads in part:

> Inasmuch as the great Father has given us this year and abundant harvest . . . has granted us freedom to worship God according to the dictates of our own conscience; now I, your magistrate, do proclaim to all ye Pilgrims . . . do gather at ye meeting house . . . there to listen to ye pastor and render thanksgiving to ye Almighty God for all his blessings.

Thus began a tradition that continues to this day.

Religion and Political Ideas in New England

A few years later came the Bible-believing Puritans to actually found the colony of Massachusetts, again with the prime goal of establishing religious freedom and democratic rights.

The founders of Connecticut, who enacted what was the first constitution in America in 1630, were strongly influenced by biblical principles and the preaching ministry of Thomas Hooker of the First Church in Hartford.

At the opening session of the General Court in Connecticut, on May 31, 1638, Mr. Hooker preached a sermon in which he maintained, "The foundation of authority is laid in the free consent of the people, that the choice of public magistrates belongs unto the people by God's own allowance," and "They who have power to appoint officers and magistrates have the right also to set the bounds and limitations of the power and place unto which they call them."

In Rhode Island Religious Freedom Blossomed

Through the leadership of Roger Williams and John Clarke, Rhode Island became a colony with very advanced religious and civil rights.

On March 7, 1638, John Clarke, with three hundred others, having left Boston by ship, composed a document signed by 19 leaders of the new colony on the Island of Aquidnick, which became known as the "Portsmouth Compact":

> We whose names are underwritten do hereby solemnly and in the presence of Jehovah incorporate ourselves into a body politick and, as He shall help, will submit our persons, lives and estates unto our Lord Jesus Christ, the King of Kings and Lord of Lords, and to all those present and most absolute laws of His given in His holy Word of truth to be guided and judged thereby."

John Clark, a Baptist minister and pastor for 40 years, a physician, scholar and business man, along with Roger Williams, strongly influenced the colony with biblical truths and virtues. It was Dr. Clarke in 1663 who secured from King Charles II a document still preserved in Providence at the capitol entitled "The Charter of 1663." It was the most liberal and democratic document issued up to that time in history by any ruler, a charter which practically guaranteed self-government and full freedoms in all areas of life, under law. The following excerpt from the document, which was written for the king by Clarke, is inscribed on the west facade of the capitol building in Providence:

> That it is much on their hearts (if they may be permitted) to hold forth a lively experiment, that a most flourishing civil state may stand and best be maintained, and that among our English subjects, with a full liberty in religious concernments.

John Clarke's political theory, based on the Bible, was a molding factor in the development of American early democracy.

Quaker William Penn, founder of Pennsylvania, likewise made his vast contribution to early American democratic and religious ideals.

Much more could be said, but space forbids citing thousands of quotations of early leaders in America who were powerfully influenced by the Bible. Regrettably, present liberal historical revisionists in many universities and centers of learning have either never studied or have chosen to ignore the deep religious and biblical roots of the great American democratic experiment of the last four centuries.

Meanwhile in England

By the early 18th century, conditions in England had deteriorated morally and religiously. Cycles of spiritual revival and moral declension have a way of recurring, as any reading of the history of ancient Israel and Judah clearly demonstrates.

This was such a time. Bishop Berkley wrote in 1738, "Morality and religion have collapsed to a degree that has never been known in a Christian country."

Into this era of spiritual darkness came a most remarkable spiritual duo, John and Charles Wesley. They were joined by a third dynamic evangelist and motivator, George Whitefield. Out of their efforts both in England and America came a great religious awakening and the birth of what we know as the Methodist Church. Again, much could be written of this history-changing religious and social revival and revolution, but consider these quotations:

> America was born in a revival of religion. Back of that revival were John Wesley, George Whitefield, and Francis Asbury.
> Calvin Coolidge

> The foundation of democracy in the sense of spiritual independence . . . it is probably that democracy owes more to Nonconformity than to any other single movement.
> R. H. Fawney

> In the vast work of social reorganization, which is one of the dominant characteristics of 19th century England, it would be difficult to overestimate the part played by the Wesleyan revival.
> Elie Hoevy in *History of the English*

> I do not know the exact figures to the debt that America owes us. Write on the balance sheet: Debtor — a thousand and ninety millions; Creditor — John Wesley and George Whitefield.
> David Lloyd George, one time Prime
> Minister of England

The widespread social reforms of the 18th and 19th centuries both in America and England were mightily enhanced by the Wesleyan revival, which involved millions of people coming to Christ on both sides of the Atlantic, as the Bible's gospel was proclaimed and its standards stressed.

It is not an exaggeration to say that much of modern democracy, capitalism, our ideals of justice, equality, liberty, and freedom, though begun early in America by the 17th and 18th-century founders of this American nation, were reinforced and adopted on an ever-creasing scale as a result of the Bible preaching of the Wesleys and their millions of hearers and followers. And what effected England in the way of just social reform was carried over to a great extent throughout the world through the British Empire.

Wherever European colonists went, from Columbus to the

explorers of the 17th century, the Bible also went.

Wesleyan Revival Sparked World Missions Outreach

Historian Robert Hastings Nichols wrote:

> Greatest of all the results of the (Wesleyan) revival was the rise of the modern missionary movement. Other influences, particularly recent discoveries in the southern Pacific had to do with this. But without the impulse to Christian service which the religious revival during the Wesley ministries gave, the missionary revival would never have occurred. The splendid honor of leadership in this awakening of missions belongs to William Carey, a cobbler and Baptist lay preacher. In the face of contemptuous opposition he pressed on his associates his vision of the conversion of the non-Christian world. Finally in 1792 he secured the organization of the Baptist Society for Propagating the Gospel among the Heathen. Its first missionary was Carey himself, whom it sent to his noble work in India. The Baptist example was soon followed. Organized were the London Missionary Society in 1799 by Congregationalists (earlier known as Puritans), and the Church Missionary Society in 1799 by the Evangelicals of the Church of England. The Methodists soon took up the cause.
>
> All the great religious bodies of England felt the missionary inspiration by the end of the 18th century. Their enthusiasm spread to Scotland, America and the continent of Europe. Throughout the 19th century the world evangelization movement continued with the spread of what became thousands of missionaries carrying the Bible and the Gospel to every continent and most of the countries of the earth. The Bible, more than ever before with the increase of literacy and the completion of more translations in more languages, became to an even greater extent the most read book in the world.

And it impacted society wherever it went.
Nichols continued:

> The foreign missions awakening in England soon won response from the newly revived Christianity in America.

Samuel Mills of Connecticut has the imperishable fame of being the first pioneer of American Christianity in the field of worldwide missions. He was the leader of five students of Williams College who are said to have considered at the Haystack Prayer Meeting the sending of the Bible and the Gospel abroad. He was the leader also of the Brethren, a society of volunteers for missions formed at Williams in 1808. The Brethren all went to Andover Theological Seminary, where Adoniram Judson joined them. Their application to the Congregational Association of Massachusetts . . . led to the formation in 1810 of the American Board of Commissioners for Foreign Missions. First composed of Congregationalists, it later chose several Presbyterian members, and for many years was the foreign missionary organization of both of these bodies.

In 1812 the American Board sent five missionaries to India. During the voyage Judson and Luther Rice adopted Baptist views, and these two separated from the others. Judson going to Burma to his great work there, and Rice returning in America to give the Baptists the vision of worldwide missions. This led to the formation of the Baptist Missionary Society in 1814.

Eventually Luther Rice not only became a great advocate and promoter of carrying out the Great Commission, but his ministry helped lay the foundation for what became the Southern Baptist Convention in 1845.

By the close of the 19th century, dozens of denominational and interdenominational missionary agencies together could count thousands of missionaries all over the world. America and the British Empire "on which the sun never set" were the leaders in this international dissemination of the Word of God and the gospel.

The Role of Bible Societies

Founded in 1816 by pastors and laymen, the American Bible Society, representing a variety of Christian denominations, gathered in New York City to establish a truly inter-confessional effort to "disseminate the Gospel of Christ throughout the inhabited world." Since that time, billions of copies of Scriptures (entire Bibles and portions) have been distributed. Other Bible societies have functioned throughout this century.

The American Bible Society declared 1999 as the "Year of the Bible." During that year the ABS urged that every American read through the New Testament between January 1 and December 31, 1999. This would require about 5 minutes a day of Bible reading.

People were urged to follow eight steps to guarantee the success of the Year of the Bible in communities all over the nation. Directors for most communities across the nation were enlisted to promote this Bible-reading program. They were (1) to pray and urge others to pray, asking God to give people a hunger to read the New Testament and that His Word would change hearts; (2) to talk to pastors and Christian leaders about the campaign; (3) to organize advertising and promotional efforts to promote the program; (4) to recruit the newspapers to run daily Bible readings; (5) to advertise through literature from the ABS; (6) to raise and budget funds for give-away New Testaments (75¢ each); (7) to arrange for New Testament distribution; and (8) to follow through with encouragement to everyone to read, read, read.

The last time a "Year of the Bible" was a national program was in 1983 when the U.S. CONGRESS DECLARED THE BIBLE TO BE "THE WORD OF GOD."

This appeared in Public Law, 97-280, October 4, 1982, 97th Congress 96 STAT. 1211:

Joint Resolution

Authorizing and requesting the President to proclaim 1983 as the "Year of the Bible."

WHEREAS the Bible, the Word of God, has made a unique contribution in shaping the United States as a distinctive and blessed nation and people;

WHEREAS deeply held religious convictions springing from the Holy Scriptures led to the early settlement of our nation;

WHEREAS Biblical teachings inspired concepts of civil government that are contained in our Declaration of Independence and the Constitution of the United States;

WHEREAS many of our great national leaders — among them Presidents Washington, Jackson, Lincoln, and Wilson — paid tribute to the surpassing influence of the Bible in our country's development, as in the words of President Jackson that the Bible is "the rock on which our Republic rests;

WHEREAS the history of our Nation clearly illustrates

the value of voluntarily applying the teachings of the Scriptures in the lives of individuals, families, and societies;

WHEREAS this Nation now faces great challenges that will test our Nation as it has never been tested before; and

WHEREAS that renewing our knowledge of and faith in God through Holy Scripture can strengthen us as a nation and a people:

Now, therefore, be it

RESOLVED BY THE SENATE AND HOUSE OF REPRESENTATIVES OF THE UNITED STATES OF AMERICA IN CONGRESS ASSEMBLED, That the President is authorized and requested to designate 1983 as a national "Year of the Bible" in recognition of both the formative influence the Bible has been for our Nation and our national need to study and apply the teachings of the Holy Scriptures.

Approved October 4, 1982

Mysteries of the Bible Now Revealed was issued in 1999, to help inspire and challenge Americans to read the New Testament this year and every year until Jesus comes.

The Bible for All Nations

According to the American Bible Society, at the close of 1997 the entire Bible had been translated into 363 languages of the world. The New Testament was available in 405 languages, while portions of Scripture, most notably one or more gospels, have been translated into a grand total of 2,197 languages. That means that 95+ percent of the world's population has at least a portion of God's Word in their native tongue. Work continues through various organizations to translate the Scriptures into the relatively few remaining languages, often tongues spoken by only a few hundred or a few thousand people in remote locales.

No other book in the world's history can match this record.

No other book has ever been so widely circulated in so many languages to so many cultures, to so many people worldwide as this one great publication, which refers to itself as THE WORD OF GOD.

And so it is.

Twentieth Century Technology Spread the Word

During the 20th century the gospel of Christ and the reading of portions of sacred Scripture have been carried on thousands of radio stations, long wave and short wave, AM and FM, in literally millions and millions of broadcasts since the 1920s.

In 1924, one of the first Christian stations ever to broadcast was in Fort Worth, Texas, and was owned and operated by the First Baptist Church, then pastored by J. Frank Norris. In the 1930s and 40s, radio programs like the Old Fashioned Revival Hour (1,000 stations) were beamed all over the world. Today there is scarcely a country in the world where the gospel has not been penetrated by radio.

Television in the last third of this century has now beamed the gospel by satellite all over the world. Trinity Broadcasting Network, with hundreds of stations, can be seen almost anywhere on earth with the right equipment.

In 1996, astronaut Dr. Shannon Lucid established a new women's record of more than six months aloft in a space vehicle, serving as a crew member on the Russian Space Station *Mir*. This great American scientist and devout believer in Christ carried with her a taped sermon by a Texas Baptist pastor, Dr. Raymond Barber of Fort Worth, a sermon entitled "God of Space."

From this former Soviet Communist and Russian space station, she played and broadcast this Bible message of the gospel from space by short wave around the world. Amazingly she could spread the gospel from a Russian space vehicle, an event never thought possible only a few years earlier.

The Oriental Factor

Over the centuries, the Bible has powerfully impacted America, Europe, England, and all of the countries once part of the British Empire, South America, Africa, and Asia. Wherever a church bell rings or a steeple rises into the blue or a group of secret disciples in a cave meets . . . the Bible has been the book responsible for every form of Christianity. While not every element of the Christian faith understands the Bible the same way, nevertheless none would even exist without this blessed book.

Jesus predicted that in the last days "iniquity would abound" and "the love of many will wax cold."

While love for and faith in the Bible has waned in much of Western civilization, there are great spiritual awakenings in the Third World.

Perhaps the most amazing spiritual awakening on earth is occurring in the world's largest country, population-wise, China.

In 1948, just 50 years ago, the Communists took control of China. All American missionaries had to flee. Churches were shut down. Religious persecution was rife. There were approximately 5,000,000 professing Christians out of a population of some 500,000,000. Many died.

One missionary and his wife, Rev. and Mrs. Oscar Wells and their daughter (who had been born in China and spent her first two years in a Japanese prison camp) were among the last to say goodbye to their Chinese Christian friends and return to America.

Oscar Wells had begun preaching in Chinese in 1940 on a Shanghai radio station. During World War II the family was repatriated to America in a prisoner exchange, but they returned for three years before the Communists took total charge. Undaunted, Wells began working with radio ministries which were beaming the gospel into China. After 50 years, he is still preaching by radio to the millions in China, always stressing the pure gospel of Christ. Many others likewise preached to the Chinese by radio. Millions of Bibles and Scripture portions have been carefully sent to China (some say smuggled).

Each night 50,000,000 radios are tuned to Wells' broadcast with as many as 5 listeners per unit. Some nights Oscar Wells, now 83, gives the biblical gospel message to 250,000,000 people out of a population of 1,200,000,000!

The Chinese Christians continued their ministry underground. "Cave churches" arose. It has been an incredible movement.

In spite of persecution, adverse circumstances, hardship, and poverty, those 5,000,000 Christians have grown to number somewhere between 60,000,000 and 120,000,000 real believers, now living in that vast nation and quietly and often secretly serving God. To serve God, when it is unpopular, when persecution looms, when there are no material advantages to being a Christian, results in genuine believers and scarcely any "hypocrites."

Oscar Wells' daughter, when but a child in China, looked up at the sky and said, "Maybe I can explore space. Everything on the earth has been found and explored." She had an adventurous and inquisitive mind, always wanting to learn something new. And she knew the Bible well.

She had a dream. It came true. That little girl, born in China of missionary parents, grew to become "space super-woman" Shannon Wells Lucid, American astronaut extraordinaire.

As for China, the Bible is continuing to have a powerful impact. Perhaps 10 percent of the population believes in Jesus. As the 19th century was a time when "the sun never set on the British Empire" and the last 100 years has been the "American Century," so the 21st will probably become the "Chinese Century."

We have yet to hear the powerful voice of a hundred million Chinese Christians and perhaps many more in the 21st century, as they glorify God and proclaim to the world the truth of the Bible. Perhaps we shall.

Perhaps it will be the Spirit-filled Chinese believers who will complete the work of the Great Commission and "this gospel of the kingdom shall be preached in all the world . . . and then the end shall come" (Matt. 24:14).

10

The Supernatural
Life-Changing Power
of the Bible

Elmer Towns

The Bible tells the old, old story of life-changing power made possible through Jesus Christ and His work on our behalf. Untold millions have experienced this power, many of them considered hopeless cases of moral failure or indifference. Some have been used of God for extraordinary works and influence.

Following are a few examples from the past and the present of the life-changing power of God's message.

William Carey (1761-1834)

William Carey, known as the "Father of Modern Missions," was born in Northamptonshire, England. Carey showed a great desire for learning early in life, but due to the poverty of the family he had to work as a shoemaker's assistant. Carey did not mind the work, and to his joy he had the opportunity to learn several languages through acquiring books on the subjects and through private tutoring by friends. He mastered Dutch, French, Greek, Latin, and Hebrew before he was 20 years of age. Two years later he joined the Baptist church and began preaching immediately, mostly on the theme of foreign missions. Carey desired to see his denomination engage in missionary activity.

Once at a ministerial meeting held at Northampton, he proposed mission work among the heathen. He was promptly told, "Sit down, young man; when God sees fit to convert the heathen, He will do so of His own accord."

Carey continued to cherish the dream of missions and wrote a treatise entitled, "An Inquiry on Missions." This was published and formed the basis for his great sermon on Christ's mission work, which he delivered on May 31, 1792, in Nottingham. This laid the foundation for Baptist mission work in India. Choosing Isaiah 54:2-3 as his text for this occasion, Carey emphasized two lessons from it — that Christians expect great things of God and that they attempt great things for God.

He helped organize the English Baptist Missionary Society and was one of its first missionaries to India. In spite of several obstacles, including scorn for being a cobbler, Carey made the voyage. His services were remarkable for their range and depth.

Carey translated the Bible into 44 languages and dialects. In addition to soul-winning, Carey founded the Serampore College. He was also instrumental in developing grammars and dictionaries in Bengali, Sanskrit, and other native tongues.

Charles Grandison Finney (1792-1875)

The United States' "new measure" evangelist was born in Warren, Connecticut, and grew up in Oneida County, New York. He taught school for a few years and studied law privately. In 1818 he entered the law office of Benjamin Wright in Adams, New York.

While reading *Blackstone's Commentaries on Law*, he noted continuous reference to the Mosaic institutions. Blackstone repeatedly mentioned the Bible as the highest authority. Finney soon bought a Bible and was reading it more than law. The Word of God brought deep conviction to his soul, and on October 10, 1821, out in the woods, he was converted to Christ. With his conversion, he became convinced that he had been given a "retainer from the Lord Jesus Christ to plead His cause," so he dropped his law practice to become an evangelist, and within two years he was licensed by the Presbyterians.

Finney's methods involved using features of frontier revivals and addressing the people as he would a jury. These methods, after being carried into the larger cities, were labeled as "new measures." He received much opposition from the trained ministers from the New England schools. However, he managed to polish his methods somewhat and was exceedingly successful in the larger cities.

The highlight of his evangelistic ministry was the "nine mighty years" of 1824-1832, during which he conducted powerful revival meetings all over the eastern cities of Gouverneur, Rome, Utica, Auburn, Troy, Wilmington, Philadelphia, Boston, and New York. During his meetings in Rochester, New York, it is reported, "the place was shaken to its foundations"; twelve hundred people united with the churches of Rochester Presbytery; all the leading lawyers, physicians, and businessmen were saved; 40 of the converts entered the ministry; and the whole character of the town was changed. As a result of that meeting, revivals broke out in fifteen hundred other towns and villages.

In 1832 he began an almost continual revival in New York City as the pastor of the Second Free Presbyterian Church. He didn't completely agree with the Presbyterian polity, and his supporters built the Broadway Tabernacle for him in 1834. Two years later he withdrew from the Presbytery, and the church became Congregational in polity. In 1835 he became professor of theology at Oberlin College, Ohio, dividing his time between the school and his New York tabernacle. In 1837 he departed from the Broadway Tabernacle to become minister of the First Congregational Church in Oberlin. From 1851 to 1866 he also served as president of the college. He died August 16, 1875.

Over five hundred thousand people responded to his public invitations to receive Christ. Finney was personal, home-spun, dramatic, and forceful, and his revival lectures are still studied by Bible-believing preachers, teachers, and evangelists.

Adoniram Judson (1788-1850)

Adoniram Judson, the son of a Congregational minister, learned to read at the age of three and by his tenth year knew Latin and Greek. A serious student of theology, Judson entered Brown University at the age of 16 and graduated three years later as the valedictorian of his class. At Andover Theological Seminary he could not get away from the words of a missionary appeal, "Go ye into all the world." This occurred after hearing a sermon entitled, "The Star in the East," which had as a text Matthew 2:2. The leading thought of the sermon was the evidence of the Divine power of the Christian religion in the East. In a letter written many years afterward, he says:

> Though I do not now consider that sermon as peculiarly excellent, it produced a very powerful effect on my mind. For some days I was unable to attend to the studies of my class, and spent my time in wondering at my past stupidity, depicting the most romantic scenes in missionary life,

and roving about the college rooms declaiming on the subject of missions. My views were very incorrect, and my feelings extravagant; but yet I have always felt thankful to God for bringing me into that state of excitement, which was perhaps necessary, in the first instance, to enable me to break the strong attachment I felt to home and country, and to endure the thought of abandoning all my wanted pursuits and animating prospects. That excitement soon passed away; but it left a strong desire to prosecute my inquiries and ascertain the path of duty. It was during a solitary walk in the woods behind the college, while meditating and praying on the subject, and feeling half inclined to give up, that the command of Christ, "Go into all the world and preach the Gospel to every creature," was presented to my mind with such clearness and power, that I came to a full decision, and though great difficulties appeared in my way, resolved to obey the command at all events.

In 1810 Judson helped form the American Board of Commissioners for Foreign Missions, and two years later he and his new wife, Ann, sailed for India. When they were refused entrance, they went to Burma, where they worked for six years before winning the first convert to Christ. During those years they were plagued with ill health, loneliness, and the death of their baby son. Judson was imprisoned for nearly two years, during which time Ann faithfully visited him, smuggling to him food, books, papers, and notes which he used in translating the Bible into the Burmese language. Soon after his release, Ann and their baby daughter, Maria, died of spotted fever. Judson withdrew in seclusion into the interior of Burma where he completed the translation of the whole Bible into Burmese. In 1845 he returned to America, but the burning desire to win the Burmese people sent him back to the Orient, where he soon died.

As a young man he had cried out, "I will not leave Burma until the cross is planted here forever." Thirty years after his death, Burma had 63 Christian churches, 163 missionaries, and over 7,000 baptized converts.

Dwight Lyman Moody (1837-1899)

Undoubtedly one of the best-known and loved American evangelists, Dwight L. Moody was born in Northfield, Massachusetts, on February 5, 1837. His father died when Dwight was four. Dwight's formal education ended at age 13, and at 17 he became a clerk in his uncle's shoe store in Boston. Edward Kimble, his Sunday school teacher, led Moody to Christ in the shoe store. Moody went to Chicago in 1856 and became a traveling salesman for a wholesale shoe firm. He did extensive Sunday school recruitment in his spare time and became affiliated with the YMCA in its early years in Chicago. He resigned from business in 1860 to devote his full time to the work of Christ. He married Emma Revell in 1862.

During the Civil War, Moody served with the United States Christian Commission, ministering to the troops on both sides, and often was found at the front of battle. Here the eternal value of individuals became clear to him and provided him with the impetus which later enabled him to preach to adults. Moody became the president of the YMCA of Chicago in 1866.

Moody organized and built an independent church in Chicago by popular demand of those he led to Christ. In 1873 he went to England with Ira D. Sankey and held a series of revival meetings which captured Britain. He left America virtually unknown in any national sense and returned as a famed evangelist. Upon returning in August of 1875 he made his home at Northfield, Massachusetts, his beloved birthplace. During the next six years he conducted revivals all across the United States. In 1879 he established the Northfield Seminary for Young Women and in 1881 the Mount Hermon School for Young Men.

In 1879 he was invited to return to England to conduct a second series of meetings. In 1884 he returned to do evangelistic work in America and Canada. In 1889 he founded the Chicago Bible Institute (now Moody Bible Institute), which has been a fountainhead for Christian workers throughout the world.

Moody was effective because of his love for the souls of men and his personal concern for their physical welfare. His preaching was known for its use of anecdotes and stories. Though not an educated man, Moody was respected by the educated. It is claimed that over one million people were converted to Jesus Christ during his ministry. His work continues today through the Moody Memorial Church and the Moody Bible Institute of Chicago.

John Wesley (1703-1791)

John Wesley, founder of the Methodist movement, was born in 1703 at Epworth, England, where his father, the Reverend Samuel Wesley, was rector. John's mother, Susanna, was most influential in shaping the lives of her children. She gave each of the children one hour per week on a fixed day for religious conversation and prayer.

John was so apt a learner that his father thought him fit for partaking of communion at a very early age. This religious training accounts for much of his later work among children.

Wesley entered Oxford in 1720, receiving a master of arts degree in 1727. At that time he was not yet converted to Christ, although he endeavored to lead a clean, moral life and pursue the subject of religion. Faith, during this period, seems to have meant little more than "right opinion."

Wesley was ordained a deacon in September 1725 and preached his first sermon at South Leigh, a small village near Witney. In March 1726 he was elected Fellow of Lincoln College. During this time he became a religious devotee and determined to give all his energy to the ministry.

Commenting on his preaching activity following his first four years at Oxford, Wesley says:

> From the year 1725 to 1729 I preached much, but saw no fruit of my labour. Indeed it could not be that I should, for I neither laid the foundation of repentance nor of preaching the Gospel, taking it for granted that all to whom I preached were believers, and that many of them needed no repentance. From the year 1729 to 1734, laying a deeper foundation of repentance, I saw a little fruit. But it was only a little — and no wonder: for I did not preach faith in the blood of the covenant."

During John's absence from college in 1727, his brother Charles (four years younger) had become serious in seeking God, along with a few undergraduates. The group came to be known as the Holy Club and later as the Methodists, because of their methodical habits. Upon John's return, he was made the head of this company. Their activities included visiting prisoners, instructing ignorant children, relieving the poor, fasting, and holding communion on a weekly schedule. Among the early members was George Whitefield, who later continued John's work in Georgia and was influential in the Great Awakening revival movement in America.

In 1735 John, along with his brother Charles, journeyed to the colony of Georgia as a missionary of the Propagation Society. Moravian missionaries in Georgia, with whom Wesley had contact aboard ship, were influential in his later conversion to Christ. He had never appropriated Christ as his personal Savior but had been a High Anglican churchman, rigidly adhering to ritual and law with a tingling mixture of mysticism. John Wesley left Georgia a failure in his ministry to the colonists and Indians.

On May 14, 1738, at a meeting of a religious society on Aldersgate Street, London, Wesley testified that, "I felt my heart strangely warmed." The following spring after hearing the account of Jonathan Edwards' success in New England and of George Whitefield's successes at outdoor preaching, Wesley obtained his first significant results. The Methodist Revival was launched, and he remained at its head for more than 50 years. He spent the rest of his life preaching in the fields, the streets, and in the Methodist preaching chapels. He was up each morning before five o'clock for prayer and Bible study, and rode on horseback 15 to 20 miles a day, preaching four or five times daily. During his lifetime Wesley traveled 250,000 miles preaching a total of 42,000 sermons. His activities and administrations are recorded in his journal and letters. He died at the age of 88 and preached up to the very month of his death.

Billy Sunday (1862-1935)

Perhaps as many as 100,000,000 people witnessed Billy Sunday's self-created down-to-earth preaching style. He was a natural actor with perfect timing and lots of body language. Preaching against sin, he said he would "kick it as long as I've got a foot, and I'll fight it as long as I've got a fist. I'll butt it as long as I've got a head. I'll bite it as long as I've got a tooth." He belted out the gospel and thundered against the saloons, but he could also make people laugh. When he did, he said he would "shove the gospel down their throats while their mouths were open."

William Ashley Sunday was born poor in Iowa and joined the Chicago White Sox baseball team when he was about 20. He excelled as a base runner and seemed destined to fame. He once won a game by stealing second, third, and home on three successive plays. He reportedly could run the bases in 14 seconds.

"But Billy got religion, and his conversion not only changed his life but his career. The baseball evangelist became an itinerant revivalist known all over the country. With his musical accompanist, Homer Rodeheaver, and his slide trombone, Billy Sunday tantalized enormous crowds, huddled together in hastily built wooden tabernacles."

About 1887 Billy and his companions went into a saloon in Chicago. It was a Sunday afternoon, and they all got "tanked up" then went outside. The following recounting of the incident is from the December 14, 1916, *Boston Herald:*

We sat down on a curbing. Across the street a company of men and women were playing on instruments — horns, flutes, and slide trombones — and the others were singing the gospel hymns that I used to hear my mother sing back in the old church, where I used to go to Sunday school.

And God painted on the canvas of my recollection and memory a vivid picture of the scenes of other days and other faces.

Many have long since turned to dust. I sobbed and sobbed, and a young man stepped out and said:

"We are going to the Pacific Garden Mission; won't you come down to the mission? I'm sure you will enjoy it. You can hear drunkards tell how they have been saved and girls tell how they have been saved from the red light district."

"I arose and said to the boys:

"I'm through. I am going to Jesus Christ. We've come to the parting of the ways," and I turned my back on them. Some of them laughed and some of them mocked me; one of them gave me encouragement, others never said a word.

Twenty-nine years ago I turned and left that little group on the corner of State and Madison streets and walked to the little mission and fell on my knees and staggered out of sin and into the arms of the Savior.

Lest the reader think that God only worked in the past, the next account demonstrates that God works today in the most hopeless cases. The story of Bill Murray's influence is still being written, but the miracle of his new birth is settled in heaven.

Bill Murray (1946-)

Which is most important, nurture or nature? Can people really escape their upbringing? What hope is there for someone trained their whole life to be a God-hater, schooled since toddlerhood to deride and mock Jesus Christ and His people?

Madylyn Murray O'Hare wanted to raise a Christian-hater, like herself. She was the exemplar of those who ruin their own life then shake their fist at God. Her bitterness and anger toward her family and anyone who spoke of God erupted continually and unpredictably in throes of violence and spasms of vituperation. She hated God and everyone else because she was poor and ignored, her "brilliance" and "gifts" unappreciated, and she indulged her "talent to infuriate people with acid-coated words" at every opportunity.

Bill met his father only once. William Murray had refused to marry Madylyn, but she took his last name anyway (she married Richard O'Hare later in life). His younger brother Garth was also illegitimate, and the burden of single motherhood and her own poor work habits necessitated Madylyn's mother, father, and brother moving in with them. This occasioned unending strife, rancor, anger, and violence.

When he was nine, young Bill was recruited to stuff Communist propaganda and distribute the envelopes on windshields. At least he got a little attention that way, although Madylyn still cursed him at the slightest provocation. But Bill got a great deal of attention from his mother when she discovered that students prayed at his school.

It was the last week of September 1960, and Madylyn and the two boys had just returned from Europe after a failed attempt to defect to the Soviet Union. With funds almost gone, the dream of Soviet defection faded and the future seemed more bleak than ever. There were no prospects for income, until she heard students praying in a classroom. Furious, she confronted a school counselor and proclaimed praying in school un-American and unconstitutional. The counselor suggested, offhandedly, that she sue the school.

She decided to change America.

Now the envelope-stuffer became the prayer-logger. Bill started logging the morning prayers, Bible readings, pledges to the flag, singing — anything remotely religious in the classroom. "At last Madylyn Murray had found her cause, one that would be noticed." So, although he longed to be a "normal" teenager, his function was, once again, to be a tool for his mother's cause.

The ensuing events — the first *Baltimore Morning Sun* article, the network coverage, the ACLU involvement, the media-covered school protest, the suit with the city, the national publicity, the appeals process all the way to the Supreme Court and the 1963 decision to remove Bible reading and prayer from public schools — consumed the teenage life of Bill Murray.

After his chaotic ninth grade year, Bill transferred to Baltimore Polytechnic, a no-nonsense technical high school with demanding standards and rigid rules. He welcomed the discipline, and no one cared about his mother. He joined the U.N. Club, earned an amateur radio operator's license, but still struggled with grades because his mother's political activities took so much time.

At 17, he began a relationship with Susan, the daughter of a prominent Jewish businessman. The father hated Bill and finally drove Susan out of the house — into Bill's house. She became pregnant, and the scandalous situation combined with the father's legal threats finally forced the entire Murray family to move away from Baltimore to Hawaii. Just before they left, Susan and Bill were married in a civil ceremony. As he recounts, "We boarded the plane . . . and as we sped westward . . . my preceding 18 years on the planet passed before my eyes, and I sunk into a depressed state of self-pity. I had been kind to no avail. I had been tolerant to no gain. I had been helpful and had received no help. I looked at Susan who . . . was no beauty queen. The child she carried had no future as far as I could see." He longed to be "just Bill Murray — not Bill Murray, son of the most hated woman in America."

In the next two years he learned to drink, smoke, get high, and steal. He had to flee to Mexico with his wife and daughter, Robin, then flee again. After all was said and done, he had left his wife and child, relatives, and obligations, and run away with Linda, a married woman. "I now cared only about feeding my own appetites. Although I was blinded to it, I represented the same picture of deceit and selfishness that I cursed my mother for."

The following years were spent on the run from one failed job to another. Linda was a heavy drug user and a drain on his finances. His daughter from his first marriage (he finally divorced Susan) had to live with Madylyn, which Bill deeply regretted. More and more, he tried to drown all this pain with alcohol.

Bill eventually began a somewhat steady career in the aviation field. He and Linda split up, and he began dating an airline secretary, Valerie. They eventually married and had a child, a girl they named Jade, and moved to Houston. He continued drinking heavily, but after a friend died in a plane crash, he entered Alcoholics Anonymous and heard about God again. By heeding the 12-step program, he was able to go four months without a drink. He relates, "As my head started to clear, I began to comprehend more of what was happening around me. My productivity at work increased. In many ways I was a new man."

He and Valerie began to drift, and one night he stormed out of the house after an argument and found a liquor store. While drunk after downing an entire bottle of scotch, he threw Valerie out of the house. She returned later with a policeman, but Bill shot at him, mistaking him for an intruder. He missed the policeman, but Bill was arrested and abused for his mistake. He decided to leave Texas and work in San Francisco, but Valerie and Jade remained in Houston.

Battling bouts of anger and depression, fighting the urge to drink, arguing violently with Valerie over the phone, Bill finally decided he could go nowhere but up. "Just days before Christmas in 1979, I finally decided to read a book I had purchased some months before, *Dear and Glorious Physician* (Taylor Caldwell). . . . I was immediately intrigued with the book and read it rapidly. I identified strongly with its main character, Lucanas. He was not an atheist but had carried anger toward God since his childhood. His anger, though, was turned to love as he searched for and found God in Jesus Christ." Bill did not yet consider Jesus as God, but "there was still a great conflict raging within me, a war over my soul."

On January 24, 1980, a vivid nightmare prompted Bill to find a Bible. He drove to an all-night discount department store near Fisherman's Wharf. There, under a stack of pornographic magazines, he found a Bible, took it home and read the Book of Luke.

"There I found my answer — not the book itself, but Jesus Christ. I had heard many times in various churches that all one needed to do was to admit guilt and ask Jesus in. I had not made that one step, to ask Him into my heart. I knew I must take that step, and I did so that night. God was no longer a distant, impersonal 'force.' I now knew Him in a personal way."

The next day he asked God to remove his desire for alcohol, and the desire left. The next to go was the three packs of cigarettes a day, and with it the bronchitis he had suffered with from youth. His hatred began to vanish as Christ's love took over, even to the point where Bill no longer hated his mother, but wanted her to know God, too.

At the age of 33, almost 20 years exactly after the prayer case had begun, Bill Murray wrote two letters. One was to the people of Austin, Texas, asking them to forgive him for building the American Atheist Center in their city. The other was to the *Baltimore Sun.* Printed May 10, 1980, it read, in part:

Being raised as an atheist in the home of Madylyn O'Hare, I was not aware of faith or even the existence of God. As I now look back over 33 years of life wasted without faith in God, I pray only that I can, with His help, right some of the wrong and evil I have caused through my lack of faith.

Our nation, our people, now face a trying time in this world of chaos. It is only with a return to our traditional values and our faith in God that we will be able to survive as a people. If it were within my personal power to help to return this nation to its rightful place by placing God back in the classroom, I would do so.

Finally, but not too late, the love of God and the transforming power of Christ had reached into the heart of another hopeless case and drawn it to himself.

11

The Mysterious Mathematical Design of the Bible

Chuck Missler

From the intrinsic evidence of his creation, the Great Architect of the Universe now begins to appear as a pure mathematician.

Sir James Jeans[1]

This chapter will explore codes involved with *numerology*, *numerics*, and *gematria*. The study of *numerology* (from the Latin, *numerus*, a number, and *logy*, science or study) is the general study of numbers, their nature, purpose, and applications. In addition to the study of *numbers* (amounts, quantity of units, or mathematical values) and *numerals* (the term designating a figure, symbol, or word expressing a number), it also includes examining the *structural* use of numbers in the design of a corpus of text.

Numerics refers to the study of symbolical, cryptic, or mystical use of numbers. *Gematria* involves the application of numerical *values* assigned to the *letters* of the alphabet. It is often, but not necessarily, associated with mysticism.

Our Numerical Universe

The universe exhibits a numerical structure that has long puzzled the scientists. This includes the nature of integers in general, and their role in the periodic table in particular; the role of 8 in the energy levels of the atom; the numerical symmetries in botany; and now, the role of

8+2 and 24+2 in the mathematics of superstrings. Scientists even use the concept of numerical "beauty" as a comfort zone in evaluating alternative theories. The elegance of the Kaluza-Klein and the Yang-Mills hyperspace models are contemporary examples.

Sir Fred Hoyle even predicted, and then discovered, in 1954, the previously unknown energy levels in the Carbon-12 atom from his sensitivity to the prevalent *patterns of numerical design* in the universe.[2] The astonishing precision of these relationships are called the "anthropic principle."

It should not surprise us that the same evidences of deliberate numerical design also appear hidden behind the biblical text.

The Heptadic Structure

The recurrence of seven—or an exact multiple of seven—is found throughout the Bible and is widely recognized. The frequent occurrence of the number seven is conspicuous even to a casual reader.

We encounter the seven days of creation in Genesis, the seven feasts of Israel, Jacob serves seven years for each of his two wives, seven kine and ears of corn in Pharaoh's dreams (seven good years and seven famine years), seven lamps of the Menorah, the seven elements of furniture in the tabernacle, seven days of the feast of unleavened bread, the repeated use of seven in the Levitical priestly instructions, the seven weeks to the Feast of Weeks, the seven months between Nisan and Tishri, (and the seven years of the sabbatical year, and the seven times seven to the Jubilee Year), the seven priests with seven trumpets circling Jericho seven times in the Book of Joshua, seven nations of Canaan, Solomon was seven years building the temple, Naaman washed seven times in the river, seven loaves fed the four thousand, etc.

In the Book of Revelation we encounter seven churches, seven lampstands, seven stars, seven seals, seven horns, seven spirits of God, seven angels, seven trumpets, seven thunders, seven crowns, seven last plagues, seven bowls, seven kings, and there are many more sevens, much more subtle in their presence.

The more one examines the text closely, the more evident is the recurrence of seven. Even in the interior design of the text, we continue to encounter this heptadic structure. Take the opening verse in Genesis chapter 1, for example:

בְּרֵאשִׁית בָּרָא אֱלֹהִים אֵת הַשָּׁמַיִם וְאֵת הָאָרֶץ:

In the beginning God created the heaven and the earth.

Number of Hebrew words:	7
Number of letters:	28 = 4 x 7
1st three words:	14 letters, 2 x 7
Last four Heb words:	14 letters = 2 x 7
4th and 5th words have	7 letters
6th and 7th words have	7 letters
3 key words: God, heaven, earth have	14 letters = 2 x 7
Four remaining words have	14 letters = 2 x 7

(Hebrew letters also each have a numerical value *(gematria)*; so even the numerical values of the letters (and words), are provocative: The numeric value of 1st, middle, last letters = 133 = 19 x 7; the numeric value of the first and last letters of all 7 words is 1393 = 199 x 7. *Gematria* will be explored later.)

We also find this in the New Testament.

A Design Challenge

Consider the following assignment: Try designing a genealogy — even from fiction — which meets the following criteria:

1. The number of *words* in it must be divisible by 7 *evenly*. (In each of these constraints, it is assumed that the resulting divisions are without any remainders.)
2. The number of *letters* must also be divisible by 7.

(Not too difficult so far? But let's include a few more constraints:)

3. The number of *vowels* and the number of *consonants* must also each be divisible by 7.

(Getting more challenging? Let's add a few more.)

4. The number of words that *begin with a vowel* must be divisible by 7.
5. The number of words that *begin with a consonant* must be divisible by 7.

(Let's add some frequency constraints:)

6. The number of words that *occur more than once* must be divisible by 7.

7. The number of words that *occur in more than one form* shall be divisible by 7.

8. The number of words that *occur in only one form* shall be divisible by 7.

(Now let's add some constraints on the grammatical structure:)

9. The number of *nouns* shall be divisible by 7.

10. Only 7 words shall *not* be nouns.

11. The number of *names* in the geneology shall be divisible by 7.

12. Only 7 *other kinds of nouns* are permitted.

13. The number of *male names* shall be divisible by 7.

14. The number of *generations* shall be 21, also divisible by 7.

A challenging assignment, indeed! Could *you* do it? Even with the aid of a computer, this is no pushover. If you encountered such a genealogy, would you attribute such characteristics as these to random chance?

These have all been met in the first 11 verses (in the Greek) in the genealogy of Jesus Christ in Matthew chapter 1.

The heptadic (sevenfold) structure of the Bible has been much studied and the subject of numerous volumes in the past,[3] but none are more provocative than the works of Dr. Ivan Panin.[4]

Dr. Ivan Panin

Ivan Panin was born in Russia on December 12, 1855. Having participated in plots against the Czar at an early age, he was exiled and after spending some years in study in Germany, came to the United States and entered Harvard University.

After graduation in 1882, he converted from agnosticism to Christianity. In 1890 he discovered some of the phenomenal mathematical design underlying both the Greek text of the New Testament and the Hebrew text of the Old Testament. He was to devote over 50 years of his life painstakingly — and exhausting his health — exploring the numerical structure of the Scriptures, generating over 43,000 detailed hand-penned pages of analysis. He went on to be with the Lord in his 87th year, on October 30, 1942.

Ivan Panin noted the amazing numerical properties of the biblical texts — both the Greek of the New Testament and the Hebrew of the

Old Testament. These are not only intriguing to discover, they also demonstrate an intricacy of design which testifies to its supernatural origin!

Vocabulary

One of the simplest — and most provocative — aspects of the biblical text is the vocabulary used. The number of vocabulary words in a passage is, of course, different from the total number of words in a passage. Some words are repeated. It is easy, for example, to use a vocabulary of 500 words to write an essay of 4,000 words.

For example, the first 17 verses of the gospel of Matthew are a logical unit, or section, which deals with a single principle subject: the genealogy of Christ. It contains 72 Greek vocabulary words in these initial 17 verses.

(The verse divisions are man's allocations for convenience, added in the 13th century.)

The number of words which are nouns is exactly 56, or 7 x 8.

The Greek word "the" occurs most frequently in the passage: exactly 56 times, or 7 x 8. Also, the number of different forms in which the article "the" occurs is exactly 7.

There are two main sections in the passage: verse 1-11, and 12-17.

In the first main section, the number of Greek vocabulary words used is 49, or 7 x 7. (Why not 48, or 50?)

The number of these 49 words which begin with a vowel is 28, or 7 x 4. The number of words which begin with a consonant is 21, or 7 x 3.

The total numbers of letters in these 49 words is 266, or 7 x 38 — exactly! The number of vowels among these 266 letters is 140, or 7 x 20. The number of consonants is 126, or 7 x 18 — exactly.

The number of these 49 words that occur more than once is 35, or 7 x 5. The number of words that occur *only once* is 14, or 7 x 2.

The number of these 49 words which occur in only one form is exactly 42, or 7 x 6. The number which appear in more than one form is 7.

The number of the 49 Greek vocabulary words which are nouns is 42, or 7 x 6.

The number of words which are not nouns is 7.

Of the nouns, 35 are proper names, or exactly 7 x 5. These 35 names are used 63 times, or 7 x 9. The number of male names is exactly 28, or 7 x 4.

These male names occur 56 times or 7 x 8.

The number which are not male names is 7. Three women are mentioned — Tamar, Rahab, and Ruth. The number of Greek letters in these three names is 14, 7 x 2.

The number which are compound nouns is 7. The number of Greek letters in these 7 nouns is 49, or 7 x 7.

Only one city is named in this passage, Babylon, which, in Greek, contains 7 letters.

Unique Vocabularies

There are some words in Matthew that *occur nowhere else* in the New Testament. There are 42 such words (7 x 6) and have 126 letters (7 x 18). Again, always an exact multiple of 7. How could this possibly have been organized?

Even if Matthew contrived to include this characteristic into his gospel, how could he have known that these specific words — whose sole characteristic is that they are not to be found in the other New Testament books — were *not to be used by the other writers*? If this was the result of a deliberate design on his part, how could he have organized this?

Unless we assume the absurd hypothesis that he had a prior agreement with all of the other writers not to use these particular words, he would have had to have the rest of the New Testament before him when he wrote his book. This characteristic would thus imply that the gospel of Matthew, then, must have been written *last.*

It so happens, however, that the gospel of Mark exhibits the *same* phenomena. This, too, suggests that the gospel of Mark would *also* have had to be written "last."

The same phenomena is found in Luke, also in the writings of John, James, Peter, Jude, and Paul. Each would have had to write *after* the other in order to contrive these vocabulary usages! You can thus demonstrate that each of the New Testament books had to have been "written last."

Was this due to "chance" or was it the result of deliberate, skillful design? There is no human explanation for this incredible and precise structure. It appears to have all been supernaturally designed or edited. We simply gasp, sit back, and behold the skillful handiwork of the ultimate Author.

Transcendent Numerical Structures

Perhaps the most provocative numerical structures are those that *bridge* the individual books of the Bible — even the Old and New

Testaments. These deliberate designs "stitch" the composite tapestry together in a manner that no living human authors or editors could have contrived. There are 36 authors who (unknowingly) maintained their composite seven-fold (heptadic) structures *across* the Old Testament and New Testament boundaries:[5]

One example is the term, *Hallelujah*, "Praise Yahweh" (Greek, *Alleluia*). It occurs 28 times (4 x 7) in the Bible, a seven-fold structure *bridging the Old and New Testaments*. It occurs 24 times in Psalms 146-150, and 4 times in the Book of Revelation.

Here are some others:

	OT	NT	Total	
"Hallelujah"	24	4	28	7 x 4
"Hosanna"	1	6	7	7 x 1
"Shepherd"	12	9	21	7 x 3
"Jehovah Sabaoth"	285	2	287	7 x 41
"Corban"	82	2	84	7 x 12
"Milk"	44	5	49	7 x 7
"Isaac"	112	14	126	7 x 18
"Aaron"	443	5	448	7 x 16
"Abaddob"	6	1	7	7 x 1
"Christ at the right hand of God"	2	19	21	7 x 3
"After Melchizedek"	1	6	7	7 x 1
"The stone which the builders refused to become headstone of the corner"	1	6	7	7 x 1
"Thou shalt love thy neighbor as thyself"	1	6	7	7 x 1
"Uncircumcision of the heart"	6	1	7	7 x 1

These patterns *do* exist. Are these patterns deliberate? How could these design motifs have been maintained? They are too consistent to have occurred by accident. They appear deliberate; and yet could not have been contrived by the authors unaided. We have 66 books, penned by over 40 authors over thousands of years – and yet there is conspicuous evidence of an integrity of design that defies any "natural" explanation. The pervasiveness and intricacy of these designed structures have significant implications. They constitute irrefutable evidence that underscores the integrity of the entire "message system," and thus also confirms its extratemporal and transfinite origins.

Secret Numbers

When Daniel was given a special prophecy by a "certain holy one" (a special angel), this special messenger was called פַּלְמוֹנִי, *palmoni*, which is annotated in the margin as "the numberer of secrets." This appears to be a specialist which has to do with numbers. Numbers as well as words appear to hold a particular significance in the works of God. Whenever we search out the secrets of God, we are doing a royal and honorable work:

> It is the glory of God to conceal a thing: but the honour of kings is to search out a matter *(*Prov. 25:2).

Ancient Numbers

Both number (quantity) and numeral (a symbol representing a number) are two concepts that have been found in every tribe and culture examined since the founding of anthropological science.[7] The Sumerians of alluvial plains of Southern Iraq apparently were among the world's first literate people. This remarkable culture evidenced addition, subtraction, multiplication, division, extraction of roots, raising to higher powers, as well as handling a number of types of fractions. The suddenness of the appearance of writing, numbers, and other concepts has given rise to the many fanciful speculations of Zechariah Sitchen, Erik von Daniken, and others.[8]

The Base 60

Have you ever wondered why there are 60 minutes to the hour and 60 seconds to the minute? The Sumerians' numerical reckoning was sexagesimal rather than decimal. The base was not 10 ($10^2=100$, $10^3 = 1,00$ etc); but 60 ($60^2 = 3600$, $60^3 = 216,000$, etc.) Fractions were also expressed with 60 as the denominator.

This may have been derived from the original 360-day year which is predominant in most of the ancient calendars. This sexagesimal system was well adapted to performing calculations on the circle as astronomical quadrants into degrees, minutes and seconds of arc. Thus, the sexagesimal system was utilized extensively for the two great proto-sciences of the Sumer civilization: astronomy and the calendrical cults (astrology).

It also proved admirably superior for weights and measures. Almost all early metrology in the Near East and the Mediterranean was sexagesimal. (There may have been a convenient method of counting on the joints of four fingers with the thumb, yielding 12; then tabulating with the other hand: times $5 = 60$.) It was also adapted by the other peoples of antiquity — Hittites, Akkadians, Greeks and others. And, of course, it remains with us today.

There is also another possibility. There may have been an earlier leadership which was *six-fingered*. The strange passage in Genesis chapter 6 indicates that there were—both before the flood of Noah and subsequently—some strange hybrids called, in Hebrew, the *Nephilim*, which were, among other things, six-fingered.[9] (For a more comprehensive discussion of the origins of these strange beings and the possible implications for today, see *Alien Encounters* by Dr. Mark Eastman and this author, available from Koinania Publishers.)

Egyptian Mathematics

The mathematics of the Sumerians predated the decimal notations and arithmetical operations of Egypt. Egyptians arrived at an approximation of B, namely 3.16, and, not surprisingly, a correct formula for the volume of a pyramid. In time, Egyptian mathematicians, the scribes entrusted with the royal enumerations, formalized the linear epigraphical script of hieroglyphics into a cursive set of ligatured signs. Numbers and their associated operations were handled in the same manner.

The increasing mood of conservatism and intransigence which characterized the last millennium of Pharaonic Egypt took its toll on the development of numbers and the understanding of the concepts of numbers. They used their clumsy system to record enumerations as high as 1,422,000. The geometry of Egypt, like that of early Ionic Greece, was based largely on construction. Even the rudiments of algebra were never approached.

The early Egyptians used a base-10 system that had a different symbol for each power of 10 up to 10^6, but it lacked a place-value notation and an explicit number zero. Zero was a later Hindu invention, which, when combined with Arabic numbers and positional notation, constituted the subsequent breakthrough. The technology of a numbering system can have a profound influence on a society. (Have you ever tried doing long division with Roman numerals?)

Babylonian Mathematics

The sexagesimal system of Sumer and the decimal system of Egypt were both known to the Akkado-Babylonians, who were dedicated businessmen and traders, and their rigorous lifestyle forced cooperation and authoritative planning for irrigation and defense. The Babylonian mathematical tablets are some of the finest exact scientific treatises from the ancient world.

(The Babylonian system was an incomplete sexagesimal [base-60] positional notation. It used only two symbols instead of the 60 distinct ones that a base-60 system could use, and thus suffered from ambiguities in representing value that could be resolved only by analyzing the context.)

Apparently on the verge of discovering some of the chief mathematical tools of later ages, such as functions and algebra, they were centuries beyond any of their contemporaries. There are texts from about 1700 B.C. that are remarkable for their mathematical suppleness. Babylonian mathematicians knew the Pythagorean relationship well and used it constantly. They could solve simple quadratic equations and could even solve problems in compound interest involving exponents. From about a millennium later there are texts that utilize these skills to provide a very elaborate mathematical description of astronomical phenomena. Under the Kassite kings, astronomy and astrology were the foremost pursuits. Under the Babylonian and Assyrian rulers, astronomical lists flourished, and great strides were made in the accuracy with which observations of the heliacal rising of fixed stars, ephemerides of the planets and eclipses of the sun and moon were recorded. With the conquest of Babylon by the Persians in 539 B.C., Babylonian mathematics passed to Iran.

A final flowering of astronomical observation, simple algebra, and the tables for lunar, planetary, and solar cycles took place after the conquest of Mesopotamia by the Greeks in 333 B.C. This led to the age of Pythagoras and his mystical school. The last vestige of the mathematical tradition was passed on in the Seleucid and Aracid era and then died out in the Medieval period.

Modern Numerical Notation

We take our modern numerical notation for granted. The distinguishing characteristics of a modern number system are its use of base position notation (place value), zero as a number, and a point or comma to separate the parts of numbers greater and less than 1.

The use of zero as a numeral appeared sporadically in Egyptian number systems. It was used, however, only between two numbers to indicate an empty position, never at the end of a number. While the early Chinese did not have a symbol for zero, the invention and use of their abacus suggests that they had an implied appreciation for positional base notation and zero as a number. The Mayans did have a zero symbol, but their inconsistency in base notation rendered it virtually useless for computations.

The bulk of the credit for our modern decimal, or base-10, number system goes to the Hindu-Arabic mathematicians of the 8th to 11th centuries A.D. The first use of zero as a place holder in positional base notation was due probably to Muhammad ibn Musa al-Khwarizmi (*c.* 780-850). This use of zero and the use of western Arabic (Gobar) numerals were spread throughout Europe in the tenth century principally by the efforts of Gerbert, who later became Pope Sylvester II.

Before the adoption of positional base notation, zero, and the point, calculations such as multiplication, division, and root extraction had to be relegated to a handful of experts. By the 1100s the algorists, using base-10 notation, were successfully challenging the abacists (those using the abacus) in the speed and accuracy of calculations and had the advantage of a permanent written record of their results. The beginning of our modern notation is attributed to the work *Liber abaci* published by Leonardo of Pisa (Fibonacci) in A.D. 1202. The development and widespread use of a number system with these components greatly enhanced the precision and ease of calculations needed in fields such as astronomy, manufacturing, and navigation. It eventually led to even more efficient forms of handling data such as logarithms, slide rules, mechanical and electrical calculators, and, of course, computers.

Biblical Accuracy

It is important to remember that regarding the biblical texts, we "see through a glass darkly," filtered by the fog of the centuries. Fortunately, the design of the text in anticipation of both noise and even hostile "jamming," was also augmented by the obsessive commitment of the scribal traditions. The diligent attention of the copyists of the biblical texts were audited by the use of numbering the sums of each of the letters for each of the pages, similar to the "checksums" and "parity checks" used in computer transmissions today.

The appearance of the large sexagesimal numbers in the early chapters of Genesis prove beyond the shadow of a doubt the antiquity of the text and the literary tradition utilized by Moses. Ancient mason's marks and tallies have also been excavated in Israel.

While there are a number of ostensible difficulties in the biblical transmission of numbers pointed to by critics, they all have substantial responses that support the fundamental accuracy of the biblical text.[10] The numbers in the biblical texts are usually spelled out phonetically, but there is no reason to assume that a more direct numeral system was not also available.

Alphanumeric Reckoning

The use of alphanumerics (using the alphabet for numbers) was employed by both the Hebrews and the Greeks.

The Alphanumeric Alphabets

Hebrew		Greek	
א	1	α	1
ב	2	β	2
ג	3	γ	3
ד	4	δ	4
ה	5	ε	5
ו	6	ς[11]	6
ז	7	ζ	7
ח	8	η	8
ט	9	θ	9
י	1 0	ι	10
כ	2 0	κ	20
ל	3 0	λ	30
מ	4 0	μ	40
נ	5 0	ν	50
ס	6 0	ξ	60
ע	7 0	ο	70
פ	8 0	π	80
צ	9 0	Χ[1]	90
ק	1 0 0	ρ	100
ר	2 0 0	σ ς[12]	200
ש	3 0 0	τ	300
ת	4 0 0	υ	400
ך	5 0 0	φ	500
ם	6 0 0	χ	600
ן	7 0 0	ψ	700
ף	8 0 0	ω	800
ץ	9 0 0	ϙ [13]	900

(For numbers 15 and 16, the combinations of 9+6 and 9+7 were often used to avoid the short forms of the divine name, יה and יו.[14])

The Romans did not use their entire alphabet: only six letters, D, C, L, V, and I, for 500, 100, 50, 10, 5, and 1, respectively. These six numbers add up to 666, incidentally. (The use of M was introduced in later years.)

An illuminating example of the Hebrew alphanumeric alphabet involves the circumference of a circle.

The Value of Pi

When I was a teenager, I was challenged by a skeptic concerning an alleged discrepancy in the Old Testament. The passage deals with Solomon's Temple and the products of Hiram the bronzeworker:

> And he made a molten sea [brazen laver], ten cubits from the one brim to the other: it was round all about, and his height was five cubits: and a line of thirty cubits did compass it round about (1 Kings 7:23).

The huge cast bronze basin was 10 cubits[15] in diameter and its circumference is said to be 30 cubits, which is mathematically inaccurate. Almost any schoolboy knows that the circumference of a circle is *not* the diameter times 3, but rather, the diameter times the well-known constant called π ("Pi"). The real value of π is 3.14159265358979, but is commonly approximated by 3 1/7.

This is assumed, by many, to be an "error" in the Old Testament record, and so it is often presented by skeptics as a rebuttal to the "inerrancy" of the Scripture. How can we say that the Bible is inerrant when it contains such an obvious geometrically incorrect statement? How do we deal with this?

In this case, the Lord ultimately brought to our attention some subtleties usually overlooked in the Hebrew text.[16] In Hebrew, it reads:

וַיַּעַשׂ אֶת־הַיָּם מוּצָק עֶשֶׂר בָּאַמָּה מִשְּׂפָתוֹ עַד־שְׂפָתוֹ עָגֹל

סָבִיב וְחָמֵשׁ בָּאַמָּה קוֹמָתוֹ [וּקְוֵה] [וְקָו] שְׁלֹשִׁים בָּאַמָּה יָסֹב אֹתוֹ סָבִיב:

A Spelling Lesson

The common word for circumference is קָו *qav*. Here, however, the word seems to be misspelled. The spelling of the word for circumference, קָוֵה *qaveh*, adds a *heh* (ה). (In the text above each word also has a leading ו as a conjunction for the masculine singular noun.)

In the Hebrew Bible, the scribes did not alter any text which they felt had been copied incorrectly. Rather, they noted in the margin what they thought the written text should be. The written variation is called a *kethiv,* (here as וּקְוֵה); and the marginal annotation is called the *qere* (here, וְקָו).

To the ancient scribes, this was also regarded as a *remez*, a hint of something deeper. This appears to be a clue to treat the word as a mathematical formula.

Numerical Values

The Hebrew alphabet is alphanumeric: each Hebrew letter also has a numerical value assigned and can be used as a number. The ק has a value of 100; the ו has a value of 6; thus, the normal spelling of this word would yield a numerical value of 106.

The addition of the ה, with a value of 5, increases the numerical value to 111. This suggests the adjustment to the ratio of 111/106, which results in 31.41509433962 cubits.

Assuming that a cubit was 1.5 ft.,[17] this 15 foot-wide bowl would then have had a circumference of 47.12388980385 feet. This Hebrew "code" results in 47.12264150943 feet, or an error of *less than 15 thousandths of an inch!*

This error is 15 times *better* than the 3 1/7 estimate that we were accustomed to using in school!

How would they even know this? This accuracy would seem to vastly exceed the precision of their instrumentation. Why was it encoded into the text?

Beyond simply these engineering insights from Solomon's day, there are more far-reaching implications of this passage.

> 1. The Bible *is* reliable. The "errors" pointed out by skeptics usually derive from misunderstandings or trivial quibbles.
>
> 2. The numerical values of the letters are legitimate and apparently can carry hidden significance.

This, in itself, is a major controversy among some. There are some who maintain that the numerical assignments in the Hebrew alphabet were borrowed from the Greek alphabet in a later period, perhaps from the influence of Pythagoras, et al. (580 -500 B.C.)[18] There are some popular references that maintain that no special signs can be demonstrated before the Babylonian exile,[19] but this has all been refuted.[20]

The Hebrew use of an alphanumeric alphabet clearly predates these assumptions.[21] It appears that all peoples in the fertile crescent area employed at least two notation systems, the symbols and the fully written words.[22]

Numerical symbolism is one of the most difficult subjects one must deal with in the science of hermeneutics. But before we get into the controversies involved, let's first explore simple numerics.

Biblical Numerics

The basic study of numerics emerges simply from the inductive inferences compiled from the occurrences and uses of numbers in the text. The conspicuous use and re-use of specific numbers in various contexts have attracted reverent minds throughout the centuries and clearly indicate that there lies a deliberate design and deeper significance behind them. Unfortunately, it is difficult to find sources that diligently draw conclusions from thorough and comprehensive examination, while yet remaining free of contrived or fanciful spiritualizations.[23] It is of paramount importance not to give up facts for theories, nor abandon truth for conjectures.

Numerous volumes have been compiled analyzing the use of numbers in the Bible. Some of these are idiomatic arrangements for rhetorical purposes;[24] others evidence the intricate numerical designs underlying the biblical text. We will simply sample a few of them.

Sevens are certainly uniquely prominent in the Scripture, and we have already noted the "heptadic" structure of the text itself.[25] Sevens occur in about six hundred passages in the Bible.[26] Sevens are so manifest — and also hidden — that they testify of a unified design of the whole, and indicate a careful and skillful editing which transcends the independent efforts of over 40 authors spanning almost two thousand years. Seven appears to imply completeness or perfection. (It is not necessarily "divine" as is often inferred; Satan has seven heads).

Six — one short of seven — also appears to be used with subtle but definable consistency. It always alludes to an inadequacy: the sinfulness of man; the evilness of Satan, etc. Examples include the six fingers of the *Nephilim* and *Anakim*; the six steps to Solomon's throne; the 666 shekels of Solomon's salary; the "seal of Solomon" itself — known today as the *Magen David*; and, of course, the 666 of Revelation.

The number two seems to point to the idea of witness, or testimony — the two witnesses of Revelation 11; the two angels at the resurrection and the ascension and at Sodom and Gomorrah; the two testaments, Old and New; the requirement for a plurality of witnesses to establish a thing before a judge,[27] etc.

Clearly the most provocative enigma of all is *three-in-one*, as it appears in what we call the "Trinity" — the concept of plurality retaining perfect unity. The presentation of the "three-in-one" pervades the entire Old Testament as well as the New, but that's a discussion for which goes far beyond our opportunity here.[28]

Caveats

On the one hand, the consistency of use of numbers and the numerical structures within the biblical text is too manifest to deny.[29] On the other hand, an over-emphasis on their mystical implications has also proven to be a quagmire that can also easily lead to doctrinal quicksand. Contrariwise, the fanciful conjectures applied to biblical numbers has also reinforced the reactions in the opposite direction, maintaining that mystical implications of numbers has no validity whatsoever.[30] Who said it would be easy?

Zealous devotees assert fanciful mystical claims, on the one hand, and skeptics go too far the other way in total denial. Clearly, these "codes" appear to be real, and yet they remain to be convincingly resolved in any systematic manner. Furthermore, numbers can play an important role in the area of hermeneutics[31] as they not only convey mathematical data, but are also important in identifying literary stylisms.

The Gnostics relied heavily on mystical numerology for their heretical views. Early Church fathers also made it part of their apologetic.[32] Irenaeus, among others, made valiant attempts to stem the tide of theological mysticism and allegorical interpretation in the Early Church.[33] Advances in mathematics, with its imaginative connotations, also had its theological impacts.

Pythagorean Influence

From the early days of the Ionian philosophers, the Greek world considered numbers as worthy of the highest and most sustained study. In the age of Plato and Aristotle (c. 300 B.C.) the great mathematical insights of the Greek civilization were brought forth. The roots of numeralogical manipulation of numbers among the Greeks is generally dated from Pythagoras (c. 582 - 500 B.C). When Pythagoras returned from travel and study in Babylon and Egypt, he founded a secret cult in southern Italy based on the numerical explanations for the phenomena of the universe.

Legend has it that Pythagoras became convinced of the primacy of number when he realized that the musical notes produced by a monochord were in simple ratio to the length of the string. Qualities (tones) were reduced to quantities (numbers in integral ratios). Thus was born mathematical physics, for this discovery provided the essential bridge between the world of physical experience and that of numerical relationships.

The Pythagoreans considered numbers to be the elements and origin of everything. This mystic brotherhood of disciples eroded whatever objective scientific value their teacher's labors may have held and plunged his name and teachings into a veritable swamp of magic and ritual. After Alexander's conquests, this residue settled upon the ancient Semitic states of the Near East.

The impact of Plotinus and Neo-Platonism energized this mystic trend to the point that gematria was practiced widely among various schools of Hellenistic thought. This numerical mysticism also was embraced in the rise of Gnostic heresies which plagued the early church and which were passed on to the post-Nicene church and the Medieval Era. Numerical mysticism is also deeply involved in Freemasonry and other occultic practices.

Ironically, it was the allegorical interpretations of Origen, and the stamp of approval by Augustine and others that led to the subsequent subjective speculations which opened the door to the twin errors of mysticism on the one hand and liberalism on the other. Having lost its moorings in the bedrock of Scripture, we should not be surprised at the diversity of views within the church today.

> Knowing this first, that no prophecy of the scripture is of any private interpretation. For the prophecy came not in old time by the will of man: but holy men of God spake as they were moved by the Holy Ghost (2 Pet. 1:20- 21).

Gematria

Compounding the numerics themselves are the speculations of *gematria.* Both the Hebrew and Greek alphabets exploited the letters for assigned numerical values.[34] *Gematria* (a corruption from the Semiticized "geometria") is the substitution of numbers for letters of the Hebrew alphabet.

There are numerous examples which clearly imply an astonishing elegance of design which integrates the Hebrew alphabet, its numerical values, and the associated sememes. The Hebrew word for "year" is שָׁנֶה, *shaneh,* which has a gematrical value of 355. Remember, the Hebrew calendar is on a *lunar* year which has 355 days! The Hebrew word for pregnancy is הריון, *haryon,* and has a gematrical value of 271; there are 271 days in a normal pregnancy.

However, gematria became a popular method exploited by the medieval Kabbalists to derive mystical insights into sacred writings or to develop new interpretations of the texts. It is the pursuit of hidden meanings — particularly when in disregard of the plain text — that this leads to subjective conjectures beyond the moorings of the directly revealed Scripture.

Gematria is widely regarded as having risen in the Hellenistic age;[35] it was the view of Hermippus that mystical numerology originated with the Jews from which Pythagoras copied it.[36] But this a scholastic presumption that appears to be without substance. The Babylonians employed "gematria" (the numerical values of letters and words) during the time of Sargon II. The wall at Khorsabad was supposed to have been built according to the numerical value of Sargon's name.[37]

The blossoming of Jewish gematria reached its seminal period during the 12th and 13th centuries. Rabbi Joseph ben Abraham Gakatilla of Castile and Segovia, published a compilation of the methods of gematria, *nokarikon* (initial letters of sentences), and *temurah* (permutation of letters) in 1274.[38] While much of the Kabbalastic literature may strike us as fanciful conjectures, there are some instances that are quite provocative. Let's review a few examples.

The Signature of God: 961

אֵל, *El*, is a Hebrew name for God. Some Kabbalists believe they have rediscovered the ancient "Law of the Square." They feel that the occurance of the *square* of a key number is especially significant. אֵל has a gematria value of 31; and $31^2 = 961$ ($13^2 = 169$: This is also curious: it is one of the very few occasions in which the reversal of the order of the integers of the root also reverses the order of the integers of its square: reversing 13 to 31 yields the squares of 169 and 961, respectively). The number 961 seems to emerge in several critical instances — so much so that some have come to call 961 "the Signature of God." As an example, when the ה was added to Abram and Sarai:

Abraham	248
Sarah	505
Isaac	208
	$961 = 31^2$, "the Signature of God"

There are other traditional examples that are a bit more specious:

Abraham's Army of 318

In Genesis 14, an alliance of four armies, led by Chedorlaomer (an Elamite, whom we know as a Proto-Persian) successfully subjugated five armies for a period of 12 years. However, in the 13th year the five rebelled. In the 14th year Chedorlaomer and his armies, after defeating the four tribes of giants, as well as the Amalekites and the Amorites, also clobbered the five rebel kings of the south. Obviously, they were a very formidable military force to be reckoned with.

In the subsequent taking of spoils by Chedorlaomer and his forces, Abram's nephew Lot was taken as a hostage. Abram, in alliance with Amorite tribes, and armed with 318 *trained* servants, took after them and succeeded where the other armies had failed. (An ancient predecessor to the more recent raid at Entebbe!)

Since Abram's headservant's name was Eliezer, which happens to have a gematria value of 318, some argue that this indicates that the "318 servants" were simply Eliezer himself.[39] This, however, contradicts the text, and the "dividing of forces" indicated in verse 15. This could be simply a coincidence; or, alternatively, it is an allusion to the involvement of the Holy Spirit: the name Eliezer means "Comforter."

The Mark of the Beast: 666

People who know little else about the Bible have heard of the "666." Even scholars who assertively deny the application of numerical symbolism in the Bible reluctantly acknowledge this declaration in Revelation 13:18 as an apparent exception.

> Here is wisdom. Let him that hath understanding count
> the number of the beast: for it is the number of a man; and
> his number is Six hundred threescore and six (Rev. 13:18).

Most authorities take for granted that this riddle is to be addressed through gematria. And libraries have been filled with volumes of speculations throughout the centuries. Martin Luther, among others, tied it to the Vatican regime.[40] There are contrived suggestions linking it to virtually every personage throughout history — and, of course, in our day as well.

Many contrive gematrical structures around English or Latin, conveniently overlooking the fact that *only* Hebrew and Greek have an alphanumeric tradition that lends itself to such practices.

The earlier occurrences of 666 in the biblical text is restricted to the tribute paid to Solomon.[41] As we noted earlier, the number six is associated with him in many other ways, and seems always to hint of a sinister character.

Furthermore, there are other ideological aspects of the history of both the numerics and the derived geometrical symbolism of the past.

The traditional Jewish hexagram — known today as the *Magen David*, or "Shield of David" — had an earlier *occult* history. It has been adopted as a symbol of Judaism only traceable since the 14th century.[42] Its earlier history was as a symbol known as the "Seal of Solomon," and was used in occultic practices.

From the context of Revelation 13:18, it is clear that the identity of the person(s) involved will be quite manifest at the time they need it. The worship and obeisance of the leader involved results in a total ineligibility for salvation. This certainly indicates that this is not likely to depend on any subtleties or mysticism. We believe, from a careful exegesis of 2 Thessalonians 3, that this identity will *not* be revealed until the post-church era.

888

Also well-known among "Gematrists" is that 888, in contrast to 666, seems to emerge in many expressions which relate to Jesus Christ. (Jesus, Iησουj = 888.)[43]

Perhaps the most provocative is the discovery that taking equidistant letter sequences at intervals of 7 also seem to result in 888 behind many of the Messianic passages.[44]

A Variety of Methods

What makes the study of gematria so subjective and inconclusive, is that, to further complicate matters, there are seven (naturally) classical methods of Gematria:

> *Ragil* (nominal) (notice that there are 27 letters, including the five "final forms").
> *Kolel,* the *ragil* values plus the number of letters in the word.
> *Katan,* small values, also called "reduced" values: all tens and hundreds reduced to 1 - 9 by summing the digits.
> *Hakadmi*, nominal values plus the values of each letter preceding it.
> *Hameruba Haklali*, the value of the word *squared.*
> *Hameruba Haperati*, the sum of the squares of each individual letter.
> *Miluy*, the sums of the values of the *names* of each letter that makes up the word. Also called "filling."

Some authorities even list 22 alternative methods of enumeration.[45] It becomes pretty obvious that one can "prove" almost anything by various manipulations. And they do.

It is somewhat reminiscent of an adage in the information processing industry: "If you torture the data long enough, it will eventually confess to anything!"

Gematria remains one of the "fringe" areas in which there so seem to be too many provocative occurrences to ignore, and yet no systematic objective methodology which yields consistent results. It is therefore no surprise that reactions tend to become polarized into two extremes: those that totally reject these techniques out of hand; and those who seem to become obsessed with them to extremes.

Perhaps more systematic investigation and objective analysis may yield more constructive fruit than the fanciful explorations to date. We have seen the use of error-correction techniques in the *lexemes* of the text; perhaps eventually we will discover that the numerical properties such as gematria may yield *sememe* redundancy as well.

But the deeper question remains: Does the Bible use numbers in a mystical sense? The Kabbalists held that every detail in the Torah was significant. So did the Lord: Matt 5:17, 18.

The Hazards of "Mysticism"

Many will, of course, accuse us of "mysticism" and we make only faint apology: Paul and John clearly were "mystics." For them the ultimate experience was union with Christ. The recurring phrase "in Christ" implies a personal union, a participation in His death and resurrection. This is especially emphasized in the farewell discourse (John 15-16) where Jesus speaks of His impending death and His ultimate return to unite himself with His followers. In his intimate prayer of John 17 He speaks of the interpenetrating union of souls in which all who are one with Christ share *His perfect union with the Father*. You can't get more mystical than that!

It will, however, prove difficult to confine our investigation to *revealed* truth and not allow ourselves to get lost in the bramble of contrived and compounded conjectures.

In instrument flying, a pilot gets his references from six basic instruments: the airspeed indicator; the altimeter; the rate of climb (or descent); the turn-and-bank indicator; the heading indicator or compass; and the artificial (gyro) horizon. The way a pilot gets into trouble is to yield to the natural tendency to fixate on any *one* of these. The well-known remedy among instrument pilots is the emphasis on "cross-check:" constantly comparing what any one instrument seems to be telling you with *all* of the others.

And this is the way we need to keep our bearings and positional attitude: by "cross-checking" everything with "the whole counsel of God."[46] We must cling to the *whole* of Scripture as our fixed point of reference.

Chapter 11 Footnotes

1 Sir James Jeans, *The Mysterious Universe* (Cambridge, MA: Cambridge University Press, 1930).

2 Chuck Missler, *Beyond Coincidence*, a briefing package from Koinonia, 1998, p.7-8.

3 R. McCormack, *The Heptadic Structure of Scripture* (London: Marshall Brothers Ltd.,1923).

   E.W. Bullinger, *Numbers of the Scriptures* (Grand Rapids, MI: Kregel Publications, reproduction from 1894).

   F. W. Grant, *The Numerical Bible*, (7 vols.); Browne, *Ordo Saeculoreium*, et al.

4 Ivan Panin, (various works), Bible Numerics, P.O. Box 206, Waubaushene, Ontario L0K 2C0.

5 Bullinger, *Numbers of the Scriptures*, p. 42-44.

6 Daniel 8:13.

7 From an excellent review by Dr. William Whit, *Zondervan Pictorial Encyclopedia of the Bible*, (Grand Rapids, MI: Zondervan Publishing House, 1975), vol 4, p. 452-61.

8 Zecharia Sitchin, *The Earth Chronicles,* Books 1 through 5; and *Genesis Revisited* (New York: Avon Books, 1990).

9 Genesis 6:1-4; 2 Samuel 21:20; 1 Chronicles 20:6.

10 Solo Baron, "The Authenticity of the Numbers in the Historical Books of the Old Testament," *Journal of Biblical Literature*, XLIX, 1930, p. 288-290.

11 The letter *vau*, with a value of 6, and *koppa,* with a value of 90, existed at one time but later became extinct. The letter *koppa* of the early Greek alphabet is replaced by *kappa* in the eastern Greek alphabet except for use as a numeral with the value of 90; it was retained in the western Greek alphabet and ultimately became the letter Q. The letter *vau*, sometimes represented by the letter *sigma*, appears in only one biblical passage: Revelation 13:18.

12 The second letter is used as the final form, the last letter of a word.

13 The letter *sampsi*, with a value of 900, also became extinct.

14 John J. Davis, *Biblical Numerology* (Grand Rapids, MI: Baker Book House, 1968), p.38.

15 Hebrew *ammah* ("mother of the arm"), the forearm, was the nominal distance from one's elbow to the fingertip; the term "cubit" is from the Latin *cubitus*, the lower arm.

16 The answer to this difficulty was discovered by Shlomo Edward G. Belaga that appeared in Boaz Tsaban's Rabbinical Math page on the Internet, <www.cs.biu.ac.il:8080/~tsaban/hebrew.html> and is also reported in Grant Jeffrey's *The Handwriting of God* (Toronto, Ontario: Frontier Research Publications, 1997).

17 There were several "official" cubits in the ancient world, varying from about 18

inches to almost two feet. Some authorities assume 20.24 inches for the ordinary cubit , and 21.888 inches for the sacred one. We have used 18 inches in the discussion.

18 Driver, *Notes on the Hebrew Text and the Topography of the Books of Samuel* (Oxford: The Clarendon Press, 1913), p. 97

R..A. H. Gunner, "Number," *The New Bible Dictionary* (Grand Rapids, MI: Wm. B. Eerdmans Publishing Co., 1963), p. 895.

19 Wiliam Taylor Smith, "Number," *The International Standard Bible Encyclopedia* (Chicago, IL: Howard-Severance Co., 1925), IV, p. 2157.

20 W. F. Albright, "The Lachish Letters After Five Years," *Bulletin of the American Schools of Oriental Researh,* No. 22, April 1941.

21 Merrill Unger, *Unger's Bible Dictionary* (Chicago, IL: Moody Press, 1957), p. 799.

22 John D. Davis, *A Dictionary of the Bible* (Grand Rapids, MI: Baker Book House, 1954), p. 546.

23 Clearly the refreshing exception are the works of E.W. Bullinger, as exemplified in his *Number in Scripture*, Kregel Publications, Grand Rapids MI, which has reproduced his classic 1894 publication.

24 The arrangement of a numeral with its sequel within a clause, (x, x+1) either syndetically or asyndetically, is a common device to express intensification or progression. Cf. Davis, p. 93ff.

25 McCormack, *The Heptadic Structure of Scripture.*

Bullinger, *Numbers of the Scriptures.*

Karl G. Sabiers, *Astonishing New Discoveries* (Los Angeles, CA: Robertson Publishing Co., 1941).

M. Mahan, *Palmoni or Numerals of Scripture* (New York: D. Appleton and Co., 1863).

Ivan Panin, "Bible Numerics," *Things to Come* (London: Horace Marshall & Sons, 1911, 1912), Vols. 17, 18.

J. Edwin Hartill, *Biblical Hermeneutics* (Grand Rapids, MI: Zondervan Publishing Co., 1947).

F. W. Grant, *The Numerical Bible*; also, Panin references in chapter 7.

26 William Taylor Smith, *The International Standard Bible Enclopedia,* p. 2159.

27 Deuteronomy 17:6, 19:15; Matthew 18:6; 2 Corinthians 13:1; 1 Timothy 5:19; Hebrews 10:28.

28 The author discusses the presentation of the Trinity in both the Old and New Testaments in his briefing package, *The Trinity — The Mystery of the Godhead*, available from Koinonia.

29 *Ibid.*

30 Davis, *Biblical Numerology.*

O. T. Allis, *Bible Numerics,* 1961.

31 *Hermeneutics* is the art of interpreting literature, especially the sacred Scriptures, and includes the recognition of the principles upon which a true analysis must proceed.

32 Davis, *Biblical Numerology*, p. 129.

33 *Against Heresies*, Book II:25:1, Alexander Robersts and James Donaldson, eds., *The Ante-Nicene Fathers* (Grand Rapids, MI: Wm. B. Eerdmans Publishing Co., 1951), Vol 1, p. 396.

34 These are in addition to their *ordinal* values, where each of the 22 letters is given an equivalent number from 1 to 22. Rarely used.

35 Davis, *Biblical Numerology*, p.125-156.

36 Origen, *Against Celsus*, Book I, chap. XV, Alexander Roberts and James Donaldson, eds., *The Ante-Nicene Fathers* (Grand Rapids, MI: Wm. B. Eerdmans Publishing Co., 1951), p. 402.

37 Vincent F. Hopper, *An Encyclopedia of Religion* (New York: Philosophical Library, 1945), p. 62.

38 Satinover p.76.

39 *Encyclopedia Judaica,* Gen. R. 43:2; Also, the *Epistle of Barnabas.*

40 Davis, *Biblical Numerology*, 132; 144ff.

41 1 Kings 10:14; 2 Chronicles 9:13.

42 W. Gunther Plaut, *The Magen David* (Jerusalem: B'nai B'rith Books, 1991), p. 37-49.

Asher Eder, *The Star of David* (Jerusalem: Rubin Mass Ltd., 1987), p. 15.

43 Jerry Lucas and Del Washburn, *Theomatics* (Lanham, MD: Scarborough House, 1977), is an example.

44 Bonnie Grant, *Jesus Christ: the Number of His Name*, points out that Isaiah 9:6 and 11:1 are conspicuous examples.

45 *Jewish Encyclopedia*, Vol. V, (New York, 1990), p. 592.

46 Acts 20:27; Hebrew 6:17.

12

The Glorious Incomparable Promises of the Bible

Thomas Ice

During the first half of World War II, General Douglas MacArthur was forced to leave the Philippines in the Pacific Theater by the Japanese. Upon his departure he made a promise to the Philippino people: "I will return." General MacArthur, through the strength and power of the American military was able to keep his promise. If humanity can make and keep promises of rescue and deliverance, how much more will our great God keep the glorious and incomparable promises He has made in His Word! Indeed, He has told us that He will one day return and fulfill the great and many promises about the glorious future in store for those who know Him as their Savior.

Why are promises important to God? Promises are important to God's plan for history, because God keeps His word. History is a record of God's faithfulness to keep His promises. Thus, God delights in making seemingly impossible promises so that He, through the most difficult circumstances, demonstrates that He keeps His promises. Think of God's record of faithfulness next time you are tempted by circumstances to go back on your word. There are three great promises that God has made to His people that I want to examine in this chapter. These promises are Israel's permanence, Christ's second coming, and eternal life to all believers.

Promise of Israel's Permanence

Scripture makes it clear that God's integrity in history revolves around His chosen people Israel. It is through Israel that God has chosen to leave His mark throughout history. It is through Israel that God gave His Law, founded a nation, caused His presence to dwell, mediated His Word, and sent the Savior of the world. It will be through Israel in the future that God will work to preach the gospel throughout the whole world, invoke the Second Coming, reign for a thousand years in Jerusalem, and place His eternal glory. Thus, God's promise to Israel is that they have an eternal permanence in history and throughout eternity. The Lord says through Jeremiah:

> Thus says the Lord, Who gives the sun for light by day, and the fixed order of the moon and the stars for light by night, Who stirs up the sea so that its waves roar; the Lord of hosts is His name: "Lord, If this fixed order departs from before Me," declares the Lord, "then the offspring of Israel also shall cease from being a nation before Me forever" (Jer. 31:35–36).

Most American evangelical Christians today have a high view of Jews and the modern state of Israel because of the positive influence of the dispensational premillennial view that national Israel has a future in the plan of God. Yet, there are those within Christendom who deny that Israel has a permanent place in the plan of God. This view is known as replacement theology.

What is replacement theology? Replacement theology is the view that the Church has permanently replaced Israel as the instrument through which God works and that national Israel does not have a future in the plan of God. Some replacement theologians may believe that individual Jews will be converted and enter into the church (something that we all believe), but they do not believe that God will literally fulfill the dozens of Old Testament promises to a converted national Israel in the future. For example, reconstructionist David Chilton says that "ethnic Israel was excommunicated for its apostasy and will never again be God's Kingdom."[1] Chilton says again, "The Bible does not tell of any future plan for Israel as a *special* nation."[2] Reconstructionist patriarch, R. J. Rushdoony uses the strongest language when he declares:

> The fall of Jerusalem, and the public rejection of physical Israel as the chosen people of God, meant also the deliv-

erance of the true people of God, the church of Christ, the elect, out of the bondage to Israel and Jerusalem.

A further heresy clouds premillennial interpretations of Scripture — their exaltation of racism into a divine principle. Every attempt to bring the Jew back into prophecy as a Jew is to give *race* and *works* (for racial descent is a human work) a priority over *grace* and *Christ's work* and is nothing more or less than paganism. . . . There can be no compromise with this vicious heresy.[3]

The Road to Holocaust

Replacement theology and its view that Israel is finished in history nationally has been responsible for producing theological anti-Semitism in the church. History records that such a theology, when combined with the right social and political climate, has produced and allowed anti-Semitism to flourish. This was a point made by Hal Lindsey in *The Road to Holocaust*, to which reconstructionists cried foul. A book was written to rebut Lindsey by Jewish reconstructionist Steve Schlissel. Strangely, Schlissel's book (*Hal Lindsey & the Restoration of the Jews*) ended up supporting Lindsey's thesis that replacement theology produced anti-Semitism in the past and could in the future. Schlissel seems to share Lindsey's basic view on the rise and development of anti-Semitism within the history of the church. After giving his readers an overview of the history of anti-Semitism through Origen, Augustine, Chrysostom, Ambrose, and Jerome, Schlissel then quotes approvingly Raul Hilberg's famous quote featured in Lindsey's *Holocaust*:

> Viewing the plight of the Jews in Christian lands from the fourth century to the recent holocaust, one Jew observed, "First we were told 'You're not good enough to live among us as Jews.' Then we were told, 'You're not good enough to live among us.' Finally we were told, 'You're not good enough to live.' "

Schlissel then comments approvingly upon Hilberg's statement:

> This devastatingly accurate historical analysis was the fruit of an error, a building of prejudice and hate erected upon a false theological foundation. The blindness of the church regarding the place of the Jew in redemptive history

is, I believe, directly responsible for the wicked sins and attitudes described above. What the church believes about the Jews has always made a difference. But the church has not *always* believed a lie.

The truth, noted by Schlissel, is what his other reconstructionist brethren deny. What Schlissel has called a lie is the replacement theology that his reconstructionist brethren advocate. Their form of replacement theology is the problem. Schlissel goes on to show that the Reformed church of Europe, after the Reformation, widely adopted the belief that God's future plan for Israel includes a national restoration of Israel. Many even taught that Israel would one day rebuild her Temple. For his Reformed brethren to arrive at such conclusions meant that they were interpreting the Old Testament promises to Israel literally, at least some of them. This shift from replacement theology to a national future for Israel resulted in a decline in persecution of the Jews in many Reformed communities and increased efforts in Jewish evangelism. Schlissel notes:

> The change in the fortune of the Jews in Western civilization can be traced, not to humanism, but to the Reformed faith. The rediscovery of Scripture brought a rekindling of the Biblical conviction that God had not, in fact, fully nor finally rejected His people.

Yet Schlissel is concerned that his Reformed brethren are abandoning this future national hope for Israel as they currently re-assert a strong view of replacement theology:

> Whatever views were maintained as to Israel's political restoration, their spiritual future was simply a given in Reformed circles. Ironically, this sure and certain hope is not a truth kept burning brightly in many Christian Reformed Churches today — In fact, their future conversion aside, the Jews' very existence is rarely referred to today, and even then it is not with much grace or balance.

This extract establishes that the "spiritualized" notion of "Israel" in Romans 11:25-26, was known to and *rejected by* the body of Dutch expositors:

Since the turn of the century, most modern Dutch Reformed, following Kuyper and Bavinck, reject this historic position.

Reconstructionist Schlissel seems to think that part of the reason why many of his Reformed brethren are returning to replacement theology is due to their reaction to the strong emphasis of a future for Israel as a nation found within dispensational premillennialism. Yet, dispensational premillennialism developed within the Reformed tradition as many began to consistently take all the Old Testament promises that were yet fulfilled for Israel as still valid for a future Jewish nation. Schlissel complains:

> Just a century ago *all* classes of Reformed interpreters held to the certainty of the future conversion of Israel *as a nation*. How they have come, to a frightening extent, to depart from their historic positions regarding the certainty of Israel's future conversion is not our subject here. . . . The hope of the future conversion of the Jews became closely linked, at the turn of the century and beyond, with Premillennial Dispensationalism, an eschatological heresy. This, necessarily, one might say, soon became bound up and confused with Zionism. Christians waxed loud about the return of the Jews to Israel being a portent that the Second Coming is nigh. It thus seemed impossible, for many, to distinguish between the spiritual hope of Israel and their political "hope." Many Reformed, therefore, abandoned both.[4]

Historical Development

As it should be, the nature of Israel's future became the watershed issue in biblical interpretation, which caused a polarization of positions that we find today. As Schlissel noted, "all classes of Reformed interpreters held to the certainty of the future conversion of Israel as a nation." Today most Reformed interpreters do not hold such a view. Why? Early in the systemization of any theological position the issues are undeveloped and less clear than later when the consistency of various positions are worked out. Thus, it is natural for the mature understanding of any theological issue to lead to polarization of viewpoints as a result of interaction and debate between positions. The earlier Reformed position to which Schlissel refers included a blend

216 • *Mysteries of the Bible Now Revealed*

of some Old Testament passages that were taken literally (i.e., those teaching a future conversion of Israel as a nation) and some that were not (i.e., details of Israel's place of dominance during a future period of history). On the one hand, as time passed, those who stressed a literal understanding of Israel from the Old Testament became much more consistent in applying such an approach to all passages relating to Israel's destiny. On the other hand, those who thought literalism was taken too far retreated from whatever degree of literalness they did have and argued that the church fulfills Israel's promises, thus there was no need for a national Israel in the future. Further, non-literal interpretation was viewed as the tool with which liberals denied the essentials of the faith. Thus, by World War II dispensationalism had come to virtually dominate evangelicals who saw literal interpretation of the Bible as a primary support for orthodoxy.

After World War II many of the battles between fundamentalism and liberalism began to wane. Such an environment allowed for less stigma attached to non-literal interpretation within conservative circles. Thus, by the 1970s, not having learned the lessons of history, we began to see the revival of many prophetic views that were returning to blends of literal and spiritual interpretation. As conservative post-millennialism has risen from near extinction in recent years, it did not return to the mixed hermeneutics of 100 years ago, which Schlissel longs for, but instead, it has been wedded with preterism in hopes that it can combat the logic of dispensational futurism. Schlissel's Reformed brethren do not appear to be concerned that, in preterism, they have revived a brand of eschatology which includes one of the most hard-core forms of replacement theology. And they do not appear convinced or concerned that replacement theology has a history of producing theological anti-Semitism when mixed with the right social and political conditions.

The Modern State of Israel

The fact that the last 50 years has seen a worldwide regathering and re-establishment of the nation of Israel, which is now poised in just the setting required for the revealing of the Antichrist and the start of the Tribulation, is God's grand indicator that all of the other areas of world development are prophetically significant. Dr. Walvoord says,

> Of the many peculiar phenomena which characterize the present generation, few events can claim equal significance as far as biblical prophecy is concerned with that of the return of Israel to their land. It constitutes a preparation

for the end of the age, the setting for the coming of the Lord for His church, and the fulfillment of Israel's prophetic destiny.[5]

Israel, God's "super-sign" of the end times, is a clear indicator that time is growing shorter with each passing hour. God is preparing the world for the final events leading up to Israel's national regeneration.

What one believes about the future of Israel is of utmost importance to one's understanding of the Bible. I believe, without a shadow of doubt, that Old Testament promises made to national Israel will literally be fulfilled in the future. This means the Bible teaches that God will return the Jews to their land before the tribulation begins (Isa. 11:11–12:6; Ezek. 20:33-44, 22:17-22; Zeph. 2:1-3). This has been accomplished and the stage is set as a result of the current existence of the modern state of Israel. The Bible also indicates that before Israel enters into her time of national blessing she must first pass through the fire of the tribulation (Deut. 4:30; Jer. 30:5-9; Dan. 12:1; Zeph. 1:14-18).

Even though the horrors of the Holocaust under Hitler were of an unimaginable magnitude, the Bible teaches that a time of even greater trial awaits Israel during the tribulation. Anti-Semitism will reach new heights, this time global in scope, in which two-thirds of world Jewry will be killed (Zech. 13:7-9). Through this time God will protect His remnant so that before His second advent "all Israel will be saved" (Rom. 11:36). In fact, the second coming will include the purpose of God's physical rescue of Israel from world persecution during Armageddon (Dan. 12:1; Zech. 12-14; Matt. 24:29-31; Rev. 19:11-21).

If national Israel is a historical "has been," then all of this is obviously wrong. However, the Bible says she has a future and world events will revolve around that tiny nation at the center of the earth. The world's focus already is upon Israel. God has preserved His people for a reason and it is not all bad. In spite of the fact that history is progressing along the lines of God's ordained pattern for Israel, we see the revival of replacement theology within conservative circles that will no doubt be used in the future to fuel the fires of anti-Semitism, as it has in the past. Your view of the future of national Israel is not just an academic exercise.

Promise of Christ's Second Coming

Even though we now live in a secular society, a recent poll by *U.S. News & World Report* found that a majority of Americans still believe that Jesus Christ will return:

218 • Mysteries of the Bible Now Revealed

Belief in apocalyptic prophecies is not just a phenomenon of the religious fringe. According to a recent *U. S. News* poll, 66 percent of Americans, including a third of those who say they never attend church, say they believe that Jesus Christ will return to Earth someday — an increase from the 61 percent who expressed belief in the Second Coming three years ago.[6]

Though many may not realize its significance, the return of Jesus Christ to planet Earth is the most important event that will occur in the future. But what do we know about the coming of Christ? Is it only a heart-felt hope and historical hype, or do we have a clear and certain word from God on this event?

The prophetic promise of the second coming of Jesus Christ to earth is the subject of many passages in both the Old Testament and the New Testament. What are some of the more prominent texts? They include some of the following: Deuteronomy 30:3; Psalm 2; Isaiah 63:1-6; Daniel 2:44-45; 7:13-14; Zechariah 14:1-4; Matthew 24–25; Mark 13; Luke 21; Acts 1:9-11; Romans 11:26; 1 Thessalonians 3:13; 5:1-4; 2 Thessalonians 1:6-2:12; 2 Peter 2:1-3:17; Jude 14-15; and Revelation 1:7; 19:11-21.

Probably the most graphic portrayal of Christ's second coming is found in Revelation 19:11-21. In this extended passage Jesus Christ is described as leading a procession of angels and saints or armies in heaven to claim the earth, destroy the armies of the world, and defeat the Antichrist and false prophet.

And I saw heaven opened; and behold, a white horse, and He who sat upon it is called Faithful and True; and in righteousness He judges and wages war. And His eyes are a flame of fire, and upon His head are many diadems; and He has a name written upon Him which no one knows except Himself. And He is clothed with a robe dipped in blood; and His name is called The Word of God. And the armies which are in heaven, clothed in fine linen, white and clean, were following Him on white horses. And from His mouth comes a sharp sword, so that with it He may smite the nations; and He will rule them with a rod of iron; and He treads the wine press of the fierce wrath of God, the Almighty. And on His robe and on His thigh He has a name written, "KING OF KINGS, AND LORD OF LORDS." And I saw

an angel standing in the sun; and he cried out with a loud
voice, saying to all the birds which fly in midheaven, "Come,
assemble for the great supper of God; in order that you may
eat the flesh of kings and the flesh of commanders and the
flesh of mighty men and the flesh of horses and of those
who sit on them and the flesh of all men, both free men and
slaves, and small and great." And I saw the beast and the
kings of the earth and their armies, assembled to make war
against Him who sat upon the horse, and against His army.
And the beast was seized, and with him the false prophet
who performed the signs in his presence, by which he de-
ceived those who had received the mark of the beast and
those who worshipped his image; these two were thrown
alive into the lake of fire which burns with brimstone. And
the rest were killed with the sword which came from the
mouth of Him who sat upon the horse, and all the birds were
filled with their flesh (Rev. 19:11–21).

The passage above shows that Christ's return will be one that
entails great physical destruction and many deaths. For those who are
not Christ's own, it will be a terrifying and terrible event. For those of
us who know Him as their Savior, it will be a time of great joy, vindica-
tion, and anticipation.

The Bible depicts the career of Christ as revolving around two
major aspects. Titus 2:11–14 speaks of Christ's two appearances on
earth.

For the grace of God has appeared, bringing salvation
to all men, instructing us to deny ungodliness and worldly
desires and to live sensibly, righteously and godly in the
present age, looking for the blessed hope and the appearing
of the glory of our great God and Savior, Christ Jesus; who
gave Himself for us, that He might redeem us from every
lawless deed and purify for Himself a people for His own
possession, zealous for good deeds (Titus 2:11–14).

The first phase is related to His coming in humiliation to die for
the sins of mankind. The second phase is when He will come in power
and glory to reign over all mankind. Hebrews 9:28 is a single verse that
explains and contrasts Christ's two comings. The writer of Hebrews
says, "So Christ also, having been offered once to bear the sins of many,

shall appear a second time for salvation without reference to sin, to those who eagerly await Him." Jesus is coming again. This is a glorious promise and hope for all believers.

The future is not all gloom and doom. It holds trials of an unprecedented nature in human history, but it also contains the glorious return of Jesus Christ to establish his righteous reign in preparation for the eternal state. The history of the Old Testament era was one of expectation for the first coming of the Messiah. The history of the New Testament and our own era is one of expectation for the second coming of Messiah. Such an expectation is voiced when we pray "Thy kingdom come, Thy will be done." His kingdom will come when Christ returns and all of creation will acknowledge Jesus Christ, the hope of history. Let's see what the Bible says about that coming!

Promise of Eternal Life

Eternal life is the gift of God given to all who believe in Jesus Christ and have accepted His offer of salvation based upon His death and resurrection (John 10:10; Eph. 2:8-9). In the Bible, eternal life emphasizes a quality of life, a quality that can only be imparted by God himself. This life does not, of course, make us God; we are and will always remain creatures. However, it is a quality of life that comes from the God who has the quality of eternality. Therefore, eternal life should not be confused with endless or eternal existence which everyone will experience. Eternal existence will be common to the redeemed and the unredeemed, but the destinies will be very different. Christians will enter into heaven and the presence of God; unbelievers will be cast into the lake of fire (Rev. 20:11-15).

For those of us who have trusted Jesus Christ as our Savior, we are given the promise of eternal life the moment we believe. John says, "The witness is this, that God has given us eternal life, and this life is in His Son. He who has the Son has the life; he who does not have the Son of God does not have the life" (1 John 5:11–13). If you have trusted in Christ, then you have eternal life in the present which will continue throughout eternity in heaven for the believer. Believers have the hope of eternal life in heaven with our Lord for eternity.

Heaven is very real. In an age of fantasy, special effects, mysticism, and spiritual apathy, it's easy for heaven to be misrepresented. Yet, the Bible is very clear about the existence and purpose of heaven. Heaven and the eternal state are part of God's plan for the ages and therefore, heaven and eternal life are integrally related. There would not be much point in experiencing eternity if the quality of life were not worth looking forward to. This will be the case for those who will dwell for eternity in the lake of fire. But since we will spend eternity living out our eternal life in heaven, free from sin, and in the presence of our Lord, then heaven and the presence of God is what makes eternal life worthwhile.

The Bible describes eternal life in heaven as full of joy, purposeful activity, and worship. When we think of eternity, it's easy to wonder if we will get bored in heaven and discontented. However, the biblical glimpses are not ones of boredom and disinterest. The Bible speaks of at least six activities in heaven: worship, service, authority, fellowship, learning, and rest. Therefore, eternal life lived in heaven will consist of worship without distraction, service without exhaustion, authority without failure, fellowship without suspicion, learning without suspicion, and resting without boredom. What glorious things our Lord has promised to His people!

Conclusion

Anyone familiar with God's word knows that He has a wonderful plan for history and His people. These are indeed glorious and incomparable promises through which He implements His plan. What should the response of the believer be to God's promises? The Psalmist rightly advises, "What shall I render to the Lord for all His benefits toward me? I shall lift up the cup of salvation, and call upon the name of the Lord" (Ps. 116:12–13).

In the New Testament, our Lord was quizzed by the multitude in Capernaum when they said as follows: "They said therefore to Him, 'What shall we do, that we may work the works of God?' Jesus answered and said to them, 'This is the work of God, that you believe in Him whom He has sent' " (John 6:28–29). Is this not what our Lord has wanted since the Garden of Eden — that we believe and trust His precious promises? Certainly He has spoken, surely it will come to pass.

When we think about the significance of the glorious promises that our Lord has in store for us as His people, we respond with a thankful heart. Let us remember that for the believer, this present life, with its good and bad, is the worst they will ever experience. But, for the unbeliever, this present life will be the best they will ever experience. Let us claim the precious promises that He has made to us in the present so that He will make us fit for eternity.

Chapter 12 Footnotes

1 David Chilton, *Paradise Restored* (Tyler, TX: Reconstruction Press, 1985), p. 224.

2 Chilton, *Paradise Restored*.

3 Rousas John Rushdoony, *Thy Kingdom Come: Studies in Daniel and Revelation* (Fairfax, VA: Thoburn Press, 1970), p. 82 and 134.

4 Steve Schlissel and David Brown, *Hal Lindsey & the Restoration of the Jews* (Edmonton, Canada: Still Waters Revival Books, 1990), p. 39-59. For a survey of the history of anti-Semitism in the Church see David Rausch, *Building Bridges: Understanding Jews and Judaism* (Chicago, IL: Moody Press, 1988), p. 87-171.

5 John F. Walvoord, *Israel in Prophecy* (Grand Rapids, MI: Zondervan Publishing Company, 1964), p. 26.

6 Jeffrey L. Sheler, "Dark Prophecies," *U.S. News & World Report*, December 15, 1997, p. 63.

Afterword

This Bible, as we have affirmed in these 12 chapters, is a masterpiece of ancient literature which is, nevertheless, up-to-date in its communication of truth today, an indestructible book, a preserved and widely disseminated literary treasure, which can still be touted as the world's best seller. This, in spite of powerful and periodic secular and religious opposition to both its circulation and total content.

It is the all time classic of civilization. No other book has been so universally adopted, so cherished and loved, so hated and rejected, yet so dynamic and enduring.

There are other "scriptures" which have been widely accepted in different countries and cultures throughout the history of civilization. But none of these other religious works contain any of the amazing and unique qualities and characteristics explained in this volume. The writers of these chapters are not ignorant of the world's religions or their writings. All of us have researched other religious traditions and studied their philosophical approaches.

Of this you can be certain: *The Bible is the only book of its kind.* None other compares.

In retrospect —

It claims to be the inspired (God-breathed) Word of God. "All Scripture is given by inspiration of God" (2 Tim. 3:16). "For the prophecy came not in old time by the will of man, but holy men of God spoke as they were moved by the Holy Ghost" (2 Pet. 1:21). We have examined much of the *internal evidence* of its divine inspiration and uniqueness.

From ancient times, the godly Jews preserved it as the Word of God, making multiple copies with meticulous accuracy; the Church has held it to be inspired of God, the foundational tenet of Christianity; and its own teachings, and especially its predictions, so clearly fulfilled, prove it to be the Word of God.

There is *external evidence*: the antiquity of the Scriptures, as proved by persons who were the immediate instruments of these revelations being contemporaneous with the events of which they wrote. The uncorrupted preservation of the Scriptures is established by Jewish history and the accuracy of the Septuagint, the Greek translation of the Old Testament from Hebrew (circa 250 B.C.), done by some 70 scholars; and by the practically identical manuscripts of the Old Testament found among the Dead Sea Scrolls (150-200 B.C.). The scrolls compare with amazing accuracy to the much later (A.D. 900) manuscripts on which our translations had been based.

From the prophecies and their fulfillments centuries later and the hundreds of distinct predictions of the birth, life, death, resurrection, and power of Jesus Christ come powerful evidences of the truth of Scripture.

There is *internal* evidence in the superior theology and philosophy and moral code of the Scriptures, plus the strong emphasis on the love of God, love for each other, and the compassion and kindness that proceeds from love. No other book, religion, or philosophy so stresses the great qualities of love, humanity, grace, forgiveness, and acceptance as does this book.

There is *collateral* evidence as we have seen. The marvelous diffusion of Christianity during the first three centuries of the Common Era and its impact on the history of the world, especially also in the last 500 years, evidences its special and divine origin.

There is *corroborative* evidence, as we have reviewed from archaeology, modern science, secular and religious history, ancient documents, and much more.

Some may characterize the more unusual and recently discovered and promoted approaches of "the secret letter codes" or the "mathematical codes" in the Bible as *controversial evidence*, but the fact is that these phenomena exist.

Now are all of these 12 aspects of the Bible's uniqueness merely a fantastic combination of a myriad of coincidences? Or does logic demand that there be a divine Designer, a great master mind, who inspired and formulated this book, guiding human writers into all truth?

Is this Bible really the REVELATION OF GOD to the human race?

You have seen the evidence. You decide.

David Allen Lewis and James (Jim) Combs

"O Lord, how great are thy works! and thy thoughts are very deep" (Ps. 92:5).

Bibliography

Chapter One: The Incredible Secret Letter Codes of the Bible

Cramer, Guy, and Lori Eldridge. "Statistical Significance Discovered in the Yeshua Codes." Internet, 1997.

Drosnin, Michael. *The Bible Code.* New York: Simon and Schuster, 1997.

Jeffrey, Grant. *The Handwriting of God.* Toronto: Frontier Research Publications, 1996.

Jeffrey, Grant R. *The Signature of God.* Toronto: Frontier Research Publications, 1996.

Kass, Robert. "Equidistant Letter Sequences in the Book of Genesis." *Statistical Science,* August 1994.

Michelson, D., "Codes in the Torah." *B'Or Ha'Torah*, no. 6 (1987): 31.

Rambsel, Yacov. *YESHUA: The Name of Jesus Revealed in the Old Testament.* Toronto: Frontier Research Publications, 1996.

Satinover, Jeffrey. *Cracking the Bible Codes.* New York: William Morrow and Co. Inc., 1997, 314.

Satinover, Jeffrey. "Divine Inspiration?" *Bible Review,* November 1995.

Chapter Two: The Amazing Literary Structure of the Bible

Bullinger, E. W. *The Companion, Bible.* London: Lamp Press 1909, reprinted by Kregel, Grand Rapids, 1990.

Pierson, A. T. *The Bible and Spiritual Criticism.* New York; Fleming H. Revell: 1905.

Unger, M. Merrill F., ed. *Unger's Bible Dictionary.* Chicago: Moody Press, 1957, rev. 1990.

Chapter Three: The Astounding Fulfilled Prophecies of the Bible

Alexander, J.A. *The Earlier Prophecies of Isaiah.* London: Wiley & Putnam, 1846, p. 170.

Beecher, Willis. *The Prophets and the Promise.* New York: Thomas Crowell, 1905, p. 394.

Culver, Robert. "Were the Old Testament Prophecies Really Prophetic?" in *Can I Trust My Bible?* Chicago: Moody Press, 1963, p. 99. His discussion of the quality of "obscurity" in predictive prophecy is excellent.

Ellison, H.L. *Men Speak from God.* Grand Rapids, MI: Eerdmans, 1952, p. 14.

Freeman, Hobart. *An Introduction to the Old Testament Prophets.* Chicago: Moody Press, 1968, p. 126.

Girdlestone, R. *Old Testament Theology.* London: Longmons, Green & Co., 1909, p. 120.

Payne, C. and J. Barton. *Encyclopedia of Biblical Prophecy.* Grand Rapids, MI: Baker Book House, 1980.

Walvoord, John. *The Prophecy Knowledge Handbook.* Wheaton, IL: Victor Books, 1990.

Water, Mark. *Bible Prophecy Made Easy.* Peabody, MA: Henrickson Publishers, 1998, p. 48-49 (Chart).

Wood, Leon. *The Prophets of Israel.* Grand Rapids, MI: Baker Book House, 1979, p. 67.

Young, Edward J. *My Servants the Prophets.* Grand Rapids, MI: Eerdmans, 1952, p. 191.

Chapter Four: The Miraculous Preservation of the Jews, People of the Bible

Fast, Howard. *The Jews — Story of a People.* New York: Dial Press, 1968.

Forrest, A.C. *Unholy Land.* Toronto: McClelland and Stewart, Ltd., 1971.

Kirschen, Ya'akov. *Trees.* New York: Vital Media Enterprises, 1993.

Lawrence, Gunther. *Three Million More?* Garden City, NY: Doubleday, 1970.

Lewis, David Allen. *Prophecy 2000.* Green Forest, Arkansas: New Leaf Press, 1987/ 1993, 6th ed.

Olson, Arnold. *Inside Jerusalem — City of Destiny.* Glendale, CA: Gospel Light/ Regal Books, 1968.

Sawicki, Tom. *The Jerusalem Report.* Jerusalem, Israel: Jerusalem Report Publications, Ltd. 1994.

St. John, Robert. *Tongue of the Prophets.* N. Hollywood, CA: Wilshire Book Company, 1952.

Chapter Five: The Fascinating Archaeological Evidence for the Bible

Albright, Prof. W. F. *Recent Discoveries in Bible Lands.* New York: Funk and Wagnalls, 1955.

Alfred, Cyril. *Egypt To The End of The Old Kingdom.* London: Thames & Hudson, 1982.

Barnett, R. D. *Illustrations of Old Testament History.* London: The British Museum, 1982 reprint.

Biblical Archaeology Review. Edited by Henshel Shanks. Washington, DC, since 1974.

Boyd, Robert T. *A Pictorial Guide to Biblical Archaeology.* Eugene OR: Harvest House, Publishers. 1981 reprint.

Bruce, F. F., *Jesus and Christian Origins Outside the New Testament.* London: Hodder & Stoughton, 1974.

_____*The Books and the Parchments,* London: Pickering & Inglis. Revised ed., 1963.

Clack, Clem. *The Bible In Focus.* Blackburn South, Victoria, Australia: Donors Inc., 1980.

Davis, John J. and John C. Whitcomb. *A History of Israel.* Grand Rapids, MI: Baker Book House, 1980.

Finegan, J. *The Archaeology of the New Testament.* Princeton, NJ: Princeton University Press, 1969.

Harvey, Jeff and Charles Pallagy. *The Bible and Science.* Blackburn, Victoria, Australia: Acacia Press, 1985.

Hindsen, Edward. *The Philistines and the Old Testament.* Grand Rapids, MI: Baker Book House, 1981 reprint.

Matthiae, Paolo. *Ebla — An Empire Rediscovered.* Garden City, NY: Doubleday, 1981.

Murphy-O'Conner. *An Archaeological Guide of The Holy Land.* New York: Oxford Jerome, University Press, 1986 edition.

Pritchard, J. B., editor. *The Ancient Near East: An Anthology of Texts and Pictures.* Princeton, NJ: Princeton University Press, 1958.

_____*The Ancient Near East: In Pictures Relating to the Old Testament.* Princeton, NJ: Princeton University Press, 1955, 2nd edition.

Price, Randall. *Secrets of The Dead Sea Scrolls.* Eugene, OR: Harvest House, 1996.

_____*The Stones Cry Out.* Euegene, OR: Harvest House, 1997.

Tenney, Merrill C. *The Bible: The Living Word of Revelation*, edited by Merrill Unger. Grand Rapids, MI: Zondervan Publishing House, 1975.

Thiele, E. R. *Mysterious Numbers of the Hebrew Kings*. Grand Rapids, MI: Wm. B. Eerdmans Pub. Co., 1951.

Thompson, Dr. J.A. *The Bible and Archaeology*. Grand Rapids, MI: Wm. B. Eerdmans Pub. Co., 1982.

Unger, Merrill F. *Archaeology and The Old Testament*. Grand Rapids, MI: Zondervan Publishing House, 1973.

Wilson, Clifford. *That Incredible Book the Bible*. Melbourne, Australia: Word of Truth, 1973.

_____*Rocks, Relics and Biblical Reliability*. Richardson, TX: Probe Books, 1977.

_____*Ebla Tablets Secrets of a Forgotten City*. Green Forest, AR: Master Books, 1979.

_____*New Light On The Gospels*. London: Lakeland, 1970.

_____*New Light On New Testament Letters*. London: Lakeland, 1970.

Wood, Leon J. *A Survey of Israel's History*, revised by David O'Brien. Grand Rapids, MI: Zondervan Publishing House, 1986.

Young, E. J. *An Introduction to the Old Testament*. Grand Rapids, MI: Wm. B. Eerdmans Pub. Co., 1950.

Chapter Six: The Awesome Ezekiel Tablets and the Bible

Elliot, Elisabeth. *Through Gates of Splendor.* Wheaton, IL: Tyndale House Publishers, 1981.

Chapter Seven: The Factual Scientific Accuracy of the Bible

Brown, Michael H. *The Search for Eve.* San Francisco, CA: Harper & Row, 1990.

Fagan, Brian M. *The Journey from Eden.* New York, NY: Thames and Hudson, 1990.

Faid, Robert W. *A Scientific Approach To Biblical Mysteries*. Green Forest, AR, 1993.

Faid, Robert W. *A Scientific Approach To Christianity*. Green Forest, AR: New Leaf Press, 1990.

Faid, Robert W. *A Scientific Approach To More Biblical Mysteries*. Green Forest, AR: New Leaf Press, 1995.

Chapter Eight: The Unique Historical Distinctives of the Bible

Delaney, C.F., editor. In *Rationality and Religious Belief.* "Moral Arguments for Theistic Belief," by Robert Adams.

Anderson, Norman. *Christianity and World Religions,* 2nd edition. Westmont, IL: Intervarsity Press, 1984.

Aquinas, Thomas. *Summa Contra Gentiles,* in *Basic Writings of Saint Thomas Aquinas*, edited by Anton Pegis. New York, NY: Random House, 1945.

Beisner, E. Calvin. *Answers for Atheists, Agnostics, and Other Thoughtful Skeptics: Dialogues About Christian Faith and Life,* revised edition. Wheaton, IL: Crossway Books, 1993.

Boice, James Montgomery. *Does Inerrancy Matter?* Oakland, CA: International Council on Biblical Inerrancy, 1979.

Brown, Colin, ed. *History, Criticism & Faith*. Westmont, IL: Intervarsity Press, 1976.

Bruce, F.F. *The New Testament Documents: Are They Reliable?* Westmont, IL: Intervarsity Press.

Craig, William Lane. *The Existence of God and the Beginning of the Universe.* San Bernardino, CA: Here's Life Pub., 1979.

_____*The Son Rises: Historical Evidence for the Resurrection of Jesus Christ.* Chicago, IL: Moody Press, 1982.

Geisler, Norman L. *Christ: The Theme of the Bible.* Wheaton, IL: Victor Books, 1990.

Harris, R. Laird. *Inspiration and Canonicity of the Bible.* Grand Rapids, MI: Zondervan Publishing House, 1957.

Jastrow, Robert. *God and the Astronomers.* New York, NY: W. W. Norton, 1978.

Johnson, Phillip E. *Darwin on Trial.* Washington, DC: Regnery Gateway, 1991.

Pache, Rene. *The Inspiration and Authority of Scripture.* Chicago, IL: Moody Press, 1969.

Parker, J. I. *God Has Spoken.* Westmont, IL: Intervarsity Press, 1979.

Radmacher, Earl D., ed. *Can We Trust the Bible?* Wheaton, IL: Tyndale House Publishers, 1979.

Unger, Merrill F. *Archaeology and the Old Testament.* Grand Rapids, MI: Zondervan Publishing House, 1954.

Van Til, Cornelius. "Apologetics." Unpublished class syllabus, Westminister Theological Seminary, n.d.

_____ *A Christian Theory of Knowledge.* Philadelphia, PA: Presbyterian & Reformed, 1969.

_____ *Defense of the Faith.* Rev. ed. Philadelphia, PA: Presbyterian & Reformed, 1972.

_____ *Jerusalem and Athens.* Edited by E. R. Geehan. Nutley, NJ: Presbyterian & Reformed, 1977.

Vos, Howard. *Can I Trust My Bible?* Chicago, IL: Moody Press, 1963.

Wilson, Clifford A. *Rocks, Relics and Biblical Reliability.* Richardson, TX: Probe Books, 1977.

Chapter Nine: The Powerful Worldwide Impact of the Bible

Asher, Louis Franklin. *John Clarke (1609-1676).* Pittsburg, PA: Dorrance, 1997.

Barfield, Kenny. *Why the Bible Is Number 1.* Grand Rapids, MI: Baker Book House, 1988.

Bready, J. Wesley. *This Freedom Whence.* New York: American Tract Society, 1944.

Connolly, W. Kenneth. *The Incredible Book.* Grand Rapids, MI: Baker Book House, 1996.

Frend, W.H.C. *The Early Church.* Philadelphia, PA: Lippincott, 1966.

Goodspeed, Edgar J. *How Came the Bible?* New York: Abingdon, 1940.

Hall, Joseph and Verna, ed. *The Christian History of the Constitution of the United States of America.* San Francisco, CA: Foundation for American Christian Education, 1966.

Leach, Charles. *Our Bible, How We Got It.* Chicago, IL: Moody Press, 1910.

Marshall, Peter, and David Manuel. *The Light and the Glory.* Old Tappan, NJ: Revell, 1977.

Nichols, Robert Hastings. *The Growth of the Christian Church.* Philadelphia, PA: Westminister, 1943.

Schaff, Phillip. *History of the Christian Church.* Grand Rapids, MI: Wm. B. Eerdmans Pub. Co., 1950.

Shelley, Bruce. *Church History in Plain Language.* Waco, TX: Word, 1982.

Wilson, Clifford A. *That Incredible Book the Bible.* Boronia Victoria Australia: Pacific Christian Ministries, 1975.

Chapter Ten: The Supernatural Life-Changing Power of the Bible

Towns, Elmer L. *The Christian Hall of Fame.* Grand Rapids, MI: Baker Book House, 1971.

Bill Murray. *My Life Without God.* Nashville, TN: Thomas Nelson Publishers, 1982.

Kerr, Hugh T., and John Mulder, editors. *Conversions.* Grand Rapids, MI: Wm. B. Eerdmans Pub. Co., 1983.

Chapter Eleven: The Mysterious Mathematical Design of the Bible

Bullinger, E. W. *Number in Scripture.* Grand Rapids, MI: Kregel Publications, reproduced from 1894 edition, 1967.

Davis, John J. *Biblical Numerology.* Grand Rapids, MI: Baker Book House, 1968.

Jeans, Sir James. *The Mysterious Universe.* Cambridge, MA: Cambridge University Press, 1930.

McCormack, R. *The Heptadic Structure of Scripture.* London: Marshall Brothers Ltd., 1923.

Missler, Chuck. *Cosmic Codes — Hidden Messages from the Edge of Eternity.* Coeur d'Alene, ID: Koinonia House, 1998.

Panin, Ivan. *The Inspiration of the Scriptures Scientifically Demonstrated.* Canada: The Book Society of Canada, Ltd., Agincourt, 1972.

Panin, Ivan. *The Writings of Ivan Panin.* Canada: The Book Society of Canada, Ltd., Agincourt, 1972.

Panin, Ivan. For a source of all of Ivan Panin's works, write to Bible Numerics, Suite 206, 121 Willowdale Ave., Willowdale, Ontario, M2N 6A3 or phone: (416) 221-7424 or Fax: (416) 221-8814.

Rambsel, Yacov A. *Yeshua: The Hebrew Factor.* San Antonio, TX: Companion Press, 1996.

Chapter Twelve: The Glorious Incomparable Promises of the Bible

Chilton, David. *Paradise Restored.* Tyler, TX: Reconstruction Press, 1985.

Rausch, David. *Building Bridges: Understanding Jews and Judaism.* Chicago, IL: Moody Press, 1988.

Rousas John Rushdoony. *Thy Kingdom Come: Studies in Daniel and Revelation.* Fairfax, VA: Thoburn Press, 1970.

Schlissel, Steve and David Brown. *Hal Lindsey and the Restoration of the Jews.* Edmonton, Canada: Still Waters Revival Books, 1990.

Walvoord, John. Grand Rapids: Zondervan Publishing Company, 1964.

James O. Combs

First enrolling as a freshman in January of 1946, James O. (Jim) Combs graduated with a diploma in 1951 and was one of the first four to receive the Bachelor of Arts in Biblical Education from Kansas City Bible College in 1952. During 1948-50, Combs, who was pastoring in Texas at the time, also completed a bachelor's degree in theology at the Bible Baptist Seminary in Fort Worth, which he also attended before returning to Kansas City.

Pastoring in California from 1953 until 1975, Jim also completed an M.A. through California Baptist Theological Seminary and Jackson College in Hawaii (1964). He earned a Doctor of Ministry from Louisiana Baptist University in 1985 and accepted an honorary Doctor of Literature in 1986 from Liberty University in Lynchburg, Virginia. Besides pastoring, Jim taught in a Bible College and at times was on radio and television.

Jim pastored for 26 years, mostly in California at one church in Lynwood and another in Costa Mesa (First Baptist Church); then ran for the U.S. Congress in 1976, winning the nomination of a major party in his California district. During his campaign, he and Jeri Marquis Combs, his wife, were guests of President Gerald Ford at the White House.

From 1977 until the present he has been an evangelist and conference speaker, majoring on prophetic subjects. In 1982 he became editor of the *Baptist Bible Tribune*, published in Springfield, Missouri, for the Baptist Bible Fellowship International (4,000 churches). Retiring from that post in 1995, he became founding editor-in-chief of Jerry Falwell's *National Liberty Journal*, serving for a year and a half.

He is the author or editor of six books, including *Mysteries of the Book of Daniel* and *Rainbows from Revelation*.

He has preached in nearly 1,000 pulpits over a 50-year ministry.

Presently, he serves as provost and a mentoring professor for an external studies school, Louisiana Baptist Theological Seminary, based in Shreveport with Louisiana Baptist University.

He and Jeri reside in Springfield, Missouri, operating out of a home office, going out to speak in various churches and writing for several publications.

Robert W. Faid

Robert W. Faid graduated from the Baltimore Polytechnic Institute. After military service, he was employed by the gerontology section of the National Institute of Health as a laboratory technician and assigned to a group investigating the effects of ACTH and cortisone on the human body in aging. This culminated in the publication of five research papers in the *Journal of the American Medical Association, Journal of Applied Psychology,* and *Experimental Biology and Medicine.*

Following another stint in the military during the Korean War, he was employed by the American Oil Company and continued his studies in chemistry at Johns Hopkins University. His work and research at the oil company resulted in developing new processes which were utilized and published through the American Chemical Society.

For many years he was involved with the W.R. Grace Company in the design and construction of commercial nuclear power plants, both in this country and abroad. He has many inventions to his credit and has written many papers and scientific articles. He was the author of *Engineering Manual for Nuclear Power Plants.* He is a member of the American Nuclear Society.

In the prime of his career he was found to be suffering from widespread terminal cancer. Unbeknownst to him, his wife and many others prayed for his recovery. One day a startled doctor came to his hospital bed to tell him they now could find no trace of his cancer anywhere in his body.

It was a miracle. The "agnostic" scientist knew something had happened and began to search for the truth about God, using the "scientific method" he had learned in his educational career, putting everything to the test. His research resulted in his accepting Christ.

His three books, *A Scientific Approach to Christianity, A Scientific Approach to Biblical Mysteries,* and *A Scientific Approach to More Biblical Mysteries,* published by New Leaf Press, contain the results of his research and his ongoing pilgrimage.

Frank Harber

Although he was taught Bible and Christian values in his childhood, Frank Harber became sceptical of Christianity and of the Bible during his college and university years. When so many brilliant professors and educators scoff at the Scriptures, it is difficult for even the most dedicated to maintain their earlier faith.

Frank decided that this Bible-based religion was not to be a vital part of his life. Nevertheless, his curiosity was piqued and his sense of objectivity led him to study seriously the claims of Christ and the nature of the Bible. After doing a well-researched scientific investigation of the historicity and record of Christ's life and ministry, Frank committed his life to the Savior and was converted.

He continued his education, earning the Master of Divinity and the Doctor of Philosophy degrees from Southwestern Baptist Theological Seminary, Fort Worth, Texas. His calling is evangelism. He now helps to equip Christians across the nation to share their faith through powerful Christian evidences.

He is the author of *Beyond Reasonable Doubt: Convincing Evidences for Christianity*, and *Reasons For Believing: A Seeker's Guide to Christianity*.

He now holds city-wide and area-wide crusades across America and is a frequent speaker at Bible and evangelism conferences. He is staff evangelist of the Travis Avenue Baptist Church in Fort Worth and Evangelist in Residence and Assistant Professor of Evangelism at Southwestern Seminary. He has worked closely with many other evangelists, including Luis Palau.

He and his wife, Becky, reside in Fort Worth with their twins, Graham and Gabrielle.

Ed Hindson

Edward E. Hindson is a pastor, educator, and author with wide-ranging abilities. In recent years, in addition to his writing and speaking ministry, he has served as associate pastor at the 9,000 member Rehoboth Baptist Church in Atlanta, Georgia, where he was also vice-president of There's Hope! ministries.

He also serves as dean of the Institute of Biblical Studies at Liberty University in Lynchburg, Virginia.

The books he has authored include: *Angels of Deceit*, *Final Signs*, *Approaching Armageddon* and *Is the Antichrist Alive and Well?*

He also served as general editor of the *King James Study Bible*, published by Thomas Nelson and the *Parallel Bible Commentary* and he was one of the translators of the New King James Version.

An executive board member of the Pre-Trib Research Center, now located in Dallas-Fort Worth Metroplex, he is also a Life Fellow of the International Biographical Association of Cambridge, England. Dr. Hindson holds degrees from several institutions: B.A., William Tyndale College; M.A., Trinity Evangelical Divinity School; Th.M., Grace Theological Seminary, THD., Trinity Graduate School; D.Min., Westminister Theological Seminary; D.Phil., University of South Africa. He has also done graduate study at Acadia University in Nova Scotia, Canada.

Ed has served as a visiting lecturer at both Oxford University and Harvard Divinity School, as well as numerous evangelical seminaries including Dallas, Denver, Trinity, Grace, and Westminister. He has taught over 30,000 students in the past 30 years. His solid academic scholarship combined with a dynamic and practical teaching style communicate biblical truth in a powerful and positive manner.

Thomas Ice

Thomas Ice is executive director of the Pre-Trib Research Center in Fort Worth, Texas, which he co-founded with Dr. Tim LaHaye in 1992 to research, teach, and defend the pre-tribulational rapture and related Bible prophecy doctrines.

Ice is a graduate of Howard Payne University (BA), Dallas Theological Seminary (TH.M) and Tyndale Theological Seminary (PH.D.).

He has served as a campus minister with Campus Crusade for Christ (1975-77); a reserve military chaplain in the Army National Guard (1981-90) and pastored for 15 years. His churches include the Grace Bible Church of Del City, Oklahoma; the Oak Hill Baptist Church of Austin, Texas, which he founded and led for 10 years; and the Trinity Bible Church in Fredricksburg, Virginia.

He has authored or co-authored four books: *Dominion Theology, Blessing or Curse?*; *A Holy Rebellion: Strategy for Spiritual Warfare*; *Ready to Rebuild: The Imminent Plan to Build the Last Days Temple*; and *The Great Tribulation, Past or Future?* (1999). He edited *When the Trumpet Sounds: Today's Foremost Authorities Speak Out on End-Time Controversies*.

He has written or co-authored over a dozen booklets in the Pocket Prophecy Series during the years of 1996-99.

He has been a contributor to numerous anthologies and several magazines and papers, including *Biblioleca Sacra*, and *Midnight Call*, plus has served as editor for *Pre-Trib Perspectives*, which he founded, and numerous other newsletters on Bible study themes.

He is a frequent conference speaker and guest lecturer at various seminaries, colleges, and institutes, and has been a guest on hundreds of radio and television shows.

Dr. Ice and his wife, Janice, now live in Arlington, Texas, with their three boys.

Grant Jeffrey

Born in a Christian home in Canada, Grant Jeffrey accepted Christ as a lad and developed a keen interest in the Bible as a teenager. In the late 1960s he attended Philadelphia College of the Bible. His facination with the prophecies of the Bible, both fulfilled and unfilled, has always been a strong factor in study of the Word.

During his twenties he became a very successful businessman with experience in real estate, insurance, investments, and sales. To further this aspect of his career he earned Certified Life Underwriter's degree through the University of Toronto.

Active as a Bible teacher in his own church and as a guest speaker in various churches and schools, he increasingly sensed the call of God to move from the secular business world to an even more challenging spiritual ministry.

He and his wife, Kaye, have traveled extensively to many countries, especially in the Middle East, where he became a diligent researcher. He examined biblical archaeological sites, museums, libraries, schools, and historic cities, scattered from England to Rome to Africa and to Iran, interviewing archaeologists, teachers, and many experts in Middle Eastern studies.

Over a 30-year period he has accumulated a library of some 6,000 books, most of which deal with prophecy and many of which are quite rare finds from antiquarian bookstores.

During the last 15 years he has written more than a dozen books on prophetic themes, which have sold over 3 million copies. He has completed a *Prophecy Study Bible*, published by Zondervan in 1999. In demand as a prophetic speaker, Grant has been called by Hal Lindsey "the most outstanding Bible researcher on prophecy in the world today."

He holds the B.A. and M.A. degrees from Louisiana Baptist University and the Doctor of Literature from Louisiana Baptist Theological Seminary.

The Jeffreys live in Mississauga, Ontario.

David A. Lewis

David A. Lewis is a clergyman, author, lecturer, researcher, publisher, and is active in national and international circles in promoting the welfare of the Church, of Israel, and the Jewish people. His ordination has been with the Assemblies of God for over 35 years.

Dr. Lewis speaks at churches, conferences, minister's seminars, colleges, camp meetings, district events, etc. He has taught short courses in eschatology and apocalyptic literature in both secular and theological colleges, also short-term seminars and spiritual life emphasis in Bible colleges.

He has traveled to the Middle East 60 times. He has visited and done research in Israel, Egypt, Turkey, Syria, Lebanon, Jordan, and Cyprus. He has also ministered in Hong Kong, Kowloon, Barbados, Virgin Islands, Iceland, Mexico, Canada, and has traveled to mainland China and many European countries.

David Lewis has conferred on numerous occasions with heads of state, including Prime Ministers Begin, Peres, and Shamir of Israel, as well as members of Israel's Parliament, Mayor Teddy Kolleck of Jerusalem, Moderate Palestinian Arab leaders, various U.S. senators and congressmen, and has met with former President Reagan.

He was invited and appeared as a witness on the Middle East before the Senate Foreign Relations Committee in Washington, D.C.

He has strong contacts with religious leaders in a broad spectrum of churches, with many Jewish religious and political leaders, and in diverse disciplines of the scientific communities.

Books by Lewis include *Prophecy 2000*, *Smashing the Gates of Hell*, *Magog Cancelled 1982*, *Dark Angels of Light*, *Coming Antichrist*, and *Holy Spirit World Liberation*.

Chuck Missler

As an expert on Russia, Israel, Europe, and the Middle East, Chuck Missler gives intriguing behind-the-scenes insight to his audiences. His more than 30 years in the corporate world as CEO of four public corporations contracting with the U.S. Department of Defense has left him with an extensive network of overseas contacts. With affiliates and associates in nine countries, Missler is a major contributor to several international intelligence newsletters. He has also negotiated joint ventures in Russia, Israel, Malaysia, Japan, Algeria, and Europe. In addition, Missler is an authority on advanced weapons and strategic resources and has participated in projects with SAMCOM-USSR, DSL, JCS, USACADA, DOJ, CCIA, and SDI. A member of the International Press Association, he is an honors graduate from the U.S. Naval Academy.

For 20 years, Chuck Missler taught a Bible study in southern California that grew to more than 2,000 attendees. In 1992, he moved to Coeur d'Alene, Idaho, where he founded Koinonia House to distribute his books, lectures, and tapes. His dynamic style, conservative values, and adherence to biblical principles have made him a highly acclaimed speaker and critic.

His newsletter, *Personal UPDATE*, a Christian prophecy and intelligence newsletter, has grown to reach more than 50,000 monthly subscribers and he has more than 8 million tapes in circulation worldwide.